The Cultural Logic of Contemporary Capitalism

Edited by Nico Baumbach, Damon R. Young, and Genevieve Yue

Jennifer Bajorek is assistant professor of comparative literature at Hampshire College and a research associate in the Faculty of Art, Design and Architecture at the University of Johannesburg, South Africa. She teaches and writes on literature, philosophical aesthetics, and photography. She is the author of *Counterfeit Capital* (2009) and *How to Write a Visual History of Liberation: Photography and Decolonial Imagination in Africa* (forthcoming).

Nico Baumbach is assistant professor of film studies at Columbia University. He holds a PhD in literature from Duke University. He is currently working on two book-length manuscripts: a study of the politics of cinema in Badiou, Rancière, and Agamben; and a rethinking of documentary theory titled "The Anonymous Image."

Jonathan Beller is professor of humanities and media studies and director of the Graduate Program in Media Studies at Pratt Institute. His books include *The Cinematic Mode of Production: Attention Economy and the Society of the Spectacle* (2006), *Acquiring Eyes: Philippine Visuality, Nationalist Struggle and the World-Media System* (2006), and *Computational Capital* (forthcoming).

Alexander R. Galloway is a writer and computer programmer working on issues in philosophy, technology, and theories of mediation. Professor at New York University, he is the author of several books, most recently *Laruelle: Against the Digital* (2014).

Sulgi Lie is a postdoctoral fellow in the School of Cinematic Arts at the University of Southern California after teaching for many years in the Division of Film Studies at the Free University Berlin. He is the author of *The Exteriority of Film: On Political Film Aesthetics* (2012) and coeditor of Jacques Rancière's film critical writings. Currently he is working on a book on slapstick comedy.

Alberto Toscano is reader in critical theory and codirector of the Centre for Philosophy and Critical Thought at Goldsmiths, University of London. He is the author of *The Theatre of Production* (2006), *Fanaticism: On the Uses of an Idea* (2010), and, with Jeff Kinkle, *Cartographies of the Absolute* (2015). He edits the Italian List for Seagull Books and sits on the editorial board of the journal *Historical Materialism*.

Amy Villarejo is professor in the Department of Performing and Media Arts at Cornell University. She writes widely on cinema, media, and queer life; her most recent book is *Ethereal Queer* (2014).

Damon R. Young is assistant professor of French and film/media at the University of California, Berkeley. His first book, *Making Sex Public* (forthcoming), examines the intertwining of sexual and social imaginaries in French and US cinema since the 1960s.

Genevieve Yue is assistant professor of culture and media at Eugene Lang College, The New School. Her essays and criticism have appeared in *October, Grey Room, Film Quarterly,* and *Film Comment.* She is a coeditor of *Discourse: Journal for Theoretical Studies in Media and Culture,* and her current projects include two books: the first is *China Girls: Film, Feminism, and the Material Image,* about gender and filmic materiality, and the second is a cultural and technical history of the blurred image.

Introduction

For a Political Critique of Culture

Nico Baumbach, Damon R. Young, and Genevieve Yue

Within the past seven years, we have witnessed what looked briefly like the implosion of the global financial system followed by a wave of protest movements challenging the neoliberal consensus, but business as usual has returned, indeed with a renewed sense of inexorability. Capitalism is both broken and all-pervasive, and while it has produced the technological conditions for a world of universal welfare and minimal work, it is at the same time the agent of ever more extreme inequality and immiseration, especially among the populations of the Global South. The global financial system to which we are all beholden has never been more opaque in its operations, or more transparent in its effects. And although the language of capitalism and class has resurfaced in public discourse—from Occupy's "we are the 99%!" to Thomas Piketty's unlikely best seller *Capital in the Twenty-First Century*—nothing seems to impede the totalizing reach of the profit motive. Capitalism has wholly saturated our world; it now threatens to extinguish it.

Meanwhile, where is theory in the American humanities? The latest violent reminders of capitalism's global dominance have coincided with various "turns": toward a "neutral" practice of description (from structure to surface); toward the empirical as opposed to the interpretive; toward an "ethics," as opposed to a politics, of reading; and toward the souls of objects, as an explicit rejection of questions of subjectivity and subjectivization. Where the stakes are higher, it is in new forms of metaphysics, revitalized vitalisms, cybernetic fantasies, or attempts by the (digital) humanities to incorporate the new "technologized scientism," as Alain Badiou has called it,[1] into its methods: to keep up with the world as it is and not be left behind. Theory today, where it still exists, often pre-

Social Text 127 · Vol. 34, No. 2 · June 2016
DOI 10.1215/01642472-3467942   © 2016 Duke University Press

sents itself as having modest or circumscribed ambitions attuned to surface effects or aiming for piecemeal results. Or, on the flip side, it invests in new kinds of ontological and metaphysical approaches that dispense with history, cultural specificity, and periodization entirely. In short, at the very moment we most need a political critique of culture, we are busy disavowing the tools that might deliver one.

The new mutations of capitalism—often associated with the economic transformations of the 1970s—have been given many names. Sandro Mezzadra and Brett Neilson's *Border as Method* catalogs some of them, including "disorganized capitalism (Lash and Urry 1987), flexible accumulation (Harvey 1989), late capitalism (Mandel 1975), the knowledge economy (Drucker 1969), post-Fordism (Aglietta 1979; Lipietz 1992), cognitive capitalism (Moulier Boutang 2011; Vercellone 2006), neoliberalism (Harvey 2005; Touraine 2001), [and] empire (Hardt and Negri 2000)."[2] Seb Franklin's recent *Control: Digitality as Cultural Logic* adds to this list the information economy (Porat 1977), the third wave (Toffler 1980), the network society (Castells 1996), the new spirit of capitalism (Boltanski and Chiapello 2005), and control society (Deleuze 1990). The list can be expanded yet further: attention economy, semiocapitalism (Berardi 2009), and the hyperindustrial epoch (Stiegler 2014). What is indexed by this "frenzy of periodization," as Franklin calls it, is not just a new form of capitalism but its extension into every aspect of our lives—our attention, our affects, our cognition, and our social relations.[3] A point made by Fredric Jameson over thirty years ago—that the logic of late capitalism has become precisely *cultural* in a new way—would appear to have been resoundingly confirmed in the period that postdates his analysis of postmodernism.[4]

Postmodernism: the term itself is conspicuously absent from the list above. In 1984, Jameson used the term to name what he called the "cultural logic of late capitalism." Since this issue endeavors to reactivate this notion of "cultural logic" and to argue for its timeliness (again or still), it is worth briefly reflecting on the demise of the cognate term with which it was originally associated.[5] *Postmodernism*, a victim of its own celebrity, was too often used to signify one of two things: an inventory of aesthetic tropes specifically associated with the last decades of the twentieth century,[6] or a reductive concept of epistemological relativism.[7] These uses of the word failed to grasp it as the cultural logic that linked aesthetics, knowledge, and political economy. They mistook its symptoms for the thing itself. Both of these (mis)uses of the word, furthermore, took postmodernism to be a relatively stable framework that could be readily applied to a given object rather than what it was for Jameson—a conceptual problem that needs to be continually reexamined in relation to emergent and frequently contradictory phenomena.

What Jameson called postmodernism was never merely a question of a particular style or, for that matter, a genre of theory. Rather, it served as a signifier for the constellation of tendencies that tied together dominant modes of cultural production against which we might begin to register genuine forms of resistance. For Jameson, one could not stand outside postmodernism; it was in some sense the name for the current conditions of thought. But this did not mean that we should embrace it uncritically. As he argued, "it was not possible intellectually or politically simply to celebrate postmodernism or to disavow it."[8] Jameson may have become associated with postmodernism, but he was also a vocal critic of what he took to be its main tendencies, reading its tropes historically albeit with the insistence that a loss of historical consciousness was a characteristic of postmodernity that infects even the discourses that try to resist it. An avowed Marxist and historical materialist, Jameson never repudiated what was one of the central metanarratives that postmodernism itself had presumably dispensed with. The famous directive with which he opened *The Political Unconscious*—"Always historicize!"—was not to be suddenly abandoned in the wake of a culture that seemed no longer to be able to think historically. On the contrary, it took on a renewed urgency.

Postmodernism, as Jonathan Beller puts it in this issue, has "lost its pizzazz." This fact risks obscuring the interest that Jameson's writings on postmodernism still have for us today, an interest that may inhere as much in what they no longer seem to adequately describe as in what still feels relevant to our current moment. If postmodernism is no longer with us, is there a better name for what we still wish to thematize, for reasons we will explain, as the *cultural logic* of contemporary capitalism? How might we distinguish the present imbrication of culture and political economy from that which Jameson described three decades ago? Does the cultural logic of the era before the fall of the Berlin Wall, the establishment of the eurozone, and the War on Terror still resemble our own? Or would an updated account of cultural logic need to take significant stock of developments such as the mass surveillance of civilian telecommunications; the ubiquity of computing devices, social media, and the cloud; the (globally uneven) mainstreaming of queerness and other reconfigurations of twenty-first-century identity; the ongoing legacies of imperialism and the violence of racialization; and the technological and economic transformations of the private and public spheres, if indeed they can still be said to be distinct? Meanwhile, what of this operation itself—the critical operation of periodization, of naming the system, locating the historical novelty of the present moment of capitalism as it is expressed in our television shows, our architecture, our technological platforms, and modes of discourse? Is this still a useful critical procedure, or is the desire for periodization itself a symptom of the cultural logic of late capitalism, as Franklin suggests?[9]

Cultural Logics

Cultural logic: the term is a theoretical provocation. Amidst the characteristic pluralism and diversity of the contemporary field of cultural production—comprising architecture, film, postbroadcast television, literature, journalism, social media, and the arts: a nonexhaustive list—can we discern an underlying logic (or logics, as the case may be), which is to say, a system of coherent patterns and relations that would be indexed to the singular economic system that currently fills all possible spaces, namely, capitalism? A cultural logic in this sense might overlap with what Foucault called a *dispositif*, or "apparatus," conditioning the field of the intelligible and perceptible and tying together, in Foucauldian terms, the discursive production of knowledge and the operations of power (or, in our own preferred terms, class interests), as well as modes of subjectivation and what Raymond Williams called "structures of feeling."[10] It might equally bear on what Jacques Rancière calls the "distribution of the sensible,"[11] especially in that it invokes the aesthetic as one of its modalities. As Bernard Stiegler, among others, has argued, capitalism works directly on the sensory or sensible life today, and "artistic and spiritual questions have become questions of political economy."[12] Like these cognate theoretical terms, the term *cultural logic* is not merely empirically descriptive. It is a term of political analysis that is precisely historical: the cultural logic that becomes "hegemonic," as Jameson sometimes puts it, under given conditions—that is, the current stage of global capitalism—is also available as a domain of contestation, resistance, and activism, even as it makes the critical distance typically implied by those terms appear outmoded.

The formidable challenge, in Jameson's account of postmodernism, was to register the unconscious attempts to think alternatives within a dominant cultural logic in which they seem unthinkable. One way this takes place in his own work is through an ongoing commitment to the notion of utopia; another is through an "aesthetic" to which he gave the name "cognitive mapping"—the necessary attempt to give form to an ungraspable world system, and itself a new form of class consciousness motivated by a utopian impulse to imagine alternatives. The gambit, both at the time of Jameson's writing and for our current and potentially distinct moment, is that the formal features that recur in current cultural production might index in some way (more complex than simply reflecting or expressing) the deeper logic of the new global system and, indeed, the tendencies that anticipate possibilities on the horizon for new modes of organization. As Jameson once put it, "All postmodern theory is . . . a telling of the future, with an imperfect deck."[13]

As familiar as these questions of base and superstructure, economy and culture may be, there has been a lack of serious interest in tackling them in contemporary theory. As we have noted, there certainly have been attempts to name what is novel about the current economy, as well as attempts to provide some kind of diagnosis of the cultural zeitgeist. But the goal, as Jameson made clear, was never "another disembodied culture critique."[14] In what follows, our contributors address these issues from two distinct angles. The first concerns the "meta" question of method, in a context of the various depoliticizing turns referred to above. Some reflect on the legacy of a Marxist cultural criticism, whose enduring—and indeed renewed—value animates their work. In his article, for example, Alexander R. Galloway offers a Jamesonian reflection on ontology and metaphysics, restoring to the latter the question of history. From a different perspective, Jennifer Bajorek, in an article on West African art, argues that an analysis of the cultural logic of capitalism today needs to reorient itself away from the Euro-American cultural reference points that, she contends, have been fundamental to the elaboration of Marxist cultural theory in the West. In his contribution, Beller reads the demise of the term *postmodernism* as symptomatic of the effacing of capitalism and its operations, an effacing that (because it is a meaningful "invisibility") clearly challenges the value of mere description. In a similar vein, Alberto Toscano's article explores the absence of an analysis of capitalism or class politics in the discourse on the Anthropocene and in contemporary photographic images of the built environment, absences that demand that we venture well beyond the surfaces of appearances. Each of these writers offers an explicit critique of current trends in the humanities while insisting on, and sketching out possibilities for, politically engaged alternatives.

The second line of inquiry attempts to delineate some of the substantive features of the cultural logic in question. The attempts at naming the new socioeconomic structure all suggest a world in which, as Franklin puts it, "a supposedly frictionless concept of information functions as a sovereign concept" at the same time as "ever-growing rates of exploitation, expulsion, incarceration, and destruction [appear] in the fissures and at the margins of this world."[15] Some of these complexities are tracked in the articles by Sulgi Lie, who identifies a shift from the economy of desire to one of drive in contemporary film, and by Amy Villarejo, who, surveying the (post)televisual landscape, addresses the new mainstreaming of queerness in the distributed forms of television across a range of digital platforms. Bajorek and Toscano, meanwhile, expand the purview of cultural logic to global and planetary arenas. Bajorek considers the reflexive awareness of the "NGO aesthetic" as it is inscribed into and challenged by African artworks that cognitively remap the terrain of contemporary cultural logic. Toscano's analysis of the trope of depopulation in manufactured landscape photography, meanwhile, offers a searing critique of the periodizing concept of the Anthropocene in its argument for a Marxist concept of human activity under capitalism, which is crucial to conceptualizing history.

Interpretive Strategies

As Galloway reminds us in his contribution to this issue, Jameson noted that "interpretation" had "fallen into disrepute" as far back as 1971. Jameson is one of the few prominent voices to consistently foreground both the value of interpretation—largely rejected by poststructuralists and analytic philosophers alike and, by his own analysis, anathema to postmodern culture—as well as its persistence even in the modes of discourse that try most strenuously to escape it.

Despite this minority position, it is a testament to Jameson's influence in American academia during the 1980s and 1990s that in Stephen Best and Sharon Marcus's 2009 introduction to a special issue of *Representations* on "The Way We Read Now," Jameson's *Political Unconscious* is taken to model the dominant reading strategy that the "now" of their title performatively dispatches to the dustbins of history. In the place of "symptomatic reading" or "ideology critique," which they place under the sign of Jameson, Best and Marcus extol the virtues of what they call *surface reading*, advocating for it by describing its rise as an empirical fact (rather than, say, a methodological commitment with ideological implications). According to Best and Marcus, Jameson is guilty of glorifying criticism as a "heroic endeavor" that requires dismissing the surface of texts and aggressively "correct[ing]" them by decoding their hidden messages. The injunction to "Always historicize!" is for its part described as a paradoxically "transhistorical imperative whose temporality matches the eternity Augustine ascribed to God."[16]

Surface reading, write Best and Marcus, "strives to describe texts accurately" and, in so doing, to avoid an "adversarial relation to the object of criticism."[17] Against the adversarial and the "paranoid," the authors advocate what they describe as an "ethical" stance of "receptiveness and fidelity to the text's surface, as opposed to suspicious and aggressive attacks on its concealed depth."[18] Here the "ethical" stands in for, and indeed displaces, the political. (Moreover, the ethical injunction is apparently not self-binding, since the authors' own reading of Jameson's *Political Unconscious* is rather more aggressive than it is accurate.)[19] In an epilogue to Best and Marcus's special issue, Emily Apter and Elaine Freedgood reiterate that "there is considerable consensus" among the issue's contributors that "symptomatic reading does not do very well as a standalone heuristic and might well be wished away."[20] Far from joining this "consensus," our own special issue is the product of a shared counterconviction that to read is already to inscribe oneself within a history that wrests from the present "a revolutionary chance in the fight for the oppressed past."[21] There is no such thing, we submit, as "simple" or "faithful" description, just as there is no act of reading that is not political. This is itself a political statement, made at a time when the stakes for how and what we read in the academy are high, and not a divine injunction or transhistorical truth. And while we think Best and Marcus offer a reductive account of the method they associate with Jameson, we are in any case not afraid to be "suspicious and aggressive," under historical conditions that call for nothing less.

In an arguably parallel development, witness the recent special issue of *differences* criticizing queer theory's investment in what the editors describe as an overattachment to the "politics of oppositionality" and to a position of "antinormativity."[22] The whole field of queer theory, the editors allege, has been based on the mistaken premise that norms are violent and that queer theory's purpose should be to resist or unsettle norms. On the contrary, they aver, norms are heterogeneous and pluralistic, even "play[ful]."[23] The implicit target of their polemic seems to be the political orientation of the field, to which one of their contributors counterposes, for example, "the value of a descriptive view of sexual practices and sexual communities" modeled on post-WWII social science.[24] This renewed emphasis on avowedly apolitical formalism in literary studies and on description in queer studies arises in tandem with object-oriented ontology and associated modes of new materialism in philosophy. These developments in contemporary theory—for all their internal heterogeneity and nuance—evince a collective desire to move away from the political investments of what is disparaged as cultural studies and from its associated practices of ideology critique and symptomatic reading. We are tempted to read this desire as itself symptomatic of the cultural logic of contemporary capitalism.

"The way we read now," to take the title of Best and Marcus's special issue, *is* changing. So too are the ways we watch, the ways we communicate, and the ways we think. What resources do the humanities afford us for understanding these changes? With new and powerful computational tools at our disposal, the possibilities of data mining or what Franco Moretti calls "distant reading"[25] are in their infancy. The turn to the social sciences as well as the hard sciences has become de rigueur in the increasingly digital humanities. Poststructuralism is out; cognitive psychology and literary Darwinism are in. On the one hand, those still committed to "the literary" take refuge in lowering the stakes—whether quarantining an analysis of form from questions of politics, or emphasizing personal experience and affect, or framing their goals in ethical (rather than political) terms, such as in the oft-pronounced preference for "reparative reading."[26] These practices cede ground to the sciences in the imperative attempt to understand the way we (as in all of us, not just academics) really do read now.

On the other hand, in committed criticism—for example, the kind regularly practiced in *Social Text*—there is increasingly an emphasis on "the social over the text," as Anna McCarthy put it in the journal's thirtieth anniversary issue in 2009.[27] Perhaps the *text* was felt to be too much a privileged object of the kind of criticism now disparaged as "postmodern" (the "text," Jameson once wrote, is a "postmodern category and phenomenon which has replaced the older one of a 'work'").[28] In *Social Text*, textual analysis has in fact suffered the same fate as the discussion of works (of art): in the same anniversary issue, Susette Min observed that "art's power as cultural resistance and convivial exchange has been viewed with skepticism and increasing cynicism . . . by the editorial board of *Social Text* in recent years, as evidenced by the virtual absence of essays that directly engage with art and aesthetics."[29] That art and literature are no longer able to offer leverage in terms of criticism or resistance is a point apparently agreed on both by those who continue to pay attention to form and textuality and by those who do not or, conversely, by those who are still invested in a politics of dissent and by those who maintain (like the advocates of surface reading) that such investments lie outside the scope of literary criticism.

The political impotence of art and aesthetics—and, presumably, of reading and criticism—under conditions of "real subsumption" has recently been celebrated by Steven Shaviro, who claims that what he calls "accelerationist art" makes good on Kant's formula for the beautiful, "purposiveness without purpose."[30] According to Shaviro, where resistance, transgression, subversion, and presumably revolution are anachronisms of the twentieth century, today all art can hope to do is to "intensify . . . the horrors of contemporary capitalism," not in order to get beyond them or even to better understand their cultural logic, but in a useless, which is to say aesthetic, gesture of empty affirmation. For Shaviro, this strategy at least "offer[s] us a kind of satisfaction and relief, by telling us that we have finally hit bottom, finally realized the worst."[31] And yet, paradoxically, contemporary art, especially the work curated under the guise of Documenta and other massive international art fairs, appears more "political" than ever. As Jameson notes in the interview in this issue, "in a sense, everybody's political. But that does not mean that our 'political' art *works* as politics." The contradiction between the avowed politicality of contemporary art and its apparent purposelessness—or indeed, its intensified circulation as a privileged form of capital—may well confirm Shaviro's point, or it may point us toward some new configuration of aesthetics and politics on the horizon. Jameson adds: "I don't think anybody knows what a successful political—truly political—art would be, one that would have an effect."

Is it possible to insist on the value of looking at art, reading texts, interpreting culture, without detaching form from politics, and without simply finding there the confirmation that things are as bad as they possibly could be? Against such dystopianism, whatever its good intentions, and against reactionary modes of formalism both old and new, we hold onto Jameson's insistence on historicizing, an insistence that keeps the dialectic (i.e., critical negativity) alive, rather than proclaiming its collapse into a airtight world of "real subsumption." After the demise of postmodernism, our issue seeks to regenerate strong interpretive strategies grounded in a philosophy of history.

What can the "formal tendencies" of the contemporary cultural landscape, to borrow Amy Villarejo's term,[32] tell us about political economy today; about history and its foreclosures and possibilities; about class relations and the exploitations that animate them as well as the utopian fantasies they harbor; about the imaginaries that order our world but only incompletely determine its horizons? We maintain that formal analysis need not be formalism, and we remain committed to the notion that form can render insights into the complex cultural conditions that produce it. In the twenty-first century, whether or not we are still "postmodern," it remains possible, and indeed an imperative, to read cultural form and political economy together in their collusions, intersections, codeterminations, and tensions.

Periodizing the Present

For Jameson, the term *postmodernism,* as the prefix *post-* implies, was also a term of periodization. In an article in the *New Left Review,* and again in the interview that appears in this issue, Jameson states that he now thinks the term *postmodernity* is less amenable to misunderstanding.[33] "It would have been much clearer," he says in the interview, "had I distinguished 'postmodernity' as a historical period from 'postmodernism' as a style." Postmodernity is not a precisely delimited historical occurrence but corresponds to the hegemonic conditions, political, economic, and cultural, that we now associate with neoliberalism, conditions that are consolidated, says Jameson, "around 1980 or so, in the Reagan/Thatcher era, with [for example] the advent of economic deregulation, [and] the new salience of globalization." Of course, the point of periodizing, which Jameson has always insisted was both necessary and necessarily inadequate, is not simply to describe or amass data: it does not mean to "recognize [the past] 'the way it really was,'" as Benjamin once put it.[34] To "always historicize!" does not enjoin us to a historicism conceived as an act of simple description. It means, rather, to understand the contingency of a set of conditions that present themselves as timeless and inevitable.

Postmodernity, the term Jameson now favors, is one possible name for the third stage of capitalism. As the story goes, sometime in the 1970s (though Ernest Mandel, it should be noted, dates the emergence of "late capitalism" to the end of WWII),[35] after the end of the Bretton Woods monetary system, and following the dissipation of the political and utopian energies of the 1960s, a new period emerged that no longer seemed adequately described by the word *modernity*. The latter corresponded to monopoly capitalism, the second stage of capitalism theorized by Lenin, marking a shift from the period of market capitalism known by Marx himself to one characterized by imperialism, Fordism, industrialization, and modernism in the arts. We have since moved to and possibly beyond the third stage, where monopolies have further morphed into transnational corporations, and in the era following decolonization, imperialism has been supplanted by new forms of neocolonialism or endocolonialism.

Postmodernity refers as well to a period increasingly dominated by a service, knowledge, or information economy, or what Hardt and Negri have called affective or immaterial labor.[36] It signals an era of finance capital increasingly untethered from production, an economic logic in which capital, as Jameson put it in 1998, "like cyberspace, can live on its own internal metabolism and circulate without any reference to an older type of content."[37] Its exemplary form is the mutant monetary entity known as the derivative. Following Giovanni Arrighi, Jameson reminds us that finance capitalism is a third stage that signals an impending crisis: capital's endless drive to expansion involves conquering or subsuming ever new regions, but once the markets of those new territories become saturated, capital resorts to speculation, leading inevitably to a crisis and a shift in the center of power. Finance capital is, of course, nothing new; as Arrighi points out, it is the third stage in a cycle that has been repeated with a series of centers from Genoa to the Netherlands to Great Britain and, from WWII at least until the end of the twentieth century, the United States.[38]

With the global saturation of capitalism seemingly complete, have we arrived at a breaking point? As Jameson puts it: "With globalization this search for fresh territory would seem to have come to an end, and thus to some well-nigh terminal crisis."[39] Is a new system that can no longer be called capitalist on the horizon? Since 2008, this is not an uncommon claim, as certain prominent left-wing intellectuals including David Graeber, Immanuel Wallerstein, and Paul Mason, and even some right-wing financial journals have argued in recent years, though of course to different ends. Jameson is often fond of reminding us that the end of the world was easier to imagine than the end of capitalism. Today, this remains true but only because the end of the world, namely, the ecological disaster wrought by the Anthropocene, is perhaps all too easy to conjure. Indeed, as Naomi

Klein has insisted, perhaps the end of capitalism is becoming easier to imagine today only because it has become clearer that it may be the only way to prevent the end of the (natural) world.[40]

As for culture in this third stage, the "make it new" of modernism, the provocations of the historical avant-gardes, and an obsession with authentic time and experience have given way, Jameson argued in his famous essay "Postmodernism, or the Cultural Logic of Late Capitalism," to the logic of pastiche and to a time sense increasingly subject to spatialization in an eternal present. The articles we have gathered address these and other formal tendencies that have emerged or been altered in contemporary culture, as well as the persistence of older forms. Sulgi Lie's article "From *Shame* to *Drive*: The Waning of Affect; or, The Rising of the Drive-Image in Contemporary Hollywood Cinema" takes up this idea of a postmodern eternal present and measures it against current formal tendencies through a close reading of two recent Hollywood films: *Shame* (dir. Steve McQueen, 2011) and *Drive* (dir. Nicolas Winding Refn, 2011). Though Hollywood, and indeed cinema itself, are no longer necessarily contemporary "cultural dominants," Lie argues that the zombie-like Hollywood film can yet tell us something about the "political unconscious of contemporary capitalism." Lie revisits Jameson's notion of the "waning of affect" (rephrased, in the interview here, as a shift from emotion to intensities), through the psychoanalytic concepts of desire and drive: according to Lie, *Shame* and *Drive* represent two different ways of managing the contemporary "rising of the drive" and the demise of what he describes as the humanist subject of desire. In both films, the drive is formally inscribed as a stasis or a "presentism": both attest to the loss of historical consciousness that Jameson already diagnosed in the 1980s. (For this reason, the films disclose that the cultural logical of contemporary capitalism is even "more postmodern that the old postmodernity of the 1980s was.") But Lie's reading demonstrates that there are political stakes to competing aesthetic strategies and, indeed, to the way criticism takes the measure of those strategies. It is critical reading that puts the negativity back into a text that otherwise seems to disclose, as Jameson observes in a discussion of Adorno, "an absolute reduction to the present and a mesmerization by the empirically and sensorially existent."[41]

Adorno is also a privileged interlocutor in Amy Villarejo's analysis of television after the digital conversion, "Adorno by the Pool; or, Television Then and Now." In surveying the contemporary media landscape, Villarejo shows how Adorno's analysis of midcentury television offers tools that remain useful well beyond their historical context. Surprisingly, the Frankfurt School theorist becomes, in Villarejo's hands, a kind of queer theorist of the televisual apparatus. Building on the argument of her 2014 book *Ethereal Queer*, she shows how desire and identification are cut to the measure of a televisual time that continues to structure ostensibly *"post-televisual"* media. Villarejo demonstrates how capital's transformations of contemporary television and digital media platforms have produced a "diffuse paraprofessional orbit" in which amateur production takes on a new salience, which in turn enables new forms of queerness to proliferate on large and small screens. This is not, to be sure, simply a form of progress—Villarejo shares Adorno's skepticism about that term. But nor is twenty-first-century televisual queerness merely a symptom of late capital's relentless domestication and appropriation of all aspects of existence. The cultural logic of contemporary capitalism is sufficiently complex and contradictory that it behooves us to remain attentive to its "unpredictable intersections rather than engag[ing] in wholesale dismissals or appraisals." Thus, Villarejo avoids a totalizing cynicism while suggesting that any grand narrative of the present will remain inadequate to the complicated nexuses of culture and capital, identity and difference, desire and its commodification that might form elements of a current cultural logic.

Jameson has frequently suggested that postmodernity might be taken as something close to a synonym of globalization. The discovery that "there is no outside" to global capitalism, as Hardt and Negri claim,[42] meant the continued reach of certain forms of Western, especially American, popular culture over the entire globe, but also that the West was no longer the West. According to Jameson, "the system of Otherness" that had emerged in that second stage of capitalism, the era of colonialism, had given way to "a world of billions of anonymous equals."[43] The initial examples of postmodern symptoms came mostly from the West, but as he expanded his work on a "geopolitical aesthetic" in the 1990s, he located many of the most promising and politically productive examples at the periphery of the world system.[44] In her article in this collection, "Beyond the 'NGO Aesthetic,'" Jennifer Bajorek considers the critical vantage afforded by the periphery at a moment of profound transformation. She explores the possibility of a Marxist cultural analysis from the perspective of West Africa, a putative "last frontier of capitalism" that, as she contends, has "leapfrogged the old, familiar forms of industrial production and of social organization." Through the work of Nairobi-based artist, Sam Hopkins and the Urban Mirror collective, Bajorek explores the trope of the "NGO aesthetic," a term used by Hopkins, to examine Africa's situatedness within a contemporary global economy. These are examples of what she calls "spatial tactics," through which these artists plot, adapt to, and make productive use of the conditions that derive from Euro-American economic and political power, variously manifested through international aid efforts, uneven commercial development, regular power shortages, digital infrastructures, and reconfigured public and private divisions in corporate holdings and urban development schemes.

An analysis of cultural logic primarily from the vantage point of the West, argues Bajorek, remains inadequate to contemporary conditions.

With "The World Is Already without Us," Alberto Toscano dilates the critical purview from a global to a planetary perspective. He challenges the periodizing concept of the Anthropocene, "this strange new name for our present" that, in subsuming all events under a geologic time scale, collapses human history into a natural event. (The end of nature, a related but not identical concept, was previously theorized by Jameson under the sign of postmodernity, when the full saturation of capitalism left no residual spaces outside of modernity.) As Toscano argues, narratives of the Anthropocene tend to exclude human activity, namely, politics and history, even as they privilege mankind as a "geological agent," quoting anarchist geographer Elisée Reclus. Tellingly, capital is absent in such notions of the Anthropocene, and Toscano, via Jameson's reading of Marx, links its occlusion to the operations of capitalism itself, which erases the traces of the past as historical occurrences, though the material remnants of past production remain. Capitalism, for Toscano, produces a "violently endless present" increasingly, though imperceptibly, occupied by dead labor: the replacement of living, human labor with machines. He reads the aesthetic trope of depopulation in the manufactured landscape photography of Lewis Baltz and Edward Burtynsky as antonymic indicators of capital's tendency to disappear itself. According to Toscano, such images reflect an ideology embedded within the natural sciences–derived notion of the Anthropocene. He describes this, following Jameson following Sartre, as an "antipraxis": "man altered, alienated by man-altered landscapes, in which all praxis seems to be snuffed out, abstracted, extinguished." In lieu of the term *Anthropocene*, Toscano favors Jason W. Moore's *Capitalocene*, which restores capitalism, instead of ecological disaster or human agency, as the central agent in historical change. Though, as he notes, the Marxist subject of history has become one of "tired mockery," replaced by the Anthropocene's subject of nature and other theoretical currents, the task of comprehending it remains politically and intellectually urgent.

It was one of the strengths of Jameson's analysis of postmodernism to consider theory itself as a symptom of the cultural logic it sought to analyze. Whether through theories of technology and new media, affect theory, theories of biopolitics and control, posthumanism, speculative realism, or accelerationism, recent philosophy has seen a turn away from critique and historicization in favor of an increasing focus on a non-Marxist form of materialism frequently framed in metaphysical terms. The theory of the Anthropocene is one example of contemporary theory that questions the distinction between nature and history that was so central to the tradition of Marxist thought exemplified by Jameson. Despite its weakness as a political slogan, as demonstrated by Toscano, it should remind us that the ontological turn in recent theory is by no means necessarily antipolitical. Quentin Meillassoux, perhaps the most influential figure in the new related movements of speculative realism and object-oriented ontology, is deeply indebted to his former teacher Alain Badiou, whose return to ontology has been in the service of a militant philosophy of the event. Meanwhile, one of the major activist theoretical texts of the recent decades, Hardt and Negri's *Empire*, rereads Marx through a Spinozist and Deleuzian ontology. On the one hand, some of these latest philosophical trends can be recognized as what Jameson has called "regressions of the current age"[45] in which pre-Marxist modes of thought are repackaged with new names. On the other hand, we must consider seriously whether some of these shifts constitute a necessary attempt to cognitively map our current moment of global capitalism, which permits no outside perspective.

In "History Is What Hurts: On Old Materialism," Alexander Galloway suggests that these new materialist philosophies call for a rethinking of "old materialism," namely, the historical materialist methodology that characterizes Jameson's writings. Rather than simply pitting historical materialism as practiced by Jameson against the idealisms of metaphysics, Galloway asks instead whether an ontology underpins Jameson's relentlessly dialectical writings, however much Jameson himself might resist the term. As Jameson himself frankly acknowledges in the interview in this issue, escaping metaphysics is easier said than done, and what gets thrown out the front door tends to creep back in through the window. Engaging with over four decades of Jameson's writings, from *Marxism and Form* (1971) up through the present, Galloway unpacks the unwavering commitment to dialectical thought, critique, and interpretation and reveals a methodology firmly marked by a modern (as opposed to postmodern) paradigm of critical and historical thought that always returns to the question of ground, or what Jameson called in *The Political Unconscious* the "absolute horizon" of the political. Having elsewhere analyzed the affinity between the ontologies of various new materialist philosophers and post-Fordist capitalism, here Galloway probes the Marxian materialism that helped shape his own intellectual trajectory and locates its difference from new materialism in its axiomatic commitment to thinking the conditions of possibility for ideology and politics.

This commitment is on full display in Jonathan Beller's wide-ranging and polemical survey of contemporary theory and the fate of postmodernism, "Texas-(S)ized Postmodernism; or, Capitalism without the Dialectic." Postmodernism, Beller argues, has lost its cachet not because it has ended but rather because it has been fully realized. The current moment is an intensification of postmodernism, but Jameson's analysis had yet to come to terms with the full implications of post-Fordist digital culture.

Mounting an impassioned argument for a revitalized Marxist cultural criticism and a renewed poststructuralism and postcolonialism adequate to our current moment of what he calls "computational capital," Beller also insists, in an implicit critique of Jameson, on the centrality of race and gender to political economy. Referring to Cedric Robinson's *Black Marxism* and Silvia Federici's "Wages against Housework," he argues that race and gender should not compete with the analysis of class, nor should they be added on to it; rather, they are constitutive of capitalism from the very start: "Maybe those who ply (and play against) the institutional and para-institutional spaces of theory might study these phrases: racial capitalism, sex/gender capitalism. They may provide tools to subvert the whitewashing of the revolutionary theory commons; they insist upon dialogue."

As these articles collectively attest, new configurations of race, gender and sexuality, information, and ecology in the twenty-first century offer critical vantage points for exploring the cultural logic of contemporary capitalism, in which they are complexly privileged terms. But their centrality to our contemporary cultural logic does not mean that they wear their meanings on their sleeve. David L. Eng, for example, has shown how a certain liberal narrative in the US maintains that the public sphere is "color-blind."[46] To challenge such narratives—to understand them as, yes, *symptomatic* of the cultural logic of contemporary capitalism—means to venture beyond "what is evident, perceptible, apprehensible in texts; what is neither hidden nor hiding."[47] Maintaining a skeptical distance from the shiny surfaces of what we still want to call postmodernity, the articles that follow aim, from a range of critical perspectives and with diverse investments, to reactivate the question of the relation of cultural and aesthetic forms to economic and political conditions, in a global context and with an eye to periodization. In so doing, they revisit, but also redefine, the possibilities for a Marxist mode of cultural analysis—in other words, for a political critique of culture.

The reason it seems to us that Jameson's *Postmodernism*—unlike the term itself—is not in fact dated is that, like Walter Benjamin's "The Work of Art in the Age of Its Technological Reproducibility," half a century earlier, it is fully aware of its own historicity. In addition to mapping emergent phenomena in the then-current moment, Jameson also maintains an eye toward what remains to be thought and is not yet fully understood: the "empty chair reserved for some as yet unrealized, collective, and decentered cultural production of the future."[48] It was with this attentiveness to historicity in mind that we organized this special issue, to sketch the variegated contours of the current cultural landscape and to reinstate the future as an open question.

The articles here do not deliver a unified analysis of a singular cultural logic. They do, however, all acknowledge that the contours of such a logic, or logics, are defined by the inexorability of contemporary global capital. And they put politics at the center of their sophisticated practices of reading. Far from presenting a unified view, the aim of this issue is to examine these questions from a range of disciplines, national locations, and critical perspectives, taking the anniversary of Jameson's postmodernism essay as an occasion to reflect, in short, on the function of criticism in the humanities today.

Notes

1. Badiou, *Second Manifesto for Philosophy*, 5.

2. Mezzadra and Neilson, *Border as Method*, 80–81. This list is referenced by Fredric Jameson in the interview in this issue.

3. Franklin, *Control*, xiii.

4. We might recall here Jameson's words of caution regarding a similar "frenzy": "The frenzy whereby virtually anything in the present is appealed to for testimony as to the latter's uniqueness and radical difference from earlier moments of human time does indeed strike one sometimes as harboring a pathology distinctly autoreferential, as though our utter forgetfulness of the past exhausted itself in the vacant but mesmerized contemplation of a schizophrenic present." *Postmodernism*, xii.

5. The decline of *postmodernism* seems to have coincided roughly with the turn of the millennium—if not specifically with 11 September 2001. It took less than two weeks following 9/11 for a writer for the *New York Times* to declare the end of the legitimacy of not only postmodernism but also postcolonialism. See Rothstein, "Attacks on U.S. Challenge Postmodern True Believers." According to Rothstein, both pomo and poco, as he abbreviated them, were philosophies dictated by moral relativism, and 9/11 (we all surely agreed) was no time for moral relativism. Tellingly, Rothstein's examples, from Edward Said and unnamed others, did not, as he supposed, corroborate the accusation of relativism. On the contrary, the unpardonable sin of these thinkers was that they denied American exceptionalism by considering the violent history of American foreign policy in their concerns for how the US government would respond to the attacks on the World Trade Center and the Pentagon.

6. For example, in the last decade, the journal *Twentieth Century Literature* has put out two special issues dedicated to the end of postmodernism: *After Postmodernism: Form and History in Contemporary American Fiction* (vol. 53, no. 3, 2007) and *Postmodernism, Then* (vol. 57, nos. 3–4, 2011); and while essays in both these issues refer liberally to Jameson, postmodernism is understood most prominently here as a literary style associated with irony, self-referentiality, and textual play.

7. While the use of the term *postmodern* within the arts has a stronger pedigree, the conflation of postmodernism with poststructuralism and, even more incoherent, with cultural Marxism has been one of its more vexing misappropriations.

8. Jameson, *Cultural Turn*, 33.

9. Jameson himself was never convinced by the lateness of so-called late capitalism but used the term merely to signal his debt to Ernest Mandel, whose book of that title was an early attempt to frame the parameters of capitalism's "third stage" (see below).

10. Williams, *Marxism and Literature*, 128–35.

11. Rancière, *Politics of Aesthetics*, 12–13.

12. Stiegler, *Catastrophe of the Sensible*, 175.

13. Jameson, *Cultural Turn*, 55.

14. Ibid., 35.

15. Franklin, *Control*, 15.

16. Best and Marcus, "Surface Reading," 5–6, 17, 15. The authors begin their analysis with the claim that the collection "represent[s] neither a polemic against nor a postmortem of symptomatic reading" (3). This is perhaps to reassure us that they are performing the respect and modesty as critics they are advocating for, all evidence to the contrary, at least where Jameson is concerned. Nonetheless, the polite surface of their text betrays a deeper investment in the demise of a "symptomatic reading" they render in caricatural terms.

17. Ibid., 16.

18. Ibid., 11.

19. Ellen Rooney makes a similar point in "Live Free or Describe." She focuses in particular on what she sees as Best and Marcus's misreading of Althusser's conception of symptomatic reading, though she also says, "Jameson's critical impact appears in some way to be the privileged object" (125).

20. Apter and Freedgood, "Afterword," 142–43.

21. Benjamin, "On the Concept of History," 396.

22. Wiegman and Wilson, "Introduction," 12.

23. Ibid., 17.

24. Love, "Doing Being Deviant," 78. (Our questioning of this move does not detract from our appreciation for Love's larger contributions to precisely the political critique of culture.) For two sharp retorts to the special issue's challenge to politicized queer theory, see Jack Halberstam, "Straight Eye for the Queer Theorist," and Lisa Duggan, "Queer Complacency without Empire," on the *Bully Bloggers* site. For a still timely critique of the "descriptive" in post-WWII sociology, see Ferguson, *Aberrations in Black*.

25. Moretti, *Distant Reading*, 47–49.

26. "Reparative reading," which Best and Marcus claim for the camp of surface readers, is what Eve Sedgwick counterposed to "paranoid"—or symptomatic—reading, in an essay ("Paranoid Reading and Reparative Reading") that is itself a masterpiece of paranoia. Like all influential concepts, Sedgwick's "reparative reading" has been taken up in a variety of ways and can thus be described, quite literally, as generative. We would submit, however, that the ethical stance of reading it propounds cannot itself be simply taken at face value, not only because it patently performs the very aggressiveness and suspiciousness it disavows, but also because its emphasis on precisely an ethics of reading (rendered in personalizing and psychologizing terms) tends to displace the question of the political. For a smart discussion, see Love, "Truth and Consequences."

27. McCarthy, "Film and Mass Culture," 131.

28. Jameson, *Postmodernism*, xvii.

29. Min, "Aesthetics," 27.

30. Shaviro, "Accelerationist Aesthetics." In an interestingly counterposed argument, Jacques Rancière has also recently returned to Kant to suggest that the discourse of art as it emerged in German romanticism has an egalitarian core, namely, that its purposelessness or uselessness for practical life is an enabling condition of its political dimension. See Rancière, "The Aesthetic Dimension: Aesthetics, Politics, Knowledge."

31. Shaviro, "Accelerationist Aesthetics."

32. Villarejo, *Film Studies*, 149.

33. Jameson, "Aesthetics of Singularity."

34. Benjamin, "On the Concept of History," 391.

35. Mandel, *Late Capitalism*, 11.

36. Hardt and Negri, *Empire*, 292.

37. Jameson, *Cultural Turn*, 161.

38. Arrighi, *Long Twentieth Century*, 27–84.

39. Jameson, "Aesthetics of Singularity," 92, 116.

40. Klein, *This Changes Everything*.

41. Jameson, *Antinomies of Realism*, 300.

42. Hardt and Negri, *Empire*, 190.

43. Jameson, "Aesthetics of Singularity," 130.

44. See Jameson, *Geopolitical Aesthetic*. It should also be noted that the formulation of Jameson's initial conception of postmodernism, as Perry Anderson pointed out at the time, emerged through an engagement with international audiences. Following a talk at the Whitney Museum in 1982 called "Postmodernism and Consumer Society," "Jameson first set out his ideas on postmodernism comprehensively in a lecture course in Beijing in 1985, and published a collection on the subject in China some years before he produced one in America. His account of 'Postmodernism and the Market' was tested out in Seoul. We owe the major text on 'Transformations of the Image' to an address in Caracas. Settings like these were not a matter of chance. Jameson's theory of postmodernity has won a growing audience in countries once of the Third or Second World." Anderson, *Origins of Postmodernity*, 75.

45. Jameson, *Singular Modernity*, 1.

46. Eng, *Feeling of Kinship*.

47. Best and Marcus, "Surface Reading," 9.

48. Jameson, *Political Unconscious*, 11.

References

Anderson, Perry. 1998. *The Origins of Postmodernity*. New York: Verso.

Apter, Emily, and Elaine Freedgood. 2009. "Afterword." *Representations* 108: 139–46.

Arrighi, Giovanni. 1994. *The Long Twentieth Century: Money, Power, and the Origins of Our Times*. New York: Verso.

Badiou, Alain. 2011. *Second Manifesto for Philosophy*. Translated by Louise Burchill. London: Polity.

Benjamin, Walter. 2002. "The Work of Art in the Age of Its Technological Reproducibility: Second Version." In *Selected Writings*, vol. 3. Translated by Edmund Jephcott et al. Edited by Howard Eiland and Michael W. Jennings, 101–33. Cambridge, MA: Harvard University Press.

Benjamin, Walter. 2003. "On the Concept of History." In *Selected Writings*, vol. 4. Translated by Edmund Jephcott et al. Edited by Howard Eiland and Michael W. Jennings, 389–400. Cambridge, MA: Harvard University Press.

Berardi, Franco. 2009. *Precarious Rhapsody: Semiocapitalism and the Pathologies of the Post-Alpha Generation*. Translated by Arianna Bove, Erik Empson, Michael Goddard, Giuseppina Mecchia, Antonella Schintu, and Steve Wright. London: Autonomedia.

Best, Stephen, and Sharon Marcus. 2009. "Surface Reading: An Introduction." *Representations* 108: 1–23.

Duggan, Lisa. 2015. "Queer Complacency without Empire." *Bully Bloggers*, 22 September. bullybloggers.wordpress.com/2015/09/22/queer-complacency-without-empire.

Eng, David, L. 2010. *The Feeling of Kinship: Queer Liberalism and the Racialization of Intimacy*. Durham, NC: Duke University Press.

Ferguson, Roderick A. 2003. *Aberrations in Black: Toward a Queer of Color Critique*. Minneapolis: University of Minnesota Press.

Franklin, Seb. 2015. *Control: Digitality as Cultural Logic*. Cambridge, MA: MIT Press.

Halberstam, Jack. 2015. "Straight Eye for the Queer Theorist." *Bully Bloggers*, 12 September. bullybloggers.wordpress.com/2015/09/12/straight-eye-for-the-queer -theorist-a-review-of-queer-theory-without-antinormativity-by-jack-halberstam.

Hardt, Michael, and Antonio Negri. 2000. *Empire*. Cambridge, MA: Harvard University Press.

Jameson, Fredric. 1981. *The Political Unconscious*. London: Verso.

Jameson, Fredric. 1984. "Postmodernism, or the Cultural Logic of Late Capitalism." *New Left Review* 146: 53–92.

Jameson, Fredric. 1991. *Postmodernism; or, The Cultural Logic of Late Capitalism*. Durham, NC: Duke University Press.

Jameson, Fredric. 1992. *Geopolitical Aesthetic: Cinema and Space in the World System*. Indianapolis: Indiana University Press.

Jameson, Fredric. 1998. *The Cultural Turn: Selected Writings on the Postmodern, 1983–1998*. New York: Verso.

Jameson, Fredric. 2002. *A Singular Modernity: Essay on the Ontology of the Present*. New York: Verso.

Jameson, Fredric. 2013. *Antinomies of Realism*. New York: Verso

Jameson, Fredric. 2015. "The Aesthetics of Singularity." *New Left Review* 92: 101–32.

Klein, Naomi. 2014. *This Changes Everything: Capitalism versus the Climate*. New York: Simon and Shuster.

Love, Heather. 2010. "Truth and Consequences: On Paranoid Reading and Reparative Reading." *Criticism* 52, no. 2: 235–41.

Love, Heather. 2015. "Doing Being Deviant: Deviance Studies, Description, and the Queer Ordinary." *differences* 26, no. 1: 74–95.

Mandel, Ernest. 1975. *Late Capitalism*. Translated by Joris de Bres. London: NLB.

McCarthy, Anna. Fall 2009. "Film and Mass Culture." *Social Text 100* 27, no. 3: 129–33.

Mezzadra, Sandro, and Brett Neilson. 2013. *Border as Method; or, The Multiplication of Labor*. Durham, NC: Duke University Press.

Min, Susette. 2009. "Aesthetics." *Social Text 100* 27, no. 3: 27–34.

Moretti, Franco. 2016. *Distant Reading*. New York: Verso.

Piketty, Thomas. 2013. *Capital in the Twenty-First Century*. Translated by Arthur Goldhammer. Cambridge, MA: Harvard University Press.

Rancière, Jacques. 2004. *The Politics of Aesthetics: The Distribution of the Sensible*. Translated by Gabriel Rockhill. New York: Continuum.

Rancière, Jacques. 2009. "The Aesthetic Dimension: Aesthetics, Politics, Knowledge." *Critical Inquiry* 36, no. 1: 1–19.

Rooney, Ellen. 2010. "Live Free or Describe: The Reading Effect and the Persistence of Form." *differences* 21, no. 3: 112–39.

Rothstein, Edward. "Attacks on U.S. Challenge Postmodern True Believers." *New York Times*, 22 September 2001.

Sedgwick, Eve. 2003. "Paranoid Reading and Reparative Reading; or, You're So Vain, You Probably Think This Essay Is about You." In *Touching, Feeling: Affect, Pedagogy, Performativity*, 123–52. Durham, NC: Duke University Press.

Shaviro, Steven. 2013. "Accelerationist Aesthetics: Necessary Inefficiency in Times of Real Subsumption." *e-flux*, no. 46. www.e-flux.com/journal/accelerationist-aesthetics-necessary-inefficiency-in-times-of-real-subsumption.

Stiegler, Bernard. 2014. *Symbolic Misery Volume 1: The Hyperindustrial Epoch*. Translated by Barnaby Norman. London: Polity.

Stiegler, Bernard. 2015. *The Catastrophe of the Sensible*. Vol. 2 of *Symbolic Misery*. Malden, MA: Polity.

Villarejo, Amy. 2013. *Film Studies: The Basics*. 2nd ed. New York: Routledge.

Villarejo, Amy. 2014. *Ethereal Queer: Television, Historicity, Desire*. Durham, NC: Duke University Press.

Wiegman, Robyn, and Elizabeth A. Wilson. 2015. "Introduction: Antinormativity's Queer Conventions." *differences* 26, no. 1: 1–25.

Williams, Raymond. 1977. *Marxism and Literature*. Oxford: Oxford University Press.

Texas-(S)ized Postmodernism

or, Capitalism without the Dialectic

Jonathan Beller

> The rhetorical strategy of the preceding [418] pages has involved
> an experiment, namely, the attempt to see whether by systematizing
> something that is resolutely unsystematic, and historicizing something
> that is resolutely ahistorical, one couldn't outflank it and force a
> historical way at least of thinking about that. "We have to name the
> system": this high point of the sixties finds an unexpected revival in
> the postmodernism debate.
> —Fredric Jameson, *Postmodernism;*
> *or, The Cultural Logic of Late Capitalism*

Rendered critical in large part because Fredric Jameson so deftly crafted
its reception as necessarily theoretical, postmodernism has, for all that,
lost its pizzazz. However, the apparent insolvency of this name for a cultural sea change that, because its author was History, intractably posed
demands for the reconceptualization of nearly everything, means neither
that postmodernism itself (or what would be the referent of the term) has
disappeared, nor that the periodizing rupture with modernism that its
gradual emergence and conceptualization signaled either did not occur
or was mistaken. Rather, as the n-grams below might suggest, the word
postmodernism has gone the way of another key word—a waning that, one
might suspect, has everything to do with persistence by other means.

    A consideration of the currency graphs (below) of the words *post-
modernism* and *capitalism* shows that *capitalism* is noticeably down from
its peak circulation in 1980, the date that, not coincidently, coincides with
the discursive eruption of *postmodernism*. Like an early tech stock, *postmodernism*, following on its IPO, continued its rapid ascent into the late

Social Text 127 · Vol. 34, No. 2 · June 2016
DOI 10.1215/01642472-3467954 © 2016 Duke University Press

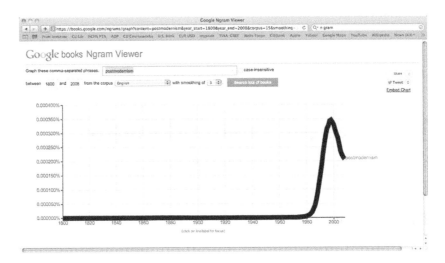

Figure 1. Google n-gram search screenshot, "Postmodernism"

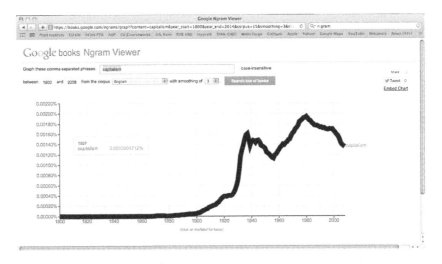

Figure 2. Google n-gram search screenshot, "Capitalism"

1990s even as the frequency of the appearance of the word *capitalism* slightly declined. And then, as the increased downward slope in the early 2000s indicates (one suspects that the dot.com bubble burst and 9/11 have something to do with this loss of interest), the frequency of the occurrence of both terms drops off steeply. Although the term *capitalism* occurs an order of magnitude more frequently than *postmodernism* (approximately 0.002 percent vs. 0.0002 percent), by 2000–2001 the frequency of the word *capitalism* is down to around its prior peak, 1929 levels—writing about capitalism declined back to the level of interest left to us in the wake of the Great Depression. This decrease in the usage of both terms occurs despite the fact that almost no one who would have published both words in the same essay believed, then or now, that capitalism is going away. Could it be, then, that the popular English-language books and articles written about the likes of postmodernism and capitalism were gradually transformed into publications weaving the mythos of tech and/or soul-searching opinion pieces around the so-poignant theme "why do they hate us?" What might it mean to suggest that today articles about capitalism and postmodernism are being written as articles about social media and the security state?

It is important to note that this terminological drift is not a matter of mere indifference, or mere technics, but a matter of history and politics. Indeed, the frequency of the occurrence of the word *capitalism* in English has been actively legislated downward. It is no secret (except from besieged students who are at once the primary target audience and among the victims of the situation) that, as in some religions in which it is impermissible to utter the name of God, *capitalism* has been banned in Texas public school history books by the Texas state legislature. In June 2012 the Texas State Board of Education decreed that the use of the word *capitalism*, because of its negative connotations, shall be banned in public school textbooks and that in all instances the word should be replaced with the palliative phrase *free enterprise system*.[1] As the incontrovertible logic behind the $1 billion textbook producers' ready market capitulation to this decree (a capitulation that, because of the massive distribution of these books, affects public education in more than a dozen states) might nicely illustrate to those who can still read, such a state-legislated dissolution of potentially critical terms is precisely one of the means by which, uhm, the "free enterprise system" functions—or is it "functions"? Beyond the banning of books (another Texan and American pastime), there is the banning of actual words in reportedly actual (Texas-shaped) history textbooks and, with that, the attempt to foreclose the younger generations' capacity to conceptualize the world situation that confronts them.

Indeed, some members of the Texas State Board of Education (the latter word belongs in quotation marks) want to take this obfuscation strategy a step further and require that slavery too no longer be mentioned in public school textbooks and that any reference to the slave trade will forthwith be called the "Atlantic triangular trade." This omission is particularly goat-getting since, as Roxanne Dunbar-Ortiz's *An Indigenous Peoples' History of the United States* tells us, Texas seceded from Mexico only after Mexico abolished slavery in 1829 and refused large Anglo landholders their "right" to continue to own slaves despite their petition to pursue their quest for plantation wealth using enslaved Africans. "They lobbied the Mexican government for a reversal of the ban and gained only a one-year extension to settle their affairs and free their bonded workers—

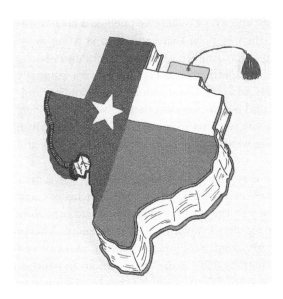

Figure 3. A textbook shaped like the state of Texas. See Isensee, "Texas Hits the Books." Image: LA Johnson/NPR

the government refused to legalize slavery. The settlers decided to secede from Mexico initiating the famous and mythologized 1836 Battle of the Alamo."[2] The disbelief produced in the historically minded (I mean "sane," for how can one study the history of a land founded on slavery and capitalism in the absence of the terms *slavery* and *capitalism*) by such grotesque cynicism makes one thing clear: Texas has taken a page out of the Orwellian playbook.[3] Totalitarianism functions by narrowing the range of thought. It liquidates history in the effort to stop time at a particular moment of hierarchical domination. Doublethink or no, rich Texans and their policy makers understand in practice that the role of their educational Ideological State Apparatus (ISA) is to produce a subject who works: the autopoesis of capitalism requires—that is, legally requires—the instrumental misrecognition of capitalism or, in other words, systematically produced stupidity.[4]

According to one only slightly exaggerated report: "In Texas, students will now be taught that slaves were not kidnapped and exploited against their will, but were actually 'unpaid interns.' 'While African workers were not compensated monetarily,' the new curriculum guidelines acknowledge, 'by working outside picking cotton, they gained valuable career experience and were provided with ample networking opportunities.'"[5] The pathological (indeed, psychopathological) absurdity of the erasure of capitalism and slavery (its history, inequality, and immeasurable violence) is here audible in a kind of *Onion*-esque Steven Colbertian hysteria. But the everyday erasure that includes the erasure of social struggle and the achievements of those striving to overcome domination means intellectual and aesthetic impoverishment through the active excoriation of the people's fundamental capacities to understand the dire stakes in the study of history—to say nothing of the study of culture, politics, and art. The once unfamiliar encounter with absurd textual practice that characterizes everyday life in the Texas classroom might have appeared only a few years ago as itself a properly postmodern bit of pastiche or blank irony, a mixing of free-floating signifiers that resulted in a form of schlock to be momentarily savored before being critically cast as symptomatic of, say, "the waning of historicity." And were it not for the waning of the sensory-affective component of a postmodernism that was both a name for a radically dehistoricizing cultural transformation and a Marxist theoretical concept that thematized history's increasingly auratic character emerging under the inexorable intensification of commodification, it still might be. At least it might be if the state had not itself been leaning on that deracinating, ahistoricizing blank-irony affect button to become one of the principal authors of pastiche and outright farce. Today farce is the very language of state power—an index of postmodern fascism.[6]

The presence of history as guarantor of traditional sense making (reason) has been going the way of Benjamin's aura, "the unique phenomenon of distance" between a given subject (a natural or historical object), for some time (toward commodity fetishism and thus spectacle, I'd say)[7]—glimpsed as it waned in the scrambled cut-n-mix meltdown of capitalized new media's global warming and recirculation of signs. The severance from "authenticity" seems at once complete and completely commodified. Three decades ago the periodizing concept of postmodernism allowed us to critically remark upon the historical disappearance of history despite the maelstrom of the repurposed space-time, affect, metaphysics, and (non)meanings of signs. Postmodernism was thus also a new type of feeling, a brush with the sublime of the "totality" that was registered in relation to the palpable perception of the evacuation of the admittedly unsymbolizable but nonetheless operative function of the Real, of the world system, of History. In a kind of intellectual bravura the concept *postmodernism* anchored simulation and virtuality to real historical process. It registered, in short, a reconstitution of knowledge via a somewhat blasé yet nonetheless enthusiastically comprehensive intellectual disposition precisely calibrated to be adequate to the now regular and unimaginably frequent experience of radical disjuncture and modern shock, and nonetheless rigorously organized through a stalwart intention to diagnose, transcode, and map. If Benjamin's waning of aura signaled the transformed perceptual dimension resulting from the liquidation of tradition and of cult brought about by the democratically aspiring potentials of technological reproducibility, along with the emergence of a set of tools to make political use of the transformation of the status and function of the work of art, then *postmodernism* signaled the new aesthetic and theoretical landscape resulting from the waning of historicity and the reformatting of culture by late capitalism. It marked and recoded the fading legibility of the contradictory record of sociality and struggle that was inscribed in the world of things by their mode of production, and it provided a riposte to the jamming of the interpretive signals, one that might communicate a dialectical knowledge of cultural forms and thus the reasons for and histories of these struggles. It historicized. The intensifying jamming of the channels of history, channels that were the very media of the proletarian revolution, has been coordinated by the same fetisistic forces of capitalism that had overtaken the democratically aspiring technologies of mechanical reproduction, particularly the cinema, that Benjamin saw "violated" and bent to the purposes of the "Fuhrer cult" by the star system.[8] Under the domination of capital, cinema did not become Vertovian but Reifenstahlian and Hollywoodized; it was made to function in service of the cults of Aryan humanism and personality. Benjamin's theses in "The Work of Art," which debunked creativity, eternal mystery, and genius, were also and self-consciously "weapons" against the "processing of data in the fascist sense" that these (outmoded) concepts for the understanding of art regularly accomplished.[9]

With postmodernism, history was bent to window dressing, and in our own day *postmodernism* itself falls under the historical erasure it was, as a Jamesonian concept at least, bent upon interrogating. The term provided a critical framework for the reception and analysis of the disappearance of metaphysical notions and therefore also of the material underpinnings of the social that nonetheless secured a relation to value, reality, history, and political praxis. *Neoliberalism, security state,* and *social media* are some of the current terms that serve as periodizing markers, but after twenty-five years of Western governments acting as if Samuel Huntington's Islamophobic policy statement "Clash of Civilizations"[10] contained in fact an essential truth that now has properly resulted in what was promised with icy glee to be an indefinite if not eternal War on Terror, no one seems particularly worried about periodization. Under digital culture, it often seems that the militarizing forces of commodification and dehistoricization have won a complete victory. With the waning even of the feeling of waning, and when the channels of history are left to the History Channel, then perhaps it really is true: upon encountering Texas textbooks of the kind mentioned above we no longer *really* feel "postmodernism." As my Althusserian allusion ("yes, it's *really* me") is meant to imply, the fact that we're not feelin' it means also that we are no longer subjected by postmodernism. But there are many who still feel the fascism. What to do with that feeling, particularly as it emerges as the enduring trait of the cultural dominant?

The analytic framework may no longer function, but the problematic remains. We do, however, confront a different moment, a transformed role for the work of theory and for the logistics of subjectification. To my mind, Jameson's great theoretical acumen relies at least as much on his extraordinary attention to form as it does on his unparalleled erudition. *Form*: "an ideology in its own right." The question of what to do with culture (and who is going to do it) is still a relevant one, particularly as culture is no longer epiphenomenal to the economy (if it ever was); rather, following on the theories of postmodernism and in accord with theories of attention economy, virtuosity, neuropower, and post-Fordism, culture has itself become a means of production. This change, *culture as a means of production within the framework of global capitalism*, was the shift in the mode of production that postmodernism, as a periodizing concept, first, if incompletely, grasped, and it is part of the problematic that confronts every would-be revolution today. Because much if not all culture making and cultural change retain something that, for the purposes of avoiding a long detour, we might hypostasize as a drive toward freedom, and indeed, while part of making involves conformity and convention, there is another element that is in close allegiance to transgression, insurrection, revolution, and communism. In today's transformed milieu, where mass culture, but also cultures, activism, and even theory, is caught in the inexorable undertow of financialization such that these pursuits also become vectors of value-extractive capitalization, *postmodernism*, like the subject itself, experiences its aphanisis. The fading of our previous period's name for its most symptomatic cultural production, whose constant if disjuncted epithet was "the cultural logic of late capitalism" (a moniker that, as Jameson taught us, was shorthand both for the transformed field of operations of late capitalism and for the formal operations themselves), in no way means that this logic of the orchestration of form by capital, which included the spatialization of linear time and flattening out of language, has abated. It has only intensified.

The technical implementation of a cultural logic that had consequences for not only sign function but also for narrative, the metaphysics of "the real," temporality, affect, and historicity continues to intensify, and indeed, it is my argument here that in a late capitalism grown even later, the disappearance of *postmodernism* marks the completion or full realization of many of the negative dimensions of this particular -ism. Postmodernism has delivered on its own threat. The crisis marked by postmodernism was not only a historical crisis; it was also the crisis of history or, rather, of its disappearance. As a heuristic device, we might add that, in postmodernism, history also always occurs twice, the first time as history, the second time as farce, with the caveat that farce is among the strategies by which history is prevented from occurring (to anyone) at all. The crisis marked by postmodernism completes itself through its own disappearance even as the very role of education, whether in the hands of large numbers of Texans or large numbers of "theorists," takes on a farcical turn.

What this means is that in order to continue to occur, postmodern-ism (or, the cultural logic of late capitalism) no longer occurs to anyone—it is history, as they say. But occur it does (and this next, to put a point on a position that I have already indicated above, is the other great sociocul-tural transformation only incompletely grasped in the theories of post-modern proper), particularly as culture has itself been seized upon by capital directly as a means of production. That perhaps is the real les-son of theories of attention economies, cognitive capitalism, virtuosity, playbor, neuropower, and the various post-Fordisms, all of which taken together could and perhaps should be understood as efforts to write the political economy of the postmodern as the financialization of culture.

Now that capital's matrix of operations is so fully dissolved in the world that its metabolic processes operate in every discursive and repre-sentational pore, not merely as superstructural symptom or free-floating commodity but as deterritorialized (social) factory; now, in short, that the capitalist state, which as the aspirations of the National Security Agency (or at least the revelations of Edward Snowden) make abundantly clear, is nearly on a continuum with social media (a term that, as I've said else-where, should always be written with a hyphen); and now that the state through its farcical utterances has shown itself to be a contender for the poet laureate of digital culture's so-called War on Terror, the waning of the periodizing concept *postmodernity* presents an occasion that ought to be clearly marked as well as theorized. Just as capitalism tends to disappear *capitalism*, postmodernism tends to disappear *postmodernism*. Without a doubt, this disappearance, a kind of discursive tactics, is a component of what Paolo Virno[11] identifies as "virtuosity," the moment-to-moment production and reproduction of capitalist society via the expropriation of the cognitive-linguistic capacities of the species. Paradoxically, in the case of both capitalism and postmodernism, the waning of the concept serves as proof of concept, which, though it should bring no particular satisfac-tion, also serves as a confirmation of both the Marcusean and Orwellian positions on the wholesale relationship of language to a fascism that is, not coincidentally, capitalist and totalitarian—and is, as importantly, through the negation of negation, the ongoing, historical negation of communism.

The death of the master narrative, Jean-François Lyotard's particu-lar claim about postmodernity, was also paradoxical in that here was the master narrative to end all master narratives. The death of the master nar-rative was, in short, the greatest story ever told, at least during that brief era, despite the fact that it still did not sell as many copies as the Bible. As it turns out, though no one feels the need to talk of it anymore, this thesis on capital's synthesis of its antithesis was also correct: we have no more master narratives, and in some respect few strong narratives of the kind that have the representational function of creating distance and a space for history-making reflection. Rather, with the foreclosure (or forestalling) of the dialectic, we have emanating from its various black holes fundamentalisms and psychosis and, in the particular genre of Marxist and post-Marxist critique—the limits of which I will come to momentarily—the following. Macropolitically, we have what Virno acerbically calls "the communism of capital," or, what Franco Berardi imagines as an "after the future," a condition that understands the totalizing historical narrative as itself a means of expropriation.[12] In Paul Virilio's terms we have, macropolitically, the markedly atemporal global "administration of fear."[13] Micropolitically, we have pathways through the database, speculative assemblages designed to configure the data flow in which we swim or drown in an intelligible way. We have McKenzie Wark's vectoral class, or, as in Hiroki Azuma's great book *Otaku*, we have "otaku culture" and (from Kojeve) "animalization," a kind of nonreflective, reality-disavowing, consumerist seeking of stimulation and intensities.[14]

If postmodernism was the concept that historicized the waning of historicity, its disappearance means that the dialectical critical practice enabling historicization is itself increasingly foreclosed. Today, consumers cannot even understand the labels that would explain what they are eating, so perhaps it is no surprise that suddenly we only hear the once resounding imperative "Always historicize," in the audio equivalent of an inverted telescope. Alberto Toscano and Jeff Kinkle's *Cartographies of the Absolute* marks a near heroic effort to walk through the culture of trash that is the Western cum universal cultural product, but it is also a book that somehow, perhaps unavoidably, reads like an excellent adventure. With genuine erudition and only a little ceremony, they cast the spell of the cognitive map on the vast storehouse of literature, films, and other junk products to show how fucked up capitalism really is. But through no fault of their own, what I get from this book and from so many others (if not nearly all books of "theory" today) is that against the onslaught what we know matters little. This is a structural problem. Increasingly, discourse itself is becoming what Bakhtin called "a tempest in a teapot" and consciousness itself a subroutine of decreasing importance.[15] Criticism, we are to understand, is at best a hobby and most often a career. The subjugation and expropriation of linguistic power by what I have come to understand as computational capital is an expression of the cultural logic. Thus, the signature of post-Fordist productivity threatens to stamp all the sentences in all the latest theory books in a way that makes writing like punching the clock and reading like paying the bills. The economic logic legible in the HMO-ization of medicine that made once (too) proudly autonomous doctors into corporately managed, informatically dressaged "hospitalists" is rapidly taking place at the university under the granular administration of omnipresent precarity for professors and students alike.

Nowadays, criticism has to take place all the way to the bank or it won't take place at all. In short, it must be civil.

Thus, it becomes clearer that the waning of postmodernism also means the waning of the dialectic—at least as a self-conscious vehicle of critique and subjectification that contains within it the persuasive promise of (non- or anticapitalist) agential transformation. Let me be clear here—I am not saying that the dialectic is done for or that Marxism is suddenly an anachronism. My position, though perhaps similar in outward appearance, is quite different from that denoted by the *Freewood Post* article showing an image of Pope Benedict XVI under the headline, "'Marxism No Longer Corresponds to Reality' Says Man in Giant Hat Who Speaks to Invisible Cloud People."[16] Rather, the disappearance of the concept of postmodernism, which in the Marxist tradition made it a point to problematize the evacuation of history from symbolic process and affective form, along with what we have seen as the capitalist-driven disappearance of capitalism as a concept, has prepared the way, not so unsurprisingly, for a return of the idea(s) of capitalism without the dialectic. The stripping of the dialectic is key to the post-Fordist functionalization of discourse. Virtuosity means that criticism is under siege. This is a structural as well as an intellectual, a discursive, and indeed a formal problem—one of manners, in all senses of that word.

For example, consider that France has recently brought to market the product of another antidialectical mind—far less compelling than, say, Jean Baudrillard. For Baudrillard, the ontological vacuum created by the materiality of simulation provided the dramatic tension of his conceptualization of the increasingly absent Real and the pursuit of a relation between the structure of the sign and that of the commodity form was immensely generative. The text in question offers a would-be universal and world-historical version of global capitalism "theorized" by someone who grew up after the 1960s and who, in his own best-selling words, has been "vaccinated against communism." It mentions neither Michael Hardt and Antonio Negri's powerful writings on empire, nor Bernard Stiegler, who proposes a dialectical method of engagement with cognitive capitalism through an examination of the technics of memory and attention. I am speaking of course of Thomas Piketty, whose book *Capitalism in the Twenty-First Century* offers organic intellectuals hydroponically cultured by the business world a chance to recalibrate their failed predictions in light of Piketty's purportedly fresh and for them seemingly astonishing conclusion that (1) capitalism creates inequality and (2) the rich have too much money.

On the one hand, the discursive insularity and naive positivism of "serious" minds are shocking: Piketty, through no fault properly his own (his research is extensive, and he might not be *Charlie Hebdo*), surprises his readers despite the writings of what must be tens if not hundreds of thousands of Marxists, anticolonialists, anti-imperialists, socialists, feminists, environmentalists, indigenous, of color, and Global South intellectuals. There are no Samir Amins, Walden Bellos, Vijay Prashads, or Vandana Shivas here. He surprises even though the latest Oxfam study (consistent with all the prior ones) reveals that sixty-two billionaires have wealth ($1.9 trillion) equivalent to the poorest 3.5 billion people on earth—and that the top 1 percent of the planet's population has wealth equal to all the rest: the other 99 percent. Economists, it seems, must not read such statistics, or somehow not allow their import to soil them, if as a group they are to be truly surprised that capitalism produces poverty, starvation, disease, fundamentalism, civil war, interstate war, terror, and genocide, or even that markets require regulation. As civility (and its paycheck) requires, it seems they do not talk to savages.

Yet despite the blockages in the free flow of economic discourse that only the class hatred and unreconstructed racism endemic to so-called civil society can really explain ("the ruling ideas are nothing more than the ideal expression of the dominant material relationships"),[17] when it comes to a consideration of the facts and the histories of inequality in the free press, it is hardly remarked upon by anyone as significant that the business pages have completely encroached on the culture pages and are now one with the pages on theater, architecture, the arts, travel, technology, and, it goes without saying, media. Or that media, as the technologies of what used to be called communication are called, is business by other means. This too is part of the completion of the postmodern condition: all the pages are the business pages. While the American economist Paul Krugman is probably the best known critic of Republican party intransigence, anti-intellectualism, instrumentality, and outright bigoted irrationality when it comes to the politics of US economic policy, no economist with a public voice in the United States worries that bankers are not interested in the dialectic, precisely because they too are in the business of suppressing it. One could say that dialectical thinking has become unconstitutional.

We might have expected more from the academy, even though from an institutional point of view the academy itself is at pains to teach us to know better—which of course means to expect less and to recognize that our debates with "civilization" are academic. Some folks have maintained a modicum of expectation despite the fact that our institutions, in a way reminiscent of the state of Texas, are increasingly in the business of mortgaging their customers' (that is, their students') brains to the banks to fund their own expansion—there are so many deans! But alas, the white people (and others and pieces of others who identify with the universal value form) who still more or less run things in the wild West cannot really be counted upon to be keepers of any other flame than that one that emanates from their cultic (or perhaps it is fetishistic) "origins." Universities, their policy making, their measurements of "outcomes," their policing of the boundaries of knowledge, their Western Civilization, their Americanism, and yes, even their "diversity" committees, to say nothing of their football teams, business schools, pentagon research partnerships, and trustees, are now dyed-in-the-wool state machines. They live parasitically on the creative powers whose autonomous flourishing they structurally exclude. Bound to markets, they bind minds to markets, flattening the dialectic. Even their discourses are bent to the purpose of value extraction. The inevitable conclusion seems to be best expressed by Fred Moten and Stefano Harney in *The Undercommons*: "The only possible relationship to the university today is a criminal one."[18]

No comfort should be derived, of course, from another, and indeed more general, great battle for the intellect: the one that so far has resulted in "cognitive and affective proletarianization."[19] To give but a single example, in the battle to stand up for "our" "rights" against the increasing encroachments on our private lives by the United States of Capitalism, our self-appointed defenders are now Google, Apple, and Facebook. Their "principled" if less than half-hearted stand against the NSA (the FBI, the pentagon, the police, etc.) to protect our privacy amounts to only a battle among the many capitals for the ownership rights to this commodity. In passing, it should be clarified that this commodity, privacy, a subset of the domain of our sensibilities that have already gone to market on the chopping block (the formal consequences of which might retroactively explain much of what postmodernism, or the cultural logic of late capitalism, was, namely, the corporate restructuring of the sensorium), is now one among a set of specialized commodities, formerly known as labor. Like labor, privacy is variable capital, distinct from the general form of the commodity in that it can be bought for less value than it produces in the free market. Like value-productive attention, my own earlier name for the more general relation to the machine-body interface with capital developed in and as cinema and that marked the beginning of the widespread deterritorialization of factory labor by the screen, *privacy*, or the pursuit of interests formerly considered personal or private, connotes a set of distributed activities pursued in ostensibly informal domains (the discursive and visual spaces of social media, the water cooler, the bedroom, your head, etc.) that by means of background algorithmic formalization (informationalization, photography, surveillance, self-help, geolocation, geomedication, mass-produced grub, digitization, monetization, etc.) are harvested as value for capital by what amounts to the technologistics of the derivative. The means and metrics here are as complex as digital culture itself—indeed they constitute "digital culture"—and are beyond the scope of this article; however, the private enterprise versus the state battle can be understood as a struggle for leveraged access to this value-productive resource. Privacy is now configured as a type of ownership; very likely you have been dispossessed of yours. While there is a question of which path privacy takes to the banks, that of social media, advertising, and the (free) attention markets or that of citizenship rights, militarization/policing, and the (coercive) attention market, as I have sketched out here, each path leads to the other: in sovereign debt, states utilize media nationalism and militarization to put their citizens on the market, and in private enterprise, shareholders depend upon these same states to hold in place the *rentier* model of the intellect and the laws, markets, and currencies that keep them owning and rich. One result is the strip-mining of traditional forms of privacy and allied forms of interiority.

This situation is of course indexed and effected by a massive mobilization and financialization of signs: capital's harvesting of cognitive activity, its cultivation of attention, its expropriation of the general intellect all made possible by the higher resolution of the computer augmentation of a universalizing digitization process that was first inaugurated by wage labor and the commodity form. Given the aphanisis of even the already becoming schizoid subject of postmodernism, along with the near total dissolution of private life and interiority, now unavoidably recomposed and made over as a source of variable capital and thus of capitalization that is conscripted in proprietary wars, what methods of analysis, what contingencies, what constituencies, what ontologies are of tactical use in the struggle for a life worth living? The question takes this form in a world rendered tactical, in a social context that Matteo Pasquinelli describes with the phrase "immaterial civil war"[20] and, I must add, so as not to elide forms of social difference that are central to the maintenance of hegemony, often includes material civil war. This latter materiality, which to some may appear dated, fated as it might seem to some observers to disappear into the inexorable movement of discrete state machines and the level playing field promised by digital culture, is by no means an ancillary or supplemental dimension to the liquidation of traditional forms of subjectivity, thought, and feeling. Material violence, racial conflict, police brutality, ethnic "cleansing," gated cities, gendered logics of expropriation, inaccessible or nonexistent hospitals and shelters, forced migration, refugeeism, camps, prisons, and genocide are fundamental vectors of the current profit system. These social mediations, and their interrelationships with banking, media companies, militaries, and states, are nearly as unconceptualizable as they are necessary to a financialized discursive context bent upon stripping consciousness of and for bodies and making it consciousness of and for capital. The accumulation of capital has resulted in an accumulation of consciousness, as well as a corresponding dispossession distributed unevenly over the general population.

· · ·

In gesturing away from certain contenders and toward others in the admittedly narrow field of cultural theory who might help to answer some of today's pressing questions regarding cultural logic, I do not claim, in this final section of this article, to be anything like comprehensive. I only hope to indicate a few qualities still in thought and practice that may extend the utopian legacies of the incomplete revolutions against the tiresome list of ills that includes capitalism, racism, sexism, homophobia, colonization, and imperialism and that foster, again in the words of Moten and Harney, "the general antagonism."[21]

One contender for attention that is to be avoided at all costs is so-called object oriented ontology (OOO). OOO rides the fading of subjectivity into yesterday's sunset in order to do away with the insights of poststructuralism, postcolonialism, critical race theory, feminism, and really all counterhegemonic discourses in toto. Yes, self-alienated mankind "can experience its own destruction as an aesthetic pleasure of the first order,"[22] and that applies here, but bracketing out the (transcendental) subject is also the most convenient way to smuggle him back in. In a not particularly promising reversal, objects (rather than other people) are pursued in an ethnographic mode. The ethos in a nutshell: create a safe space for unmarked philosophers ("white dudes," in Mark Driscoll's fine phrase)[23] to philosophize freely about things—to keep on talking all the way to the bank. Often, these are not self-identified white men (really, who in their right mind would self-identify as white?), but their utter disavowal of embodiment and of the situatedness of their utterances, if not their ostensibly depoliticized ontologies, makes them easily identifiable as such. We have a word for these endeavors, and I offer a mild one: reactionary.

The disappearance of poststructuralism, and what I really mean by this is postcolonial poststructuralism, is one of the great casualties of the generalized disappearance of postmodernism. Put another way, it is one of the great victories of white supremacy. The current depletion of language by capital, states, and capitalist states seems to include a depletion (by legislation, by automation) of the consciousness of the operations of language that at the theoretical level included an understanding of the means by which language posited being and presence. These insights were gleaned precisely at the moment when Western language was put under siege. On the one hand, it was put under siege by the various apparatuses, programs, and scripts that began the colonization of interiority and imposed what Brian Holmes, following Gilles Deleuze and Félix Guattari, calls an "overcode,"[24] which subjugated and repurposed prior codifications, and, on the other hand, it was seized by a world that was fed up with Western metaphysics: as Frantz Fanon famously wrote, "The black man has no ontological resistance in the eyes of the white man."[25] Poststructuralism was the awareness of the recession of, that is, the auratic character of, being as posited by language, and the growing awareness that "natural" language, inseparable from technics and power, was, at the end of the day, in no sense natural. Language was a medium, a signifying chain, a movement of signs—a technics. Metaphysical instantiations and the positing of ontologies was always/already politics. This recognition, arguably made possible by the growing material evidence that language was also one medium among many, as well as by its deployment nearly everywhere from Ireland and Spain to colonial Africa and the Philippines as an instrument of war, registered the weakening of linguistic purchase on truth. Poststructuralism meant the abstraction of the structural limits of abstract structures, and therefore the abstraction of countertruth. Thus, poststructuralism also recognized the positing of metaphysical entities as at once a mode and an artifact of linguistic function. Terrifying as it may be, the fading of being, again like the withering of aura, had (and has) a radically decentering, radically democratizing side. Indeed, the dissolution of metaphysical entities and their related hierarchies (white/black, male/female) arguably emerges not only from the growth of potentially democratizing technologies but also from the associated anticolonial struggles against the West, and Western metaphysics. Both of these shifts index an emergent understanding of the materiality of distributed production and reproduction—itself an argument against unitary sovereignty.

In this gradual awakening of an awareness of the consequences of redistribution, of the distributed production and reproduction of reality, whether along signifying chains, commodity chains, or media pathways, poststructuralism had the benefit of vitiating any theory reliant upon linguistic transparency or a metaphysics of essence and, as a corollary, cast any and all truth claims as always already political. Most suspect, of course, were utterances that disavowed or, worse, denied their political intentions and spoke "truth." Thus, it became (and remains) a categorical mistake for an anthropologist (even for Dave Graeber) to look at, say, non-Western "egalitarian societies," such as the Piaroa, the Tiv, and the people of Highland Madagascar in what had been a Malagasy state and merely observe debt relations without any apparent awareness that the framework of his perception is also an encoding: the result of histories of commodification, patriarchy, colonization, and racialization.[26] We may develop our relationship to the outside, but strictly speaking, we do not know the outside. Perceptual reality is not existential reality—particularly because both, but here especially the latter, are metaphysical artifacts.

One perceives neither facts nor truth but mediations—assuming (albeit incorrectly) that one perceives at all; rather, perception, not reality—and actually, as in the most exciting passages of *Of Grammatology*, not even perception, merely language and ultimately ~~language~~. It could be said that, with poststructuralism, Marx's understanding that the alienation of labor to capital brings about the loss or reality for the worker found its corollary in the critique of metaphysics—the generalized and historically speaking irreversible loss of reality resulting from a history of commodity production that itself gave rise to mass media and the generalized demotion of language. Historicizing slightly, let's say that the proletarian alienation, worked up in the 1844 manuscripts, from product, self, man, and species, that is, the alienation of life and therefore of reality under wage labor, manifested at a higher level in the (now) always deferred arrival of being and presence in the signifying chain, and again in the rupture and fragmentation of signifying chains in what Deleuze and Guattari called "schizophrenia." Dialectically considered, these new formations were testaments to a new order of domination via the alienation of language and the general intellect, by capitalism, which is also to say monetized media, but also, when grasped as sites of struggle, they suggested forms of revolution. As moments in generalized postmodernization, these theoretical interventions were exemplary efforts of thinking making itself adequate to its new conditions and conditions of possibility.[27]

In counterrevolutionary (essentialist) theory since postmodernism, it was, and arguably remains, the work of phallogocentrism to reinaugurate the forgetting of the suddenly perceptible modality of linguistic movement, the forgetting of what Derrida called *différance*, the always already differed and differential arrival of closure and hence meaning that, while in hindsight was perhaps a provincial European abstraction of social difference (written in a universal key) that registered the antidialogical foundation of Western ethnocentrism, precisely marked the linguistic situation that emerged for the condition of European thought and metaphysics being placed under siege, refusing both transcendence and the unmarked site of the utterance. But today, with the uncritical return of phallogocentrism, what is not to be forgotten is that phallogocentrism has also become, invariably, a financial instrument. This financialization of language, and by extension of conceptualization, critique, and subjectification, can be observed in its particular affects by considering for a moment another would-be contender for pride of place in the institutional vacuum left by the aphanisis of postmodern theory and its historicizing subject. Here I have in mind the minor but disconcertingly turgid German approach summarized in the phrase *cultural techniques*. According to its own mythology, the study of cultural techniques has emerged victorious in a war that has been raging since the critique of reason became the critique of media. This war that "pits culture against media" is for "nothing less than the throne of the transcendental that has remained vacant since the abdication of the 'critique of reason.'"[28] Advertising itself as the latest Mercedes Benz in the marketplace of theory, the method described in the institutional "promotion" of media "to the status of cultural techniques"[29] is actually more akin to IKEA, whereby using a few very basic tools a reader can (re)assemble anything—anything at least that can be assembled by an algorithmic method requiring zero innovation, a modicum of elbow grease, a few standardized brackets, and a bunch of nameless workers disappeared into the precut plywood program of history. This deracinated materialism, which extirpates conflict and struggle in its neo-Kittlerian comprehension of the technics of cultural history and form, is an indirect, though no less intentional, attack on the institutional space and resources won by materialist feminism, queer and critical-race theory, postcolonial theory, and Marxism. Through the violence of its Heideggerian abstraction, the cultural technique of cultural techniques strains to separate the insights regarding the material-technical articulation of cultural form from the fundamental historical antagonisms that inform knowledge practices: race, class, gender, nation, colonialism, capitalism, imperialism. It is a would-be movement that, in eliminating the considerations just indexed, is quite literally an occupation, a kind of settler colonialism intent upon occupying the institutional spaces necessary for the practice of the critical methods and techniques capable of resolving both the historicity of social form and the violent materiality of "the human," and developed precisely through historical and institutional struggle against oppression. It would also eliminate, by virtue of the smug transcendence of its comprehensive program, the legitimacy, positions, and perhaps the existence of those who waged those struggles. In this "cultural techniques" is a perfect expression of German neoliberal accounting—which, it should be remembered, has today accomplished what Hitler never could: the takeover of Europe.

Even someone as comprehensive as David Harvey seems at times not to understand that the abstractions operative in capital evolved and were constituted through the mediation of social difference. Capital is not indifferent to the incidentals of race and gender but is in fact a formation that is bound up in these. Slavery and colonialism are not incidental to the emergence of use value and exchange value, or to what we call class. The classical categories in Marxism, such as they are, have been constituted via these material mediations that are themselves part of the development of capital, even if all aspects are not resolved—and are indeed subsumed and repressed—in classical Marxism.

Retrospectively, then, it may be that one significant factor in the defeat of postmodernism as an analytic can be gleaned from a monumental study released a year before Jameson's landmark work on postmodernism and then largely ignored. I am speaking here of Cedric Robinson's *Black Marxism* (1983), a book that embarks on an exhaustive and very likely irrefutable demonstration that capitalism is itself a racial formation. "We begin to perceive that the nation is not a unit of analysis for the social history of Europe," writes Robinson.[30]

> The tendency of European civilization through capitalism was not to homogenize but to differentiate—too exaggerate regional, subcultural, dialectical differences into "racial" ones. As the Slavs became the natural slaves, the racially inferior stock for domination and exploitation during the middle ages, as the Tartars came to occupy a similar position in the Italian cities of the late Middle Ages, so at the systemic interlocking of capitalism in the late sixteenth century, the peoples of the Third World began to fill this expanding category of a civilization reproduced by capitalism.[31]

Capital develops not only through class differentiation but also through racialization. As Robinson expressed it:

> What concerns us is that we understand that racialism persisted, rooted not in a particular era, but in civilization itself. And though our era might seem a particularly fitting one for depositing the origins of racism, that judgment merely reflects how resistant the idea is to examination and how powerful and natural its specifications have become. Our confusions, however, are not unique. As an enduring principle of European social order, the effects of racialism were bound to appear in the social expression of every strata of every European society no matter the structures upon which they formed. None was immune. . . . [T]his proved to be true for the rebellious proletariat as well as the radical intelligentsias. It was again, a quite natural occurrence in both instances. But to the latter—the radical intelligentsias—it was also an unacceptable one. Nevertheless it insinuated itself into their thought and their theories. And thus, in the quest for a radical social force, an active historical subject, it compelled certain blindnesses, bemusements which in turn systematically subverted their analytical constructions and their revolutionary project.[32]

Perhaps Robinson's understanding of "racial capitalism," recognized early on by Cornel West and by Robin Kelley, and now an informing concept recently brought to fuller public discussion by Ruth Wilson Gilmore and Nikhil Singh, is part of what is needed in support of other work such as that of Angela Davis, Gina Dent, Avery Gordon, Dylan Rodriguez, Gilmore, and others on prison abolitionism and abolition feminism, and also an emergent queer Marxism such as that which arguably informs the late José Esteban Muñoz's *Cruising Utopia*.[33] This is work that understands that to change anything you have to change everything, but it is not thus prevented from creating community along lines of social fracture that do not appear as class in the first (or last) instance. For Angela Davis, prison abolition is not just an issue of race, gender, and class oppression; it is also an issue of history and the imagination, since, as she notes in *Are Prisons Obsolete?*, before the abolition of slavery, many people, including some black slaves, could not imagine the tyranny of slavery ever coming to an end.[34] In my own partial view, any cultural work whatever always negotiates social difference whether it knows it or not; therefore, in a Gramscian sense, it makes a prediction with respect to social difference and thus has a program. It therefore must train its attention to the lines of violence and possibility in any social formation under study (and this includes the situation of its own utterance) if it would critically engage and successfully confront a cultural logic that while one of financialization, virtuosic virtualization, and, in agreement with David Golumbia, computation and programming,[35] is also one of widespread racialized and gendered dispossesion.

Axiomatic, then, is the engagement with social difference. Only when difference's omnipresent social engines are attended to might one understand the constant remaking of race and class as, for example, Silvia Federici does with her framing of contemporary capitalism as "the system of global apartheid." This coarticulation of race and class emerges, not coincidentally, from Federici's 1975 analysis of "reproductive work" in her now classic "Wages against Housework":

> It should be clear, however, that when we struggle for a wage we do not struggle to enter capitalist relations, because we have never been out of them. . . . To say that we want wages for housework is to expose the fact that housework is already money for capital, that capital has made and makes money out of our cooking, smiling, fucking. At the same time it shows that we have cooked, smiled and fucked throughout the years, not because it was easier for us than for anybody else, but because we did not have any other choice. Our faces have become distorted from so much smiling.[36]

Angela McRobbie has also remarked on the continuing failure of (post-) Marxism to seriously address the fact that labor and class sustain "always existing entanglements with gender and ethnicity."[37] As in Mark Driscoll's "Looting the Theory Commons" (a bitter critique of Hardt and Negri's Eurocentric citational politics with respect to postcolonial theory and Global South intellectuals in *Commonwealth*), McRobbie pointedly remarks on the unacknowledged debts and lacuna with regard to materialist feminism in *Operaismo*.[38] Given these Other Marxisms, one might suspect that every time a Badiou or an Agamben gets a shout-out for a presumably radical thought, a woman or a person of color is subsumed and erased. One would not be wrong.

Maybe those who ply (and play against) the institutional and para-institutional spaces of theory might study these phrases: racial capitalism, sex/gender capitalism. They may provide tools to subvert the whitewashing of the revolutionary theory commons; they insist upon dialogue.

In his study of language, psychoanalysis, and capital, Jean-Joseph Goux writes of the amortization of consciousness in the historical working up of the transcendental abstractions. The "I," the phallus, the value form—these are the results of practical activities that are amortized and thus encrypted in the abstractions that they dialectically engender.[39] With Robinson, and with work devoted to marshaling the currently untranscendable horizon of race against the failings endemic to those who would leave racialism as is or ignore it completely, we can begin to sense and perhaps grasp the violent amortization of racialization in our abstractions, our categories, and our objects. With Federici and materialist feminism, we should be aware of the gender dynamics of the value form and of domination by cultures and states, and of the heteronormative assumptions of so much of revolutionary Marxism.

Confronted with our reifications (and the fact that, conveniently or not, we also belong to them), we must reopen the ledger and reexamine the debts. For me, now, not only is capitalism, that first universalizing digital culture that gives rise to the current one, a racial formation and a sex/gender formation, but so also are its machines. Contemporary technologies, and by this I include computers, rather than being value neutral, are thus also racial and sex/gender formations. How could it be otherwise, since the discrete state machine that is today at the heart of digital culture is at once the result and the condition of possibility for globalization? Computers are algorithmically driven, high-resolution difference engines. The ongoing decryption of what in my current work I call computational capital would yield an analysis of both racial capitalism and racial computing. Simultaneously, it would reverse engineer digital culture as sex/gender capitalism and sex/gender computing. In tracing the amortized subjectivities and, indeed, lives constitutive of present objects, objectives, and presumed objectivities, it would be part of an ongoing struggle to combat the multiple downsides of the reigning cultural logic: the practical deconstruction not only of the historical fabric of our lived connections but also of their very substrate, which, to name it here, could only be planetary life itself.

Notes

1. Riley, "Messing with Texas Textbooks."
2. Dunbar-Ortiz, *Indigenous Peoples' History*, 127.
3. "Who controls the past controls the future: who controls the present controls the past" (Orwell, *1984*, 32). Another gem, relevant to educators everywhere: "Stupidity was as necessary as intelligence, and as difficult to attain" (229).

4. This discussion is ongoing; a complete list of 2011–12 stipulations may be found at Texas Education Code, "Texas Essential Knowledge," among them:

(9) Economics. The student understands the various ways in which people organize economic systems. The student is expected to:

(A) compare ways in which various societies organize the production and distribution of goods and services;

(B) compare and contrast free enterprise, socialist, and communist economies in various contemporary societies, including the benefits of the US free enterprise system;

(C) understand the importance of morality and ethics in maintaining a functional free enterprise system; and

(D) examine the record of collective, non-free market economic systems in contemporary world societies."

5. Partridge, "Texas Board of Education Revises Textbooks." It's satire, but barely.

6. Farce has become the language of fascism in the United States. In the time between the writing and copyediting of this essay, the world has seen the ferocious, farcical, yet frightening rise of Trump's phallic white supremacy. With respect to the topic at hand, Texas education, the *New York Times* reports on Mary Lou Bruner's bid to represent thirty-one East Texas counties for a seat on the fifteen-member Texas board that sets curriculum standards and that ranks, reviews, and adopts textbooks. Bruner, despite or because of her anti-Obama, anti-Islam, anti-evolution, and antigay Facebook posts, has 48 percent of the vote and faces a runoff with another Republican. "On her Facebook page, Ms. Bruner called Mr. Obama 'Ahab the Arab,' and wrote that he 'hates all white people and all wealthy people because to him wealthy means white.' Although she condemned the Ku Klux Klan in one posting, she wrote positively of its roots, writing that it started 'as citizens trying to fight back against a corrupt government when there were corrupt officials or no officials at all to keep law and order in the rural areas.' Of Mr. Obama's youth, she wrote: 'I heard from a reliable source that Obama was also a male prostitute for a while when he lived in New York with his male "partner." How do you think he paid for his drugs?'" ("Texan Seeking a Say," A17).

7. For Benjamin, mechanical reproduction's capacity to wither the cultic relation to the original comes from its ability "to pry the original from its shell, to destroy its aura [a]s the mark of a perception whose 'sense of the universal quality of things' has increased to such a degree that it extracts it even from a unique object by means of reproduction" (Benjamin, "Work of Art in the Age of Mechanical Reproduction," 223). But the demolition of the cultic relation to authenticity that, from a utopian point of view, seemed to promise "the universal equality of things" in the democratic sense of equality seems rather to have resulted in their equality as commodities that are denominated in the general equivalent: money. For capital commodities may differ in the quantity of exchange value they represent but are nonetheless all the same in their quality of being exchange values. In this case, equality would mean that all things, including people, are equally exchangeable in the calculus of capital.

8. Benjamin, "Work of Art in the Age of Mechanical Reproduction," 222.

9. Ibid., 218.

10. Huntington, "Clash of Civilizations?," 22–49.

11. Virno, *Grammar of the Multitude*.

12. See Virno, *Grammar of the Multitude*; Berardi, *After the Future*.

13. Virilio, *Administration of Fear*.

14. See Wark, *Telesthesia*; Azumu, *Otaku*.

15. "The internal bifurcation (double-voicing) of discourse, sufficient to a single and unitary language and to a consistently monologic style, can never be a fundamental form of discourse: it is merely a game, a tempest in a teapot" (Bakhtin, *Dialogic Imagination*, 325). This description well characterizes the internal discourse of commodities as they/we make our way through the post-Fordist environment of cognitive capital, commanded as they/we are to perform our part of its distributed monologue within the parameters of its unitary language. Sadly, the university is no longer an exceptional space in this regard.

16. The text reads, "Pope Benedict XVI criticized Cuba's Marxist system earlier today, saying he and the all-powerful being he personally represents find it backwards and out of step with common sense. Denouncing the Cuban regime in a language that's been dead for centuries, Benedict noted that Marxism's focus on state control of the means of production would actually work quite well if—like the Pope—Raul Castro was incapable of making mistakes." Murphy, "'Marxism No Longer Corresponds to Reality.'"

17. Marx, "German Ideology," 172–73.

18. Moten and Harney, *Undercommons*, 26.

19. Stiegler, *New Critique of Political Economy*, 30.

20. Pasquinelli, "Immaterial Civil War."

21. Moten and Harney, *Undercommons*, esp. "The General Antagonism: An Interview with Stevphen Shukaitis," 100–159.

22. Benjamin, "Work of Art in the Age of Mechanical Reproduction," 242.

23. Driscoll, "White Dude's Burden."

24. Holmes, *Escape the Overcode.*

25. Fanon, *Black Skin, White Masks*, 110.

26. Graeber, *Fragments*, 26–29.

27. Deleuze and Guattari's schizophrenia famously produced "the line of flight," and French Algerian Jacques Derrida's formulation "The inside is the outside" at once announced the limit of and offered a challenge to writing. Hortense Spillers's category of "the flesh" proclaims the always/already historical and political character of categories along with their tendencies to erase their histories of violence. See Spillers, "Mama's Baby, Papa's Maybe," 67.

28. Siegert, "Cultural Techniques," 49.

29. Ibid., 54.

30. Robinson, *Black Marxism*, 24.

31. Ibid., 27.

32. Ibid., 29.

33. See Muñoz, *Cruising Utopia.*

34. Davis, *Are Prisons Obsolete?*, 25.

35. See Golumbia, *Cultural Logic of Computation.*

36. Federici, "Wages against Housework," 19.

37. McRobbie, "Reflections on Feminism," 61.

38. See Driscoll, "Looting the Theory Commons."

39. See Goux, *Symbolic Economies.*

References

Azumu, Hiroki. 2009. *Otaku: Japan's Database Animals.* Translated by Jonathan E. Abel and Shion Kono. Minneapolis: University of Minnesota Press.

Bakhtin, Mikhail. M. 1981. *The Dialogic Imagination.* Translated by Caryl Emerson and Michael Holquist. Austin: University of Texas Press.

Benjamin, Walter. 1969. "The Work of Art in the Age of Mechanical Reproduction." In *Illuminations*. Translated by Harry Zohn. New York: Schocken.

Berardi, Franco. 2011. *After the Future*. Oakland, CA: AK Press.

Davis, Angela Y. 2003. *Are Prisons Obsolete?* New York: Seven Stories Press.

Derrida, Jacques. 1974. *Of Grammatology*. Translated by Gayatri Chakravorty Spivak. Baltimore, MA: Johns Hopkins University Press.

Driscoll, Mark. 2009. "White Dude's Burden." *Cultural Studies* 23, no. 1: 100–128. dx.doi.org/10.1080/09502380802016238.

Driscoll, Mark. September 2010. "Looting the Theory Commons: Hardt and Negri's *Commonwealth*." *Postmodern Culture* 21, no. 1. dx.doi.org/10.1353/pmc.2010.002.

Dunbar-Ortiz, Roxanne. 2014. *An Indigenous Peoples' History of the United States*. Boston: Beacon.

Fanon, Frantz. 1967. *Black Skin, White Masks*. Translated by Charles Lam Markham. New York: Grove.

Federici, Silvia. 2012. "Wages against Housework." In *Revolution at Point Zero: Housework, Reproduction, and Feminist Struggle*, 14–22. Brooklyn, NY: PM Press.

Golumbia, David. 2009. *The Cultural Logic of Computation*. Cambridge, MA: Harvard University Press.

Goux, Jean-Joseph. 1990. *Symbolic Economies: After Marx and Freud*. Translated by Jennifer Curtis Gage. Ithaca, NY: Cornell University Press.

Graeber, David. 2004. *Fragments of an Anarchist Anthropology*. Chicago: Prickly Paradigm.

Holmes, Brian. 2009. *Escape the Overcode: Activist Art in the Control Society*. Eindhoven, Netherlands: Van Abbemuseum, in collaboration with WHW.

Huntington, Samuel P. 1993. "The Clash of Civilizations?" *Foreign Affairs*, Summer, 22–49.

Isensee, Laura. 2014. "Texas Hits the Books." *NPR-Ed*, 23 November. www.npr.org/blogs/ed/2014/11/21/365686593/texas-hits-the-books.

Marx, Karl. 1978. "The German Ideology." In *The Marx-Engels Reader*. 2nd ed. Edited by Robert Tucker, 146–200. New York: Norton.

McRobbie, Angela. 2010. "Reflections on Feminism, Immaterial Labor and the Post-Fordist Regime." *New Formations* 70, no. 4: 60–76.

Moten, Fred, and Stefano Harney. 2013. *The Undercommons: Fugitive Planning and Black Study*. New York: Autonomedia.

Muñoz, José Esteban. 2009. *Cruising Utopia: The Then and There of Queer Futurity*. New York: NYU Press.

Murphy, Kyle. "'Marxism No Longer Corresponds to Reality' Says Man in Giant Hat Who Speaks to Invisible Cloud People." *News That's Almost Reliable*. www.freewoodpost.com/2012/03/25/marxism-no-longer-corresponds-to-reality-says-man-in-giant-hat-who-speaks-to-invisible-cloud-people.

Orwell, George. 1981. *1984*. New York: Signet Classic.

Partridge, Chris. 2012. "Texas Board of Education Revises Textbooks: Slaves Were 'Unpaid Interns.'" *Postindustrial Ethics–Morality* (blog), 27 September, drsundjataatwvsu.blogspot.com/2013/08/texas-board-of-education-revises.html.

Pasquinelli, Matteo. 2006. "Immaterial Civil War: Prototypes of Conflict within Cognitive Capitalism." European Institute for Progressive Cultural Politics, November. eipcp.net/policies/cci/pasquinelli/en.

Piketty, Thomas. 2014. *Capitalism in the Twenty-First Century*. Cambridge, MA: Harvard University Press.

Riley, Theresa. 2012. "Messing with Texas Textbooks," *BillMoyers.com* (blog), 29 June. billmoyers.com/content/messing-with-texas-textbooks.

Robinson, Cedric. 1983. *Black Marxism: The Making of the Black Radical Tradition.* London: Zed.

Siegert, Bernard. 2013. "Cultural Techniques: Or the End of the Intellectual Postwar Era in German Media Theory." *Theory, Culture, and Society* 30, no. 6: 48–65.

Spillers, Hortense J. 1987. "Mama's Baby, Papa's Maybe: An American Grammar Book." In "Culture and Countermemory: The 'American' Connection," special issue, *Diacritics* 17, no. 2: 64–81.

Stiegler, Bernard. 2010. *For a New Critique of Political Economy.* London: Polity.

"Texan Seeking a Say on Textbooks Pushes the Boundary of the Far Right." 2016. *New York Times*, March 13.

Texas Education Code. 2010. "Texas Essential Knowledge and Skills for Social Studies, Subchapter B, Middle School, Chapter 113," ritter.tea.state.tx.us/rules/tac /chapter113/ch113b.html.

Toscano, Alberto, and Jeff Kinkle. 2015. *Cartographies of the Absolute.* Winchester, UK: Zero Books.

Virilio, Paul. 2012. *The Administration of Fear.* Translated by Ames Hodges. Los Angeles: Semiotext(e).

Virno, Paolo. 2004. *A Grammar of the Multitude.* Los Angeles: Semiotext(e).

Wark, McKenzie. 2012. *Telesthesia: Communication, Culture and Class.* London: Polity.

From *Shame* to *Drive*

The Waning of Affect; or, The Rising of the Drive Image in Contemporary Hollywood Cinema

Sulgi Lie

Any attempt to periodize contemporary Hollywood cinema after Fredric Jameson is faced with the question of what comes after postmodernism. If this article suggests a somehow tautological answer that it is still postmodernism that follows postmodernism, it is precisely because I believe that the very historicity of our cinematic present arises from the (film-) historical moment of the 1980s that Jameson identified as postmodernism. If the concept of *postmodernism* has gradually disappeared from the critical vocabulary of film and cultural theory over the last decades, it is not because it has proven wrong but, in a way, "too true." To remain faithful to the Jamesonian dictum "Always historicize"[1] thus means not to hectically abandon old concepts in favor of new ones but to reanimate postmodernism again as a Marxist theoretical tool to illuminate a present that is more postmodern than the old postmodernity of the 1980s was. The Freudian name for this retroactive epistemology is, of course, *Nachträglichkeit*, respectively translated as "afterwardness," "belatedness," or most commonly "deferred action." In the nonlinear temporal structure of deferred action, the unknown meaning of a past event waits to be deciphered in the future, while the present cognitions reversely alter the symbolization of the past. This dialectical historicity of deferred action might help us to approach not only the belatedness of late capitalism in general but also the retroactivity of cinema in particular: at least for the two emblematic films of recent Hollywood cinema discussed in this article, it is of importance not to confuse this retroactive causality with the usual mode of, let's call it, *retropassive* nostalgia. In mediating their absolute contemporaneity

Social Text 127 · Vol. 34, No. 2 · June 2016
DOI 10.1215/01642472-3467966 © 2016 Duke University Press

with phantasmagoric allusions to the 1980s, both films achieve an immanent periodization of their own postmodernist aesthetics, a historicizing operation in the precise Jamesonian sense: "Historicity is, in fact, neither a representation of the past nor a representation of the future . . . : it can first and foremost be defined as a perception of the present as history; that is, as a relationship to the present which somehow defamiliarizes it and allows us that distance from immediacy which is at length characterized as a historical perspective."[2] This includes the paradox that the cinematic history of our present can only be written as a history without history, as the persistence of a posthistorical history, a "new historical period we had begun to enter around 1980."[3]

While in Steve McQueen's *Shame* (2011) the visual depiction of New York's spatial system almost seems like a cinematic commentary on Jameson's famous analysis of postmodern architecture, Nicolas Winding Refn's *Drive* (2011) evokes a hallucination of the 1980s as an eternal posthistorical presence of the past. What Jameson in perhaps the most notorious phrase of his 1991 *Postmodernism* called the "waning of affect" is accomplished in both films to a degree that in retrospect a 1980 film like Lawrence Kasdan's *Body Heat* (1981), which Jameson discussed as an advanced example of postmodernist Hollywood, appears as a pre-postmodernist prototype. If the process has come to an end, if the affect is not in the waning but has finally waned, the drive takes over. In psychoanalytically transcoding Jameson's "waning of affect" as the rising of the drive, I understand the drive image as generative for the aesthetic and social form of contemporary Hollywood cinema in full postmodernity. Both films register the withering of the old modern forms of sociality and subjectivity (the law, the public sphere, the bourgeois citizen) as the very form of sociality in late capitalism in tracking down its "structure of feeling," to invoke Raymond Williams's classic term:

> The unmistakable presence of certain elements in art which are not covered by . . . other formal systems is the true source of the specializing categories of the "aesthetic," "the arts," and "imaginative literature." We need, on the one hand, to acknowledge (and welcome) the specificity of these elements—specific feelings, specific rhythms—and yet to find ways of recognizing their specific kinds of sociality, thus preventing that extraction from social experience which is conceivable only when social experience itself has been categorically (and at root historically) reduced. We are then not only concerned with the restoration of social content in its full sense, that of a generative immediacy. The idea of a structure of feeling can be specifically related to the evidence of forms and conventions—semantic figures—which, in art and literature, are often among the very first indications that such a new structure is forming.[4]

This great passage may serve as a methodological reminder how the aesthetic articulation of social forms can anticipate and grasp a structure of feeling that withdraws itself from the immediacy of social experience—a very Jamesonian idea indeed, only with the slight difference that Williams turns Jameson's epistemology of mapping from cognition to feeling. But the structure of feeling mapped by both films under discussion can hardly be described as feeling anymore, or as emotion or affect: I claim that the drive constitutes the predominant structure of feeling after the end of feeling.

Far away from being an interior feeling, a moving emotion, or an expressive affect, the drive is not a biological instinct but, rather, a parasite alien force that is more alive than the subject itself. In his most recent inquiry of the ancient musical predecessors of postmodernity (Wagner, Mahler), Jameson himself stresses the essential in- or even superhumanity of the drive: "In Lacan, the 'death wish' is in fact the force of the drive . . . , which acts through us even when our personal desires and wishes are exhausted, indeed even when our own individual energies are virtually at an end."[5] That this "too-muchness" of the drive, its excess of quantitative energy is inherent to the self-referential and recursive nature of capitalism has been pointed out by the Japanese philosopher Kojin Karatani—capital (and especially finance capital) is self-increasing money in the process of endless expansion: "This is equal to the drive to attain the *right* to consume anywhere and anytime, instead of consumption at this moment. . . . What I would like to focus on here is not how capital's self-reproduction is possible but why capital's movement has to continue *endlessly*. Indeed this is *interminable* and *without telos*."[6] The drive drives itself, which also means that the self-driven capital knows no outside of itself. Driven by the compulsion of endless accumulation, the antiteleological temporality of late capitalism is haunted by what Hegel calls "bad infinity."[7] The bad infinity of sheer quanta addition ($n + 1$) forms the drive matrix of endless capitalist oversaturation, economic as well as psychic: "One fix after another, one purchase after another; for there is no end to the accumulation: 'the lonely hour of the "last instance" never arrives' (Althusser)."[8] Translated back to Jameson's term, this infinite seriality of the drive is to be understood not as a temporal continuum but as an atemporal discontinuum of what he newly calls singularities: "The world of finance capital is that perpetual present—but it is not a continuity, it is a series of singular events."[9] Not at least, this discontinuity of the drive has important ramifications for the temporality of cinema as a narrative medium in general and for the Hollywood code of continuity editing in particular. Whereas of course contemporary mainstream Hollywood cinema as a whole symptomatically acts out this end of temporality in one way or another, I locate the aesthetic and epistemic superiority of both *Shame* and *Drive* in their abstract formalizing tendencies, in shaping a specific rhythm of the drive in Williams's sense. Confronted with the atemporality of the waning of affect—whether we call it intensity, singularity, or presentism (as Jameson does in the interview with the editors in this issue), the formal mutations of narrative time and cinematic montage in *Shame* and *Drive* are symptomatic of a regime of the drive that structures the libidinal economy of the "forever and ever" of late capitalism. An allegorical reading of cinematic forms still seems indispensable to me for any attempt of mapping, cognitive or otherwise. However, historicizing Jameson also implies acknowledging the relative denial of his work to connect his Marxist classism to the overdeterminations of race and gender. Mirroring this structuring absence in Jameson's theory, the two post-postmodernist films discussed design their drive images in apparently exclusively white male settings. Although a nuanced account of both films' racial and sexual politics is not what this article can fully elaborate, at least some scattered hints in this direction are insinuated.[10] As I hope to show below, the political failure of *Shame* (despite its success in formalizing the drive image) is intrinsically bound to its gender conservatism, whereas the utopian (however weak it may be) success of *Drive* lies precisely in its projection of a feminine signifier against the fascist white male rampage unleashed in this film.

If my article is driven by the conviction that the aesthetic analysis of Hollywood cinema still offers us a major key to the unlocking of the political unconscious of contemporary capitalism, it is not because I believe that cinema is yet the cultural dominant of our period in a way it was when Jameson was writing about films in the 1980s, but precisely because cinema has somehow become an anachronistic medium in the cultural logic of the present. Cinema attempts to narrativize what withdraws itself from narrativization—the drive.[11]

The Desublimated Beautiful: *Shame*

"The visual is *essentially* pornographic, which is to say that it has its end in rapt, mindless fascination,"[12] Jameson once famously claimed. Understanding pornography ontologically rather than generically may also help to dialectically approach Steve McQueen's *Shame*, a film at once totally complicit in the visual commodification of the world into a naked body and formally reflexive and austere enough to "draw [its] energy from the attempt to repress [its] own excess."[13] This formal repression of excess, the taming of the pornographic fascination is achieved by a distinctive (neo) classicism of cinematic style—in some ways the signature style of Steve McQueen's feature films from *Hunger* to his recent *12 Years a Slave*. It remains to be seen if the retreat to classicism is able to pacify the pornographic regime of the visual or, to put it differently, to sublimate it.

Because sublimation is something the protagonist of *Shame*, the sex-obsessed Brandon (Michael Fassbender), is precisely not capable of. Trapped in the prison house of his body, Brandon is the opposite of a balanced classicist in his uncontrollable greed for sex. Brandon is the negation of Casanova: in the contemporary meat market of late capitalism, the art of seduction has withered and has been replaced by a generalized autoeroticism, with masturbation as its dominant sexual matrix. Brandon is not a pickup artist but essentially a masturbator, hence the recurrence of masturbation scenes throughout the film: Brandon in the shower, Brandon in the office restroom, Brandon in front of his laptop. Even his real sexual encounters with women (mostly prostitutes) are marked by the exchangeability of each of them. As if the market economy of supply and demand is short-circuited in his own body, Brandon's sexuality narcissistically revolves only around himself. To illustrate his concept of the drive, Jacques Lacan refers to the paradoxical image of a mouth kissing itself.[14] Slavoj Žižek comments: "It may appear that drive is the paradigmatic case of the closed circle of auto-affection, of the subject's body affecting itself within the domain of Sameness."[15] Moving away from the order of desire (which in Lacanian terms is both a desire of/for the other and the desire to desire) to the order of the drive, Brandon is an autoerotic monad who thrives from his own narcissistic ego-libido rather than from object-libido. "The insertion on one's own body, . . . the departure and the end of the drive,"[16] is also echoed in the departure and end of the circular trajectory of *Shame's* atemporal narrative form. The short-circuited and closed-circuited autoaffectivity of the drive causes the collapse of a chronological and linear cinematic temporality into the hallucinatory intensity of an eternal present that Jameson so vividly described as the effect of a schizophrenic breakdown of signification: "If we are unable to unify the past, present, and future of the sentence, then we are similarly unable to unify the past, present, and future of our own biographical experience or psychic life."[17] The vicissitude of the drive manifests not only in the symptom of *Shame's* protagonist but also in the very "linguistic malfunction" of cinematic syntax itself, which is not able anymore to articulate a "certain temporal unification of past and future with one's present."[18]

Shame departs and ends with two extended montage sequences mirroring each other in which the signifying difference between flashback and flash-forward is rendered indistinguishable. The opening sequence alternates between scenes of Brandon in his apartment and his hunt for new sexual prey during a subway ride. The temporal relation between both scenes is distorted by a strange parallelism that the apparently classical form of cross-cutting evokes: Brandon seems to be at both places at the same time. Is the aggressive flirtation in the subway a former or a future event in relation to the apartment scene? A further complication is added by the fact that the temporal duration of the apartment scene is also blurred by repetitive and recursive patterns. Brandon's awakening in the morning is intercut by an orgasm at night, while the morning itself seems doubled by the recurrence of the same shot of Brandon going to the toilet. As if rotating in an endless loop of an engulfing present, the logic of the montage points to the dissolution of past and future into a total simultaneity of present moments or, to use Jameson's phrase, "a series of pure and unrelated presents in time."[19] When cross-cutting is disconnected from the chronology of temporal succession in this way, the result is a pure parallelism of sameness that hollows out the narrative perspectivism of cinematic montage. One may call it "postcontinuity editing" with Steven Shaviro;[20] I prefer to call it drive montage,[21] the drive becoming montage, the montage becoming drive, also because there is nothing essentially postcinematic or digital about this editing style. The classicism of cross-cutting is driven to the point of implosion, muting into a narcissistic feedback loop of present layers. The drive, Freud and Lacan teach us, is characterized by its inhuman "constancy," a strange inertia without temporal ebbs and flows: "The first thing Freud says about the drive is, if I may put it this way, that it has no day or night, no spring or autumn, no rise and fall. It is a constant force."[22] This machinist force of the drive also invades the underlying elegiac music score with a quiet but constant noise of what sounds like the ticking of a metronome. Pointing toward a beyond of biological life, the drive montage of *Shame* consequently begins with a mortified negation of motion and emotion: the first image of the film is a fixed overhead shot of Brandon lying motionless in his bed, staring off with empty eyes, a beautiful male corpse drained of any signs of vitality. It could almost be mistaken for a photographic still until the blinking of his eyelids signals a glimpse of movement. The moving image is no longer the image of movement, so it allegorically seems—the image does not animate the human body anymore rather than arresting, paralyzing, and transfixing it. What this motionless image reveals is that Brandon the drive-creature is a veritable zombie. For Shaviro the zombie is the very form of subjectivity or subjection that corresponds to the regime of the drive in late capitalism: "Zombies are no longer alienated workers, producing value but excluded from its enjoyment. Instead, they are already-exhausted sources of value, former vessels of creative activity and self-reflexivity that have been entirely consumed and cast aside. No longer capable of living labor, they are not a renewable resource."[23] In contrast to the vampire, who still needs the blood of the other, the zombie is doomed by the bad infinity of the drive in his addictive hunt for enjoyment.

Zombified and subjected by this mindless, headless, *acephale* drive, in one particularly intense shot during the subway sequence the X-ray–

Figure 1. Still from *Shame*

like blur on Brandon's face distorts it to a skull without eyes. Despite its all too human title, from the very beginning *Shame* registers what Rem Koolhaas referred to as the "delirious New York" of late postmodernity,[24] a site of an anthropological mutation. Like Koolhaas already predicted in 1978, New York always was a laboratory for the end of civilization. No longer the living space of human beings, the city has become the habitat of a new kind of species that may wear a human mask but—almost like the body-snatched consumer-aliens in John Carpenter's classic *They Live* (1988)—is devoid of any depth, expressivity, and interiority. The "glacéd X-ray elegance"[25] Jameson detected in Andy Warhol's pictures is the very substance the driven zombie-monad Brandon is made of. In perfect analogy to this "glacéd" subject, in *Shame* the entire architectonical object world of delirious New York in the twenty-first century seems to be wholly made of glass. Both Brandon's apartment and the offices in the media company (with typical neoliberal flat hierarchies) he's working in are composed of glass windows, skins, and screens that promote a total pornographic visibility of bodies. The totally glazed late-capitalist city privatizes the urban public sphere to an advertising space of sexual exhibition values. Window shopping is window sex: after watching a couple having sex pressed against their giant apartment window, Brandon later mimics this glassy skin flick with a prostitute.

While by means of the Bonaventura Hotel Jameson allegorized the ubiquitous spectacle of glazing as the spatial triumph of a depthless surface in postmodernity,[26] I suggest a somehow forgotten concept of a Frankfurt School thinker Jameson is indebted to: repressive desublimation. Herbert Marcuse's notion for the unleashing of the drive in late capitalism may sound a bit old-fashioned now because it somehow naively presupposes a natural nonalienated libido, but this lengthy passage from his *One-Dimensional Man* reads not only like a forerunner of Jameson's diagnosis of a postmodern vitrification of affects and things but also as a perfect description of *Shame*'s shift toward a desublimated drive:

> The environment from which the individual could obtain pleasure—which he could cathect as gratifying almost as an extended zone of the body—has been rigidly reduced. Consequently, the "universe" of libidinous cathexis is likewise reduced. The effect is a localization and contraction of libido, the reduction of erotic to sexual experience and satisfaction. For example, compare love-making in a meadow and in an automobile, on a lovers' walk outside the town walls and on a Manhattan street. In the former cases, the environment partakes of and invites libidinal cathexis and tends to be eroticized. Libido transcends beyond the immediate erotogenic zones—a process of nonrepressive sublimation. In contrast, a mechanized environment seems to block such self-transcendence of libido. Impelled in the striving to extend the field of erotic gratification, libido becomes less "polymorphous," less capable of eroticism beyond localized sexuality, and the latter is intensified. Thus diminishing erotic and intensifying sexual energy, the technological reality limits the scope of sublimation. It also reduces the need for sublimation.[27]

To resublimate and thus to redeem this decathected drive by aesthetic sublimation is what *Shame* ultimately seems to strive for. Two correlating strategies are mobilized for this project: (1) at the plot level a rather traditionally gendered tale of moral awakening, Oedipally initiated by Brandon's psychically vulnerable sister, Sissy (Carey Mulligan), and leading to Brandon's temporary heteroaffection by the other; and (2) at the formal level a pronounced classicism of cinematic style, which—following an insightful article on Steve McQueen by the Austrian art historian Markus Klammer[28]—could be defined as the organizing principle of an idea of the "beautiful" expressing itself in the careful image compositions and well-tempered music (J. S. Bach's *Goldberg Variations*). Aesthetic and moral distance promises to be the remedy for the destructiveness of the drive, or in other words, pornographic desublimation is countered by sublimation as classicist contemplation. The glassy (sex) screens "totally incapable of serving as a conductor of psychic energy"[29] are dereified and recoded as cinematic mediums of cathartic reflection as Klammer argues:

> The appearance of glass planes in *Shame* achieves an additional function: They put the film spectator in a position of reflexive distance towards the screened events, they prevent an all too strong identification with the character of Brandon and produce a separation between the body of the spectator, the projection screen and the projected bodies. Thus, by means of their specific aesthetic use, these vitreous and specular objects of alienation are transformed to mediums of reflection and distance.[30]

But *Shame*'s aesthetic repression of repressive desublimation, to speak with Marcuse and Jameson, is not without its own aporias: not only since Steve McQueen's authorial classicism depends on spectacular sensationalism and a problematic mixture of voyeurism, empathy, and reflection,[31] *Shame*'s idealist pastiche of the beautiful is hardly convincing. I would argue that the film's failure results in its inability to analyze the intrinsic entanglement of classicism and reification. Far from recathecting the glass surface of the body-commodity with healthy libido, cinematic classicism is itself a catalytic converter in desublimating the beautiful, as Sean Cubitt convincingly claims:

> Thus the importance to classicism of the seamless fabric, the integral surface, of film's body, the body without orifices. There is no body here to penetrate, no reality to be laid bare, no concept to reveal itself, but only an ideal glassy smoothness, the gaze of a lens rather than an eye, the sheen of the screen rather than a Cartesian space. . . . Classicism instead mobilizes fantasy, but does so in order to satisfy it. It evokes desire to display it, to mirror desire back onto itself and in that reflection to complete desire as a closed and narcissistic loop.[32]

If nonsatisfiable desire is satisfied, it precisely mutates into the closed narcissistic loop of the drive. In a dialectical sense, the failure of *Shame*'s commodified classicism is also its success: classicism's cathartic cathexis immanently collapses. In the final drive montage of the film (Brandon in alternating stages of his voyage into an orgiastic sexual netherworld), which exactly mirrors the confusion of flashback and flash-forward of the beginning, catharsis is claimed but simultaneously undermined by the atemporal autoaffection of looped cross-cutting. Near the end of a delirious threesome scene with two prostitutes, an artificially yellow filtered close-up captures an expression of despair on Brandon's face as if the agony of affect breaks through the surface of his character mask. After he finds out about Sissy's suicide attempt, he melodramatically cries in the rain, but again, this apparent catharsis is put into question by the becoming drive of the narrative. Thus, in the last sequence of *Shame*, the beginning returns when Brandon meets the same woman in the subway. Something has changed, it seems—the drive seems to have shifted to the woman; now it is she who stares at him, and for a moment the expression on Brandon's face seems to actualize the Sartrean title affect of the film, "because an affect is what shame is":[33] "shame"—that is released by the traumatic look of the other—"that which puts me into question in my very being, and with which, in one way or another, I must come to terms."[34] However, the indifferent flattening of the classical shot/reverse-shot pattern makes it impossible to decide if this scene finally stages an encounter with the other or is just the repetitive "return into circuit"[35] of what Lee Edelman graphically calls "the arbitrary, future-negating force of a brutal and mindless drive."[36] Anyway, in the final shot the character mask of the zombie-monad is readjusted again: this is the shameless drive image of *Shame*.

The Superficial Sublime: *Drive*

Design and/is crime—Hal Foster's well-known polemical coupling of glossiness and gore could be converted to the interlocking of design and drive. In the contemporary cinema of the drive, destructive desublimation displays itself as design deluxe: "Design is all about desire, but strangely this desire seems almost subject-less today, or at least lack-less; that is, design seems to advance a new kind of narcissism, one that is all image and no interiority—an apotheosis of the subject that is also its potential disappearance."[37] Once again, desire is subsumed by drive, lack by excess, and subjectivity by surplus-enjoyment. Nicolas Winding Refn's *Drive* (2011) is such an exercise in ornamental designer violence, too, its title literally exposing the film's mechanism: the signifier *Drive*, I want to suggest, means not "to drive" but "drive." Released in the same year as *Shame*, *Drive* feels like an uncanny West Coast double of *Shame*, sharing not only Carey Mulligan as the supporting actress but also the distortion of narrative temporality into a flat plateau of drive-montage sequences. But, in contrast to Steve McQueen's neoconservative designer classicism, the Danish director is deeply rooted in genre filmmaking, fusing action, horror, and most notably film noir into a mythopoetic universe far away from a psychological realism even a highly formalist film like *Shame* is still indebted to. One of the immediate theoretical temptations when writing about *Drive* (to which in fact many film critics have succumbed) is to understand it as prototypical example of the Jamesonian "nostalgia film" in which the dense pastiche texture of film historical allusions tends to replace the "real historical time"[38] of a referential outside. In this sense, *Drive* would figure not only as a prime instance of a film noir pastiche (like Kasdan's early 1980s film *Body Heat* for Jameson) but as a doubled simulacrum, a pastiche of a pastiche, remade and remodeled after Walter Hill's similarly titled *Driver* (1978), itself a pastiche of historical film noir and of Jean-Pierre Melville's French noir nostalgia of *Le Samouraï* (1967).[39] Against this all too evident attempt to reduce the film to an obsessive, cinephile nostalgia for nostalgia, I argue that, at the formal level of its drive logic, *Drive* is an absolute contemporary film that works through its own screen memories toward a rigorous self-destruction of nostalgia. Rather than nostalgia for nostalgia, the film carries out nostalgia without nostalgia. To put it more precisely, in *Drive* the apparent fetish for film noir functions not as a ideological veiling of its lack of real historicity but as the unveiling, the laying bare of what could be called film noir's materialism. This noir materialism is nothing other than a materialism of the drive prefiguring the emergence of postmodernity's monadic sociality. At least, this is Joan Copjec's crucial insight in her brilliant text about the vanishing of public space in film noir: far from naming a pathology of the individual, the shift from desire to drive has to be understood as a fundamental change in the social formation of capitalism: "Lacan has argued that this shift describes a general historical transition whose process we are still witnessing: the old modern order of desire, ruled over by an oedipal father, has begun to be replaced by a new order of the drive, in which we no longer have recourse to the protections against *jouissance* that the oedipal father once offered. These protections have been eroded by our society's fetishization of being, that is of *jouissance*."[40]

In actualizing film noir, *Drive* seismographically and graphically registers the erosion of the (old) symbolic order of Oedipal desire and patrimonial law in its recent late capitalist state. While a film like *Shame* nostalgically mourns the waning of desire, the success of *Drive* is exactly its lack of lack, its refusal to reroute drive back to desire that *Shame* at least partly tried to achieve. Delirious Los Angeles set in some eternal 1980s is ruled by an order of the drive in which the law is radically absent from the very beginning: in this universe of crime, the police has ceased to exist. The opening precredit car chase sequence is the only moment in the film where the presence of the police is abstractly evoked by the sound of sirens and helicopters. But Ryan Gosling in the role of the nameless driver manages to hide in the darkness of the night. The police then disappear from the nocturnal stage of *Drive*'s drive world and is allegorically substituted by a Hollywood pastiche of the police: working part-time as a stunt driver for film productions, the driver puts on a police uniform and an uncanny latex mask before performing a particularly risky car crash. He is asked by a member of the crew to sign a contract that releases the production company of any legal responsibility in case of his death.

In this postlegal regime of the drive, the subject is released into a realm outside the social, literally turning the law into trash. Subjected and excluded by this total privatization of the law, the driver is forced to inhabit an asocial state of emergency somewhere between low-level service staff and *lumpenproletariat*. But far away from a raising of class consciousness from below, the driver is identified and identifies himself with the boundless violence of a pastiche police gone berserk: in the violence to come, the driver fills the empty place of the law with his own private version of punishing police power as if the police props of the film set would have sealed his drive destiny forever. The victim of the trashed law imaginarily (mis)identifies himself as the killer in the name of law and

Figure 2. Still from *Drive*

order. Yet this ostensibly right-wing projection must not be misunderstood as the ideological project of a reactionary or even fascist film, but as the disclosure of a class consciousness or class unconsciousness from above that paradoxically seduces and interpellates the very victims of capitalist class antagonisms. Jameson has demonstrated this in his reading of Stanley Kubrick's 1980 *The Shining* in which the proletarized Jack Nicholson beams himself back to the ruling classes of the Roaring Twenties.[41] The law and order delirium of the driver is the ideological symptom of its exact opposite: a law *out of* order, yet as class-stratified and racialized as the older order, as the peculiar whiteness of the latex mask unmistakably signifies. In *Drive* the disorder of the law signals not its malfunction but its excess beyond any justice—a phenomenon Bernard Stiegler recently described in Marcusean psychoanalytical terms as the becoming drive of the superego in late capitalism: "The law, when it is imposed, or compulsively endured, when it is not desired as the idea of what is just, ceases to be the law, becoming merely a sterile order, that is, without future, and thus a factor in the serious disorders to come."[42] If the law is absorbed by the drive, as this sequence of *Drive* shows us, its collective intelligibility as part of a public sphere is swallowed up by private (business) transactions and private (revenge) actions—hence, capitalism and its monads.

A further malicious irony is added by the fact that the name of Irene's (Carey Mulligan) ex-con husband is Standard: crime is standard and perversion is norm. What appears in place of the empty position of the Lacanian "name of the father" (the *nom du père* homonymous with the *non du père*) is a regime of pervert gangsters, a post-Oedipal "regime of the brother":[43] grouped around the evil mob boss Bernie Rose (played by comedian, writer, actor, and director Albert Brooks), the drive creatures of the film all are incarnations of an obscene jouissance beyond the law.[44] Especially Bernie Rose is revealed as an aestheticist of sadistic violence who almost passionately succumbs to idiosyncratic ways of killing and treasures his exquisite collections of different razor blades and knives. This is an allegorical autoportrait of the director Nicolas Winding Refn himself as a cinematic designer of ultraviolence. As a consequence of this mesmerizing fusion of design and crime, speech is reduced to minimum, almost giving *Drive* a silent film's atmosphere with long passages of ambient music muting down all diegetic sounds. In strict equivalence to these drive sounds in the diegesis, the opening track by the Chromatics mechanically repeats the "Tick of a Clock" of its title, followed by the credit pop song, Kavinsky's "Nightcall," whose lyrics call up the drive of the driver: "There's something inside you. It's hard to explain. They're talking about you boy. But you're still the same." There's nothing inside you: the sameness of the driver is the sameness of the drive. Since the drive is driven not by motion but by stasis, similar to the opening of *Shame, Drive*'s belated credit sequence begins with a slow dissolve of delirious Los Angeles's nocturnal skyline to the static image of the driver sitting motionless in his car, filmed from below. Again, the moving image bleeds out to an apparent freeze frame until minimal body gestures vivify this zombie of cool.

In this succession of shots, the driver is less a human figure than an asubjective aggregate state of the noirish sublime of the city. Another dissolve from an ornamental overhead panorama shot of night traffic to the figure in the car testifies as well to the incommensurability of urban hyperspace and the human body Jameson hinted at: the driver maps and is mapped by the city, obviously different than in the Hegelian/Lukácsian cognitive mapping Jameson hoped for but, rather, in the mode of a libidinal mapping of structures of (non)feeling, of drive intensities inherent both to object and to subject. Let's stay for a moment at the side of this subjectless subject, perfectly embodied by a new generation of (non)actors like Michael Fassbender or Ryan Gosling: their petrified character masks mark the latest stage of what Jameson in a scattered series of remarks about the mutation of Hollywood acting in postmodernity referred to as the ongoing crisis of method acting.[45] Writing about *Body Heat*, he characterizes William Hurt's acting as follows: "The latest generation of starring actors continue to assure the conventional functions of stardom (most notably sexuality) but in the utter absence of 'personality' in the older sense, and with something of the anonymity of character acting."[46] Though compared with Fassbender (whom Ridley Scott consistently cast as an android in *Prometheus*) and Gosling (whose gentle boyishness all too often tilts over to borderline states; see *Murder by Numbers, Stay, All Good Things*, and of course Winding Refn's *Only God Forgives*), William Hurt in *Body Heat* is never endangered to become a drive-creature, maybe because he remains vulnerable, not to say—hurt. "History is what hurts,"[47] as Jameson is not tired to remind us, but hurt is absent in *Drive* despite the orgies of violence in which the driver immerses himself. In the post-post-method acting era that Fassbender and Gosling are emblematic of, drive-induced coldness and cruelty seal the ultimate "waning of affect" on the level of acting. Acting is replaced by acting out, and Hurt is lost.

The relationship between drive and affect is a rather complicated issue in psychoanalytical theory and too difficult to be tackled here in detail. Yet there are good theoretical arguments for thinking of the Jamesonian waning of affect as correlative to the rising of drive, if drive is precisely understood as a quantitative rather than qualitative category, or what Adrian Johnston in an extensive study named "negative affect": "Pressure registers itself as 'negative affect,' that is, an unpleasurable sensation resulting from the accumulation of tension when demands of the drive-source make themselves felt."[48] Drive is pure quantitative intensity, a negative affect in the double meaning of negativity and negation, hence also a disappearance or a waning of qualitative affect.[49] Surprisingly for his usual contempt of psychoanalysis, in his first cinema book Gilles Deleuze gives a very similar definition of the drive in his taxonomy of the "drive image," which is translated from the French "image-pulsion" as "impulse image."[50] According to Deleuze, the drive occupies a hybrid position between affection and action, the drive being a "degenerate affect" and an "embryonic action."[51] The drive is a deformed affect unable to facially transcend the body, stuck in the "frontier between the somatic and the mental,"[52] in the classical Freudian notion of the drive. The drive, Deleuze insists, is not affect, emotion, or feeling: "An impulse is not an affect, because it is an impression in the strongest sense and not an expression. But neither is it like the feelings or emotions which regulate and deregulate behaviour. Now we must recognise that this new set is not a mere intermediary, a place of transition, but possesses a perfect consistency and autonomy, with the result that the action-image remains powerless to represent it, and the affection-image powerless to make it felt."[53] This means that the drive image is not an inferior version of the affection image, because the drive's degeneration is its very generic form, the positivity of a negative/negated affectivity.

In *Drive* this impression of the drive has its formal signature in the dissolves mentioned above. Whereas in classical cinematic syntax dissolves usually are markers of narrative transition, in the hallucinatory simultaneity of *Drive* dissolves gain a pictorial autonomy beyond any narrative caesura. While in *Shame* the atemporal cross-cuttings impose stasis over movement, in *Drive* the atemporal layering of shots impose "Cronos and not Chronos,"[54] devouring cinematic time and releasing the short circuit of classical cinematic "fort/da."[55] Montage gives way to a superimposition

Figure 3. Still from *Drive*

of presentness, whether in the hard montage of *Shame* or the soft montage of *Drive*. The recurrent simultaneous dissolves are symptomatic of a superimposition of sameness suspending the temporalization of presence and absence, on-screen and off. Under the impression of the drive, the cinematic image turns to an imprint of constant and permanent layers—an interface.[56] In a particularly impressive dissolve, the close-up of the driver's leather-gloved hand forming a fist and his motionless face are overlaid by a long shot of him entering a nightclub to act out his neverending series of gory vengeance.

The interface of autoaffection is the autoaffection of the interface: sameness dissolves into sameness rather than otherness, charging the action-inhibited drive image with an immanent virtual violence Deleuze hinted at: "It is a violence which is not merely internal or innate, but *static*, whose only equivalent is that of Bacon in painting, when he summons up an 'emanation' which arises from an immobile character, or that of Jean Genet in literature, when he describes the extraordinary violence which can be contained in a motionless hand at rest."[57] However, in *Drive* this static statics of violence is driven to the point of implosion/explosion in the second half of the film: being a strictly split film, the first part of the film almost appears to be a somnambulant romance movie in which Gosling and Mulligan exchange shy gestures of amorous affection, behaving like two inhibited teenagers. In the first half *Drive* stages a world of asexual sublimation in which the highest of feelings is a tender touch of their hands during a nightly car ride. If inhibition is an effect of prohibition, the law must somehow be present as a standard, and so it's no other than Standard (Oscar Isaac), Irene's husband and father of their little son, who incarnates a (per)version of the law that prohibits the romance of boy and girl. But the (gold) Standard has always already eroded in the regime of the drive, and it is Standard himself who releases the first eruption of violence after being shot in a failed robbery of a pawnshop. But far away from realizing their desire after the removal of the obstacle, the exact opposite happens in the film: the production of the heterosexual pair is impossible not despite the elimination of symbolic law but, rather, because of it. In a degenerated, desublimated displacement of repressed sexuality to excessive violence, in strict rotation the driver exterminates all the gangsters who may menace the life of his beloved. Retroactively, the first part of the film is recoded as the staging of a faked, simulated world of temporalized desire, if desire is understood as the expectation and anticipation of an open futurity in the sense of Todd McGowan's useful delineation of a contemporary cinema of the drive: "Desire exists in the interval between an initial awareness of the object of desire and the moment of obtaining that object. This temporal distance is essential for nourishing desire because it allows the subject to believe that the realization of desire is a future possibility. I recognize that I don't have what I want right now, but I can see the realization of my desire in the future."[58] In *Drive*, drive disguises itself as desire, the cinema of drive in nostalgia for a lost cinema of desire.

In what is perhaps the decisive moment in the film, the destruction of this nostalgic design of desire is consummated within a shock moment of acted out violence: "This is no longer an acted, but a compressed violence, from which only abrupt, effective and exact, often terrible acts which show a raw impulse, derive."[59] It's the first and last kiss of the film: gloriously illuminated by the elevator's light and hypnotically transubstantiated by an extreme slow motion, all of the sudden this kitsch kiss is followed by graphic gore of the most disgusting kind when the driver turns the villain's head into a bloody sludge with his sledgehammer boots. It is important to interpret this extreme moment not just as the self-destruction of romance by horror, lack by excess, desire by drive, but precisely as its perverse fulfillment: the killing is the *real* love act; the kiss, just foreplay—*Kiss Me Deadly*. To put it in a dialectical formula: the *dérive* of drive from desire is one and the same with the completion of desire by drive. The drive is both problem and solution to a deadlock immanent to desire. Lacan always insisted that the psychotic's phantasmatic delusion is a (re)solution in the realm of the real, a kind of remedy for the failure of symbolization that is to be distinguished from the neurotic's struggling with the reality principle: "In neurosis, inasmuch as reality is not fully rearticulated symbolically into the external world, it is in a second phase that a partial flight from reality, an incapacity to confront this secretly preserved part of reality, occurs in the subject. In psychosis, on the contrary, reality itself initially contains a hole that the world of fantasy will subsequently fill."[60] In spite of the danger of oversimplifying these complicated clinical matters, and for the sake of aesthetic analysis, I propose to classify *Shame* as a neurotic version of the drive image, while *Drive* is the

Figure 4. Still from *Drive*

psychotic version of it. *Shame* nostalgically mourns the waned (neurotic) affect of shame in sexual desublimation, whereas *Drive* positively affirms the risen (psychotic) nonaffect of drive in violent desublimation. The violence of sex (*Shame*) and the sex of violence (*Drive*) are dialectically interlocked as two fundamental formations of the contemporary drive image.

After having sent his bloody love letter to Irene, in the most hallucinatory allegorical shot of *Drive*, the already pop-iconic scorpion bomber jacket of the driver slowly pulses under the impulse of raw drive energy—*Scorpio Rising*. Alluding to the homoerotic fetish world of Kenneth Anger's avant-garde classic movie, this drive image literally animates an undead animal: the scorpion is a totem of the drive, an ornament of circular forms in which the deadly sting of the tail autoaffectively heads toward the head. As already shown, this circular closure of the drive is the reason for the *dérive* from goal to aim. The drive's aim is the constant conservation of itself—the drive drives itself: "For the subject of the drive, the means becomes the end."[61] In the second half of the film, the unleashing of excessive violence mutates from means to end. And this is why it cannot end. If violence is disarticulated from the action image, it loses its redeeming potential, hence its causal, cathartic, and cathectic quality—it ceases "to be a reaction linked to a situation: [it] become[s] internal and natural to the character, innate."[62] Thus, the drive image is tied to a paradoxical logic in which the accumulation of violence is structured not by a steady rising toward an orgasmic climax but, rather, by a serial flatness or repetitive sameness. Accumulation merges with repetition, movement with stasis, speed with inertia, excess with entropy. The drive, writes Deleuze, "accelerates in undoing itself."[63] The cartography of the contemporary drive image could be imagined as an endless plateau, a posthistorical (Hollywood) flatland populated by neurotic and psychotic monads of jouissance.

If in the following of the formerly mentioned dissolve from close-up to long shot the driver appears as a doppelgänger of himself in simultaneous sameness to threaten the gangster Cook, the psychotic ambience of the film is audiovisually rendered by the heightening of fragmented partial objects. In an important passage Deleuze defines the close-up in the drive image as the exceptional case in which partiality is magnified and totalized: "So that the impulse-image is undoubtedly the only case in which the close-up effectively becomes partial object: but this is *not* because the close-up 'is' partial object; but because the partial object being that of the impulse then exceptionally becomes close-up. The impulse is an act which tears away, ruptures, dislocates. Perversion is therefore not its deviation, but its derivation, that is, its normal expression in the derived milieu."[64] Not deviation but derivation, *dérive*.

The impression of drive pressure overcharges and "overcathects" the partial object with (psychotic) enjoyment beyond the pleasure principle. The hand with the archaic hammer trembling with tactile acoustic jouissance, the driver is autoaffected by his own drive. Meanwhile, a group of ornamentally arranged strip dancers observe this brutal acting out with lifeless coldness, circularly closed by a mirror image of the driver. To return to Jameson's notion of the waning of affect: the dummy-like posture of the models not only recalls the window-shopped superficiality of Andy Warhol's *Diamond Dust Shoes*; it is an allegory of reified spectatorship in the cinema of late capitalism. The waning of affect has finally petrified the aesthetic experience of the spectator who consumes designer violence with utter unaffectedness in a perversion of the Kantian notion of the beautiful as purposiveness without purpose. The negative affect of the drive has finally sealed the negation of affect—the desublimated beautiful, once again, without shame, but also without the "decorative exhilaration"[65] Jameson still detected as a relic of pastiche affect in the Warhol picture: "Nothing in this painting organizes even a minimal place for the viewer,"[66] so nothing in this film does. The waning of affect seems synonymous to the waning of the cinematic spectator: the implied audience of the drive image is an (un)dead one, forever glacéd by the reified fetish of a visuality that does not return the gaze.

In one gruesome moment during the concluding half-hour orgy of automated violence, *Drive* consequently recalls the famous (non)ending of the most apocalyptic of all film noirs, Robert Aldrich's *Kiss Me Deadly* (1955), when the latex-masked driver drowns Bernie Rose's companion Nino (Ron Perlman) in the open sea. The deadly radiation of atomic light in *Kiss Me Deadly*'s apocalyptic blast is echoed here in the pulsing of the searchlights overexposing the extreme darkness of the image with flashes of X-ray–like neon lights. This is the noirish return of the Jamesonian "hysterical sublime" after the end of nature, "an experience bordering on terror, the fitful glimpse, in astonishment, stupor, and awe, of what was so enormous as to crush human life altogether."[67] Yet in the drive image the sublime as much as the beautiful falls under the doom of the desublimation of what I call a superficial sublime, a sublime bereft of (oceanic) deepness and (affective) depth. In such a desublimated sublime, if you like, the Kantian negative pleasure has been absorbed by the drive: this sublime is superficial, stump, even stupid, or "stuplime," to cite Sianne Ngai's fine neologism she implicitly links to the circular "stuplimity" of the drive itself: "Yet this preference for the cycle, an endless round of driving excitations and fatigues."[68] In assigning *Shame* to a classicist and *Drive* to a romanticist version of the drive image, I am also tempted to split the title of Žižek's book on David Lynch's *Lost Highway* as a double aesthetic category[69]—*Shame; or, The Art of the Serious Beautiful*, and *Drive; or, The Art of the Ridiculous Sublime*: "Sublimity should *follow* Beauty because it is the point of its breakdown, of its mediation, of its self-referential negativity. . . . Beauty calms and comforts; Sublimity excites and agitates."[70]

I insist that these categories are for all their utter reification still aesthetic and not technological: despite the fact that *Shame* was actually shot with traditional 35-mm film and *Drive* with a digital ARRI Alexa camera not at all marks a media-ontological difference between the two films. Rather, it is a difference of degrees, the digital *Drive* only heightening the sterile superficiality of the visual that *Shame* is likewise indebted to. Yet *Drive* more explicitly highlights a specific (in)difference of the digital image that could be described as a strange bifurcation of the classical Bazinian congruency of deep focus and deep space. The high-definition images of *Drive* are simultaneously deep and flat or, to phrase it differently, visual depth itself is an effect, a mirage, a simulation staged by an antecedent depthlessness. Thus, *Drive* digitally demystifies its apparent nostalgia for film noir without taking refuge in the (neo)classicist illusion to reroute drive back to desire. This nostalgia is most evident in *Shame*'s contrived, pretentious long-take affection image of Carey Mulligan singing an ultravulnerable, quasi-naked version of Sinatra's "New York, New York," moving even stone-cold Brandon to tears. This mannered pastiche of bigger-than-life emotion reveals the film's classicist nostalgia for melodrama as utterly conservative, not to say reactionary.

What at first seems to be a rather common heterosexist feature, both films stage a purified feminine desire image as a redeeming counterpole to the destructive masculine drive image, once again articulating a decisive difference between *Shame* and *Drive*. Sissy's desire for a memory against the blind drive of Brandon in *Shame* (her voice mail words "we are not bad people, we just come from a bad place" linger over the sexual frenzy of the final threesome) remains a purely private plea against the amnesia of acting out, whereas the desire image of Irene in *Drive* can be decoded in

Jamesonian terms as a political allegory of class: as a single mother working as a waitress in a diner, Irene is as subjected to the underpaid service economy as the driver, but she's not giving in to the delusions of the driver's drive, insisting in her opaque yet gentle desire, a desire to desire. In one of the many acoustic mise-en-abyme moments of the film, Irene's desire finds its musical expression in the "Under Your Spell" song of the band Desire, in which the lyrics seem to ask the driver: "Do you know the difference between obsession and desire?" In asking this question, Irene resists the regime of the drive, "invaginating the airless space of the zombie-monad," as Tavia Nyong'o writes, "by way of her reflective, acoustic image of her desire, a desire that brings 'the whole absent world and earth into the revelation around itself,' as Jameson puts it, within the silent tread of the single mother, the loneliness of her kitchen vigils."[71] In deprivatizing the desire image of Carey Mulligan by way of a class-political antagonism, *Drive* "against the grains of dystopic claims"[72] enshrines a feminine utopian impulse of a nonnostalgic desire that is not swallowed up by the drive, a desire incarnated in the sublimated yet touchingly "common" beauty of Carey Mulligan's indeterminate yearning face.[73]

The aesthetic and political superiority of *Drive* over *Shame* rests upon *Drive*'s radical negation of defensive nostalgia that also proves in my (polemical) opinion the superiority of genre filmmaking over auteur cinema—at least in Hollywood. In laying bare what Copjec in an astonishing dialectial inflection called the "ersatz representation of depth" in film noir, *Drive* destroys the phantasmatical protective screen of visual depth as the very ideology of film noir and its nostalgic neopastiches: "The visual techniques of *film noir* are placed in the service of creating an artificial replication of depth *in the image* in order to make up for, to compensate for, the absence of depth *in the narrative spaces*; that is, these techniques are placed in the service of a defense against the drive."[74] In the digital quasi depth of *Drive*'s images this ersatz representation of depth ceases to be a compensatory lure for the waning of desire, because in the fully unfolded drive image there is no longer an antinomy between image and narrative, the image becoming as flat as the narrative on a plateau of sameness. In the superficial sublime, sublimity has lost its enigmatic force. The digital short-circuit of deception and disclosure exposes a (cinematic) world completely lacking any mysterious depth, "a world in which nothing can lie hidden, everything must come to light. This is really the dark truth of *film noir*."[75] Visual and narrative mystery is replaced by a constant, flat, and uniform "undeadness" of what is finally disclosed as the ultimate death drive of *Drive*: the driver is someone who is not capable of dying. This is a paradox Žižek repeatedly hinted at: "In this precise sense, the death drive stands for its exact opposite, for the dimension of the 'undead,' of a spectral life which insists beyond [biological] death."[76]

In the final confrontation with Bernie Rose, the ending of *Drive* nearly symmetrically echoes the ending of *Shame*, dissolving and cross-cutting between flashback (Irene listening to the driver's voice mail message), diegetic presence (the driving to and meeting with Bernie Rose in a Chinese restaurant), and flash-forward (the knife stabbing in the parking lot in broad, "secretless" daylight turning the characters into ghostly silhouettes). Again, the startling similarity of both film's final drive montages reveals a minimal yet pivotal difference in their respective audiovisual rendering of the antagonism between drive and desire. While the acousmatic voice mail message of Sissy haunts the drive montage of *Shame* with the vague memory of the other, in *Drive* it is the voice of the driver that sends Irene the message of abandonment ("I have to go somewhere now; I don't think I can come back"), while a dissolve unites them across their spatiotemporal distance. Faithful to the romanticism of the film, this gesture is the tender reversal of the former deadly kiss: love is loss, so the drive has literally to drive away from desire, paradoxically self-sublimating itself,[77] to enable utopian (feminine) desire to rebuild a world from the ruins of the dystopian (masculine) drive netherworld.

Figure 5. Still from *Drive*

After the driver stabs Bernie Rose to death, a frozen close-up of the (mortally) wounded driver's apparently dead face lingers for almost half a minute until, in exact symmetry to the beginning of the film, the slow wink of his eye signals his undead resurrection as a zombie who has survived his own biological death: "He exists as a kind of self-vampire or self-parasite, sucking life from his own steady dissolution, languishing in some twilight region between the living and the dead."[78] Totally possessed by the undead death drive, this interminable ending circles back to the beginning. Dispensing with beginnings and endings altogether, the driver drives along the lost highway of the drive as if nothing ever happened. The driver is now the exact negation of what the refrain line from the concluding pop song proclaims him to be: "A real human being." *Drive* ends with an interminable ending.

A few final words on Jameson: "But one cannot awake until one has first measured the extent and the intensity of the nightmare,"[79] he concluded his chapter on Sartre in *Marxism and Form*. It's better to suffer through the enduring nightmare of our posthistorical present than to promise a false awakening, a false consciousness. History hurts with a vengeance even if/because history seems to have disappeared in the "bad infinity" of Hollywood cinema. The absolute contemporaneity of *Shame* and *Drive* "is to be found in this aesthetic of an absolute present, where, as Adorno warned about late capitalism, all negativity has been tendentially reduced and extirpated—and this not only in his sense of the distances still maintained by critique and 'critical theory,' but even in the temporal sense of the gaps left by the past and the mirages fitfully generated by the future: an absolute reduction to the present and a mesmerization by the empirically and sensorially existent."[80]

But this is not as sad as it sounds. At least for the two films discussed it is imperative not to forget a famous phrase by Joseph Conrad that Jameson dialectically reminded us of: "In the destructive element immerse."[81] Or, don't be ashamed of drive.

Notes

1. Jameson, *Political Unconscious*, 9.
2. Jameson, *Postmodernism*, 284.
3. Jameson, "Aesthetics of Singularity," 104.
4. Williams, *Marxism and Literature*, 133.
5. Jameson, *Ancients and the Postmoderns*, 128.
6. Karatani, *Transcritique*, 209.
7. See Hegel, *Science of Logic*, 228.
8. Shaviro, *Doom Patrols*, 2.
9. Jameson, "Aesthetics of Singularity," 122.
10. For a queer critique of Jameson's *Postmodernism*, see Merck, "Figuring Out Andy Warhol."
11. "The death drive is not a purposeful narrative, but the ruin of all narrative." Eagleton, *After Theory*, 215.
12. Jameson, *Signatures of the Visible*, 1.
13. Ibid.
14. See Lacan, *Four Fundamental Concepts of Psychoanalysis*, 179.
15. Žižek, *Ticklish Subject*, 370.
16. Lacan, *Four Fundamental Concepts of Psychoanalysis*, 183.
17. Jameson, *Postmodernism*, 27.
18. Ibid., 26.
19. Ibid., 27.
20. See Shaviro, *Post-cinematic Affect*, 123–30.
21. "Let me say that if there is anything resembling a drive it is a montage. It

is not a montage conceived in a perspective referring to finality." Lacan, *Four Fundamental Concepts of Psychoanalysis*, 169.

22. Ibid., 165.

23. Shaviro, *Connected*, 168, 169.

24. Koolhaas, *Delirious New York*, 9–28.

25. Jameson, *Postmodernism*, 9.

26. Ibid., 38–45.

27. Marcuse, *One-Dimensional Man*, 62. About the sexual effects of glazing Marcuse writes: "Functionalism, going artistic, promotes this trend. Shops and offices open themselves through huge glass windows and expose their personnel; inside, high counters and non-transparent partitions are coming down. The corrosion of privacy in massive apartment houses and suburban homes breaks the barrier which formerly separated the individual from the public existence and exposes more easily the attractive qualities of other wives and other husbands." Ibid., 63.

28. Klammer, "Ideas Not Medium."

29. Jameson, *Marxism and Form*, 105.

30. "In Shame jedoch erfüllen die in der filmischen Diegese auftauchenden Glasflächen eine zusätzliche Funktion: Sie versetzen die Zuschauer im Kinoraum in eine reflexive Distanz zu dem gezeigten Geschehen, unterbinden eine allzu starke Identifikation mit dem Charakter des Brandon und sorgen für eine Scheidung von Betrachterkörper, Projektionsfläche und projizierten Körpern. So werden diese gläsernen, spiegelnden Versatzstücke der Entfremdung durch ihren spezifischen ästhetischen Gebrauch zu (Heil-)Mitteln der Reflexion und Distanzierung umfunktioniert" (translation mine). Klammer, "Ideas Not Medium," 103, 104.

31. Most notably in the orgiastic threesome at the end of *Shame*, but also in the stylistically virtuous long-take torture sequence of *12 Years a Slave* (2013). See also Rebhandl, "Atrocity Exhibition," 4–7.

32. Cubitt, *Cinema Effect*, 169, 180.

33. Copjec, "May '68, the Emotional Month," 92.

34. Jameson, *Marxism and Form*, 304.

35. Lacan, *Four Fundamental Concepts of Psychoanalysis*, 179.

36. Edelman, *No Future*, 127.

37. Foster, *Design and Crime*, 25.

38. Jameson, *Postmodernism*, 21.

39. See Žižek, *Looking Awry*, 112, 113.

40. Copjec, "The Phenomenal Nonphenomenal," 182.

41. See Jameson, *Signatures of the Visible*, 112–34.

42. Stiegler, *Lost Sprit of Capitalism*, 91.

43. See McCannell, *Regime of the Brother*.

44. "The neutral, dead system of symbolic community and exchange that had supported the classical world has given away in *film noir* to a world that crawls with private enjoyment and thus rots the old networks of communication." Copjec, "The Phenomenal Nonphenomenal," 194.

45. The first piece of this series is Jameson's ideology critique of Al Pacino's performance in Sidney Lumet's *Dog Day Afternoon* in *Signatures of the Visible*, 47–74. See also my commentary of this crucial text in Lie, *Die Außenseite des Films*, 171–79.

46. Jameson, *Postmodernism*, 20.

47. Jameson, *Political Unconscious*, 102.

48. Johnston, *Time Driven*, 273.

49. Jameson's confrontation of affect and intensity hints at this direction.

50. Deleuze, *Movement-Image*, 123–40. Most scholarly discussions of Deleuze's cinema books tend to neglect the impulse image in favor of the more accessible chapters on the affection image.

51. Ibid., 123.

52. Freud, "Instinct and Their Vicissitudes," 122.

53. Deleuze, *Movement-Image*, 123.

54. Deleuze, *Time-Image*, 81.

55. Freud, *Beyond the Pleasure Principle*, 8–10.

56. This formal device is reminiscent of the delirious dissolves in the famous opening sequence of Francis Ford Coppola's *Apocalypse Now* (1979), with its blurring of beginning and end, left and right, down and under, internal and external, subjective and objective, a film that seems to have very much influenced Winding Refn, regarding the even more obvious pastiche of this film in his *Only God Forgives* (2013). For a theory of the interface as short-circuit of shot and reverse shot, see Žižek, *Fright of Real Tears*, 55–75.

57. Deleuze, *Movement-Image*, 136.

58. McGowan, *Out of Time*, 26.

59. Deleuze, *Movement-Image*, 135.

60. Lacan, *Psychoses*, 45.

61. McGowan, *Out of Time*, 16.

62. Deleuze, *Movement-Image*, 135.

63. Ibid., 126.

64. Ibid., 128.

65. Jameson, *Postmodernism*, 10.

66. Ibid., 8.

67. Ibid., 34.

68. Ngai, *Ugly Feelings*, 295. The "stuplime" is a flat, fatigued degeneration of the sublime: "This term allows us to invoke the sublime—albeit negatively, since we infuse it with thickness or even stupidity—while detaching it from its spiritual and transcendent connotations and its close affiliation with Romanticism" (271). I thank Damon Young for advising me to read Sianne Ngai's work in relation to Jameson.

69. See Žižek, *Art of the Ridiculous Sublime*.

70. Žižek, *Sublime Object of Ideology*, 228.

71. Nyong'o, "Response to the Author."

72. This quasi-Jamesonian phrase is from the song "A Real Hero" by College Feat. Electric Youth.

73. On the distinction between drive creatures and desire creatures, see also Elsaesser and Buckland, *Studying Contemporary American Film*, 238–48.

74. Copjec, "The Phenomenal Nonphenomenal," 102.

75. Ibid.

76. Žižek, *Puppet and the Dwarf*, 93.

77. See Copjec, *Imagine There's No Woman*, 30–33, for a more complicated account of the relationship between drive and sublimation.

78. Eagleton, *On Evil*, 70–71.

79. Jameson, *Marxism and Form*, 319.

80. Jameson, *Antinomies of Realism*, 300.

81. This is the title of Fredric Jameson's essay on Hans-Jürgen Syberberg's films in his *Signatures of the Visible*, 86–111. The ambivalent implications of this phrase were recently (albeit critically) discussed by Benjamin Noys in the context of accelerationism in *Malign Velocities*, 6–8.

References

Copjec, Joan. 1992. "The Phenomenal Nonphenomenal: Private Space in *Film Noir*." In *Shades of Noir*, edited by Joan Copjec, 167–97. New York: Verso.

Copjec, Joan. 2002. *Imagine There's No Woman: Ethics and Sublimation.* Cambridge, MA: MIT Press.

Copjec, Joan. 2006. "May '68, the Emotional Month." In *Lacan: The Silent Partners*, edited by Slavoj Žižek, 90–114. London: Verso.

Cubitt, Sean. 2004. *The Cinema Effect.* Cambridge, MA: MIT Press.

Deleuze, Gilles. 1986. *The Movement-Image.* Vol. 1 of *Cinema.* Minneapolis: University of Minnesota Press.

Deleuze, Gilles. 1989. *The Time-Image.* Vol. 2 of *Cinema.* Minneapolis: University of Minnesota Press.

Eagleton, Terry. 2001. *On Evil.* New Haven, CT: Yale University Press.

Eagleton, Terry. 2003. *After Theory.* New York: Basic.

Edelman, Lee. 2004. *No Future: Queer Theory and the Death Drive.* Durham, NC: Duke University Press.

Elsaesser, Thomas, and Warren Buckland. 2002. *Studying Contemporary American Film: A Guide to Movie Analysis.* London: Arnold.

Foster, Hal. 2002. *Design and Crime (and Other Diatribes).* London: Verso.

Freud, Sigmund. 1957. "Instinct and Their Vicissitudes." In *Standard Edition of the Complete Psychological Works of Sigmund Freud*, edited by James Strachey, vol. 14, 117–40. London: Hogarth.

Freud, Sigmund. 1962. *Beyond the Pleasure Principle.* Edited by James Strachey. New York: Norton.

Hegel, Georg Friedrich Wilhelm. 1969. *Science of Logic.* New York: Humanities Press.

Jameson, Fredric. 1971. *Marxism and Form: Twentieth-Century Dialectial Theories of Literature.* Princeton, NJ: Princeton University Press.

Jameson, Fredric. 1982. *The Political Unconscious: Narrative as a Socially Symbolic Act.* Ithaca, NY: Cornell University Press.

Jameson, Fredric. 1991. *Postmodernism; or, The Cultural Logic of Late Capitalism.* Durham, NC: Duke University Press.

Jameson, Fredric. 1992. *Signatures of the Visible.* London: Routledge.

Jameson, Fredric. 2013. *The Antinomies of Realism.* London: Verso.

Jameson, Fredric. 2015. "The Aesthetics of Singularity." *New Left Review* 92: 101–32.

Jameson, Fredric. 2015. *The Ancients and the Postmoderns: On the Historicity of Forms.* New York: Verso.

Johnston, Adrian. 2005. *Time Driven: Metapsychology and the Splitting of the Drive.* Evanston, IL: Northwestern University Press.

Karatani, Kojin. 2003. *Transcritique: Kant and Marx.* Cambridge, MA: MIT Press.

Klammer, Markus. 2013. "Ideas Not Medium: Von den Film- und Videoinstallationen zum kinematografischen Werk Steve McQueens." In *I Want the Screen to Be a Massive Mirror: Vorträge zu Steve McQueen*, edited by Stephan E. Hauser and Tom Bisig, 83–108. Basel: Laurenz-Stiftung, Schaulager.

Koolhaas, Rem. 1997. *Delirious New York: A Retroactive Manifesto for Manhattan.* New York: Monacelli Press.

Lacan, Jacques. 1981. *The Four Fundamental Concepts of Psychoanalysis.* Book 11 of *The Seminars of Jacques Lacan.* London: Norton.

Lacan, Jacques. 1993. *The Psychoses.* Book 3 of *The Seminars of Jacques Lacan.* London: Norton.

Lie, Sulgi. 2012. *Die Außenseite des Films: Zur politischen Filmästhetik*. Zurich: Diaphanes.

Marcuse, Herbert. 1964. *The One-Dimensional Man: Studies in the Ideology of Advanced Industrial Society*. New York: Routledge.

McCannell, Juliet Flower. 1991. *The Regime of the Brother: After the Patriarchy*. New York: Routledge.

McGowan, Todd. 2011. *Out of Time: Desire in Atemporal Cinema*. Minneapolis: University of Minnesota Press.

Merck, Mandy. 1996. "Figuring Out Andy Warhol." In *Out Warhol*, edited by Jennifer Doyle, Jonathan Flatley, and José Esteban Nuñoz, 224–37. Durham, NC: Duke University Press.

Ngai, Sianne. 2005. *Ugly Feelings*. Cambridge, MA: Harvard University Press.

Noys, Benjamin. 2014. *Malign Velocities: Accelerationism and Capitalism*. Winchester, UK: Zero Books.

Nyong'o, Tavia. 2015. "Response to the Author." Paper presented at the workshop "The Cultural Logic of Contemporary Capitalism: Jameson and After." The New School, New York, 21 February.

Rebhandl, Bert. 2013. "Atrocity Exhibition." *Cargo: Film/Medien/Kultur* 20: 4–7.

Shaviro, Steven. 1997. *Doom Patrols: A Theoretical Fiction about Postmodernism*. New York: Serpent's Tail.

Shaviro, Steven. 2003. *Connected; or, What It Means to Live in the Network Society*. Minneapolis: University of Minnesota Press.

Shaviro, Steven. 2010. *Post-cinematic Affect*. Winchester, WA: Zero Books.

Stiegler, Bernard. 2014. *The Lost Sprit of Capitalism*. Cambridge, MA: Polity.

Williams, Raymond. 1977. *Marxism and Literature*. Oxford: Oxford University Press.

Žižek, Slavoj. 1989. *The Sublime Object of Ideology*. London: Verso.

Žižek, Slavoj. 1991. *Looking Awry: An Introduction to Jacques Lacan through Popular Culture*. Cambridge, MA: MIT Press.

Žižek, Slavoj. 2000. *The Art of the Ridiculous Sublime: On David Lynch's Lost Highway*. Seattle: University of Washington Press.

Žižek, Slavoj. 2001. *The Fright of Real Tears: Krzysztof Kieślowski between Theory and Post-theory*. London: BFI.

Žižek, Slavoj. 2001. *The Ticklish Subject: The Absent Centre of Political Ontology*. New York: Verso.

Žižek, Slavoj. 2003. *The Puppet and the Dwarf: The Perverse Core of Christianity*. Cambridge, MA: MIT Press.

Adorno by the Pool

or, Television Then and Now

Amy Villarejo

Where is queer television, now? Not just the nagging ontological question, what is television now?, but where? Where should we look for it and its consequences? I play on the title of a recent conference, "Where Is Frankfurt, Now?" that interrogated the legacy of the Frankfurt School for the present moment.[1] And by "present moment" the conference organizers meant a number of things: the state of film and media theory in the twenty-first century, media and culture in post-1968 Europe and North America (institutions, media technologies), and social movements and shifts that prominently included feminist and queer art and theory, as well as postcolonialism and critiques from the Global South. Think of the names of those Frankfurters: Horkheimer, Adorno, Kluge, Habermas, Marcuse, Benjamin, Kracauer, and a host of others whose names swirl in connection to them (Brecht, Sergei Eisenstein, Heiner Müller, Heidegger, Kittler, Godard, etc.). Now match up the names to the themes or topics above.

If you're like me and you seek to revisit some of these important questions about politics and aesthetics raised by the Frankfurt School, you think, for a start, you have to say why Herbert Marcuse (the theorist most easily identified with questions of gender and sexuality) isn't necessarily helpful to feminist and queer media theory today (I do that in the next section). And then you have to say why you think Theodor Adorno continues to be the most helpful thinker of what he called the culture industries, not because they betray some essential continuity over the period from the mid-twentieth century when he wrote cogently about them to today, but precisely because Adorno remains an agile and remarkable theorist of how to produce ensembles of technocultural production as objects of located

Social Text 127 · Vol. 34, No. 2 · June 2016
DOI 10.1215/01642472-3467978   © 2016 Duke University Press

thought. My object in this article, as it has been before, is television, then and now. I begin with a word about how this article departs from the extended reflection on Adorno I offer in my book *Ethereal Queer*.[2]

Ethereal Queer is organized to address shifts in the temporal organization of the television apparatus over the period of its coherence as a broadcast technology in the United States, roughly the 1940s to the first decade of the twenty-first century. It moves from the network era to the introduction of consolidated public television and then cable television systems (or multiplatform delivery), and, I confess, I then simply stop, baffled a bit by the digital conversion and its ramifications. The book's argument is simple: as television makes and takes our time in different ways, with ever-changing relationships to what it means to belong (appear, endure, attach) to normative social types and groups, television changes what we understand to be queer, and we, in turn, change television's capacities to take and make queer time.

In the book's first chapter, Adorno becomes my guide for understanding the television apparatus in the network age, so let me say why and how. I read closely a single essay by Adorno, "How to Look at Television" (published in English in the United States in 1954), to derive Adorno's view of the television apparatus as particularly responsive to feminist and queer dynamics. This surprised me, and I hope that it surprises my readers in turn—Adorno is not widely appreciated for nuanced writing about these issues. And yet there it is: his essay is itself an extended close analysis of how television—particularly the sitcom, and the sitcom importantly made in Los Angeles in the new three-camera studio environment of the postwar period—constructs imprisoning stereotypes for its women viewers, stereotypes of female power and sexual possibility that it then contains and, what's worse, offers as *negative* poles of identification for the overwhelmingly female viewership of the era.

Television constructs images of ourselves by which we become more imprisoned through the assent television demands through its mode of address, a mode that involves a presumptively female viewer whose labor time is coextensive with television time and whose attention television commodifies as it simultaneously constrains the viewer's imaginative possibilities. That's his take on *Our Miss Brooks* and the other sitcoms and anthology dramas whose scripts he assessed for his essay. In that sitcom (itself adapted from radio), television shows us a spunky and witty schoolteacher (Eve Arden as Connie Brooks, the titular character), and then it punishes both the character and our identificatory affection for the very bid for freedom it showcases.

What immediately appeals to me about this understanding of television is that it hardly depends upon the exemplary program or particular generic codes of freedom and constraint integral to midcentury television;

to the contrary, it is an analysis, if not a wholesale indictment, of how the apparatus functions to make our leisure time into (active and productive, not simply negative) assent to capitalist imperatives and conformity to social norms. And it seems right about *Our Miss Brooks*: somehow, no critic had gotten around to analyzing what Adorno was actually watching (or reading in the way of scripts) while he was in exile in California, and so it seemed important to me to gauge whether his eyes and ears were any good, watching these foreign programs in a foreign tongue on alienating soil. It turns out that he nailed the program's appeal and dynamics, appreciating its regular characters' personalities and Eve Arden's delicious star persona.

For Adorno, the television apparatus belonged to a larger group of phenomena he and Max Horkheimer famously dubbed and treated in the "culture industries" chapter of *Dialectic of Enlightenment*. It is to this chapter, and not to the essays on television and popular culture published and collected elsewhere, that his readers most often return to assess the relevance or longevity of his thought in relation to contemporary cultural formations or, conversely, to test the utility of the "culture industry" label for technocultural assemblages of the present moment. I wish to do neither, however, in what follows. Instead, in the first section below, largely following Fredric Jameson, I underscore how the culture industries could emerge as theoretical objects in the first place, always in relation to those historical constellations of art, freedom, thought, and rationalization (or unfreedom) that calibrated Adorno's thought (both on his own and with his collaborator, Horkheimer). In the second section, I begin to describe contemporary queer television in its digital forms, taking the step I resisted so heartily in *Ethereal Queer*. This is no mere matter of resolve or nomenclature but instead a matter of materiality, access, and selection, as I detail. In the concluding section, I bring Adorno and queer digital culture together anew, that is, now.

But why "queer" as the optic through which to assess television's transformations? If we can meaningfully still refer in this early twenty-first century to an entity called "television," it remains, I would argue, the most significantly potent force in implanting social lifetimes, sexualized and gendered, normative and contested. On our screens, we continue to see ourselves doubled and miniaturized: not reflected but refracted and dispersed, assembled into desiring machines that are at once contained and full of potential. What Adorno calls "mimetic comportment" is precisely this active capacity to become something "other" in watching: "Ultimately, aesthetic comportment is to be defined as the capacity to shudder, as if goose bumps were the first aesthetic image."[3] In relation to the schemas and stereotypes of gendered and sexual life on television, we quiver and respond, and it is in this spectrum that I locate queer television.⁴ It is not, then, merely a choice to write about queer television. It is an imperative of the apparatus, an imperative Adorno recognized a half-century ago that has been long ignored by the industry's most able critics, including those few Frankfurters who wrote about desire and sexuality.

Television as Culture Industry

Reading Marcuse today, like reading the crazier Wilhelm Reich, one is still struck by the energy of the 1960s sexual revolution and its proto-queer possibilities. Nonrepressive genital sublimation—right on! But one is also taken aback by how limited the theoretical domain is in *Eros and Civilization*: how the task really is the opening of specifically male desire, specifically heteropatriarchal modes of affiliation, within an aesthetic-political horizon that also remains pretty much untransformed by critical theory, still mired in idealism.⁵ Not so with Adorno, whose reflections on the culture industries are rooted in a number of extremely far-reaching aesthetic and theoretical commitments that undergird and frame his analysis of the nefarious effects of midcentury television, radio, cinema, and music.

In his helpful gloss on Adorno and Horkheimer in *Late Marxism*, Jameson characterizes these effects as belonging to some degree to conceptions of "manipulation, in which a passive public submits to forms of commoditization and commercially produced culture whose self-identifications it endorses and interiorizes as 'distraction' or 'entertainment.'"⁶ In fact, it's better to say that Jameson *historicizes* a particular view of reception and spectatorship attributed to Horkheimer and Adorno that emerged in academic cultural studies and media studies in the 1980s, writing that was keen to validate ideas of resistance against manipulation. If the extreme versions of that strain of criticism (John Fiske's *Reading the Popular* would be my primary example) caricatured and rendered mechanistic the experience of mass culture described in the *Dialectic of Enlightenment*, it did so in part because it misunderstood or ignored these broader concerns elaborated among others by Jameson, namely, the historical convergence of the industrialization of American-style mass culture with Nazism, the historical legacy of and commitment to European modernist art, and the position and task of philosophy, the "thinking subject" whose emancipatory movement is always the horizon of Adorno's thought.

I won't rehearse Jameson's contextual discussion, which I find extremely helpful in situating Adorno's thoughts about American mass culture, except to emphasize how television in particular emerges as a theoretical object within this matrix. In their condemnation of the industrialization of culture, Adorno and Horkheimer in fact elaborate a subject who is not exactly passive but whose intellectual functions and judgment have been replaced by a priori stereotypicality and schematization:

Kant's formalism still expected a contribution from the individual, who was thought to relate the varied experiences of the senses to fundamental concepts, but industry robs the individual of his function. Its prime service to the customer is to do his schematizing for him. Kant said that there was a secret mechanism in the soul which prepared direct intuitions in such a way that they could be fitted into the system of pure reason. But today that secret has been deciphered.[7]

The culture industries implement, extend, and sharpen the logic of abstraction (Max Weber's rationalization, Georg Simmel's intellectualization, György Lukács's reification), and they do so by organizing the world into schemes of equivalence, which, as Jameson notes, banish difference and heterogeneity, "transforming the unlike into the same."[8] Adorno's emphasis on the use of stereotypes in television characterization helps us to see this process in a medium-specific environment, but this limited view of American midcentury television is linked to a wider and historically significant shift in perception and experience codified by late capitalism. In understanding industrialization, therefore, Horkheimer and Adorno are not, as Jameson has importantly observed, theorizing culture per se, much less the dynamics of spectatorship, but processes of transformation observable in the form of cultural objects.

This is not to say that Horkheimer and Adorno are uninterested in the experiential dimensions of art and culture. Adorno himself was steeped in music from childhood onward, and he sustained passionate, if desperate, attachments to the experiences of "genuine art" or autonomous art throughout his writings. The industrialized cultural objects Adorno encountered in exile in America—radio, television, cinema, music—take shape against his deep existential investments in art, but high art and modernism never found themselves simply opposed to the products of mass culture. Instead, the culture industries bring the liquidation of autonomous art, as it were, to light, calling forth the separation of the thinking subject from art. Autonomous art "has been attended through bourgeois history by a moment of untruth, which has now culminated in the social liquidation of art."[9] As in much of Adorno's thinking, the new mode of transformation (that of the commodity form that *is* mass culture) retrospectively reveals the character of autonomous art, that which is now lost and yet still hoped for. The last point is significant, for *promise* and *hope* are meaningful terms in the analysis of mass culture's contradictions; they are precisely what oppose naive utopianism and cynical despair. It is true that Adorno's conception of experience, loaded onto the category of high art, arrests the oscillation between mass culture and autonomous art in a particularly bleak historical moment. As Miriam Hansen puts it, in her extended introduction to Oskar Negt and Alexander Kluge's

Public Sphere and Experience, we might explore the possibility, denied by Adorno, that "new forms—and other kinds—of experience, new modes of expression, self-reflection, and intersubjectivity might emerge from the same cultural technologies that were destroying the old."[10] (Hansen also has pointed out that, late in Adorno's life, his attitudes toward the culture industry shifted, and he saw in film music and German cinema new possibilities disclosed to him by Kluge himself.[11])

What is beginning to emerge from this mere sketch of Adorno's thoughts on mass culture is a picture of one of the culture industries, television, which (1) does not induce passivity in its spectator but, rather, offers her predigested types and categories; (2) does not simply oppose genuine or high art but instead reveals something about what we miss or gain in aesthetic experience; and as I will now want to discuss further, (3) does not limit itself to a particular genre or historical moment but instead is understood as a particular technical-aesthetic mode of mediation. Here I therefore take issue with Jameson's periodization, in which he alleges to have found the objects proper to Adorno and Horkheimer's characterization of the culture industries: "Standard Hollywood Grade-B genre film (before the latter's reorganization by *auteur theory*) . . . radio comedy and serials of a thirties and forties variety ('Fibber McGee' and 'Molly' for example)."[12] He allows that maybe their analysis "anticipates"[13] later 1940s television programming but offers no historical argument about what might have shifted and why. (One could add that the parenthetical reference's erroneous punctuation tells all: it's *Fibber McGee and Molly*, one of the best-known radio comedies of the era, not two separate programs.)

This is more, I think, than a quibble: it's the heart of the (wrongly formulated) question of whether Adorno's thought is pertinent to contemporary (digital, or what Jameson calls "technically expert" and "elegant")[14] television of the twenty-first century. It's the wrong question because it presumes that we know in advance what the differences are, that we have some rigorously historical understanding of what has changed or how we have changed, politically, intellectually, aesthetically in relation to that object we are calling television. Let's look, then, at what we think we are referencing when we talk about the domain of the digital.

Eros and Digitalization: Uneven Development

Here, then, is an attempt to read off the location of queer television from today's hyperindustrial, fragmented, and uncertain landscape—not, that is, by adding some sociological factors but by understanding the micropolitical horizons immanent to its current forms, forms indexed by my term *digitalization*. I want to stipulate a few starting points before addressing a phenomenon we confront in this mediascape, a loosening of professional borders, that I think demands our collective attention. In the section that follows this one, I argue that the current configuration presents us with emergent forms of amateur and paraprofessional production that solicit our attention beyond textual analysis and beyond recognizable aesthetic precedents. Here, though, I sketch out what we might mean by queer television, in its most capacious definition: *Transparent*, *Orange Is the New Black*, *Glee!*, *American Horror Story*, *Looking*, *The Rachel Maddow Show*, *Anderson Cooper 360*, *The Fosters*, *RuPaul's Drag Race*, *How I Met Your Mother*, *The Ellen DeGeneres Show*, *Modern Family*—maybe these are obvious; but also *Lost Girl* and *Pretty Little Liars*, *Falling in Love . . . with Chris and Greg*, *The Slope*, *The Outs*, *F to 7th*, *Little Horribles*, and hundreds of serial narratives and queer topical content available on platforms ranging from television stations to YouTube to dedicated websites.

Where is television now, if not streaming across our screens and loaded onto our flash drives, as many would emphasize the shifts wrought by narrowcasting, multiplatform delivery, endless bandwidth, and new modes of monetizing attention? First, it seems important to put counterpressure on the discourse of convergence and its *ruptures* by noting formal continuities, even regressions, between television of the national, broadcast, and restricted variety of the mid- to late twentieth century and that of the broadband, global, and multichannel platform variety of today. This is to oppose the halfhearted periodization offered by Jameson with an assessment of the wildly uneven nature of contemporary infrastructure and programming across an industry marked by narrowcasting, shrinking market shares, and unpredictability. The conventions, for example, of the three-camera, studio-recorded sitcom obtain as much in the aforementioned *Our Miss Brooks* as in the current ITV program *Vicious* (distributed in the United States by BBC America). The latter, which was originally titled more clearly *Vicious Queens*, circulates these stereotypes with a renewed queer urbane archness, one that is just as at home in the contemporary BBC studio sitcom as its unreconstructed predecessor *Our Miss Brooks*. Briefly, *Vicious* pits Ian McKellen as Freddie against his longtime partner of fifty years, Stuart, played by Derek Jacobi, creating an unrivaled (if often unfunny) camp pas de deux. Comedic foils and deflections are provided by the best friend Violet (Frances de la Tour, who is wonderful despite the excesses of her character) and naive young neighbor Ash (Iwan Rheon), who populate each episode in story arcs more predictable and dependable than those in early American sitcoms.

Although the two programs, *Our Miss Brooks* and *Vicious*, are sixty years apart, they obey precisely the same televisual conventions from the framing of faces to the use of laughter, take place in precisely similar middle-class domestic interiors, and trade in a kind of knowing humor that partakes of a long tradition of queer comedy. Nothing about the form of the sitcom prevents some mobility in its content, but conversely, nothing about the vast shifts in the industrial infrastructure of today's digital environment prevents the successful circulation of age-old queer aesthetics, including camp. Here, then, we have to concede that television found in London in the twenty-first century models itself on the centralized industrialization of mid-twentieth-century American networks, despite the changes wrought by digital platforms. This weird throwback is what many seem, in my view inaccurately, to be calling "global" television, mainly because it is more easily accessed around the world (here through BBC America's streaming) than terrestrial broadcasts. The effects of the British 1990 Broadcasting Act, which enabled the Thatcherite privatization and deregulation (and, many would argue, Americanization) of the British television industry, are still felt in this type of programming, which harbors the sea changes of the British communications industries of the past several decades.[15]

Let's remain for a moment with this example of *Vicious* and tease out its implications. I am arguing that this program is one index of why the term *posttelevisual* is inadequate to designate our uneven environment. The queens' banter on *Vicious* is so close to the measured beats on 1950s American sitcoms as to seem an uncanny double. There is nothing "post" about it. Take this one-minute snippet of dialogue from the fifth episode of the first season, entirely representative of the series as a whole. Ash introduces his new girlfriend Chloe to Freddie and Stuart:

> Chloe [gazing at Ash]: I love you so much.
> Ash [gazing at Chloe]: I love you so much more.
> Stuart: Jesus Christ!
> Freddie [fondling his drink]: It's like a car crash. You can't take your eyes
> off it.
> Chloe: It's so inspiring you've both been together so long. How do you do it?
> Freddie: Well, I mostly attribute it to the fact that he won't leave.
> Stuart: When the time comes, I'm going to so enjoy unplugging you.
> [Freddie sips drink]
> Chloe: You're joking again.
> Stuart [sarcastically]: Yes. Ha. Ha.
> [Chloe laughs, gratingly and uproariously]
> Freddie: What a delightful laugh you have. It isn't irritating at all. Are you
> sure we can't get you a proper drink?
> Ash: Oh no. She never drinks. Isn't that right, Chloe?
> Chloe: It's true. And nothing could give me more of a high than being with
> Ash.
> Freddie: Have you tried cocaine?[16]

Add camp and stir—there's the recipe for this form of biting exchange, fueled by booze and a laugh track. If *Vicious* is formally identical to its mid-twentieth-century predecessors, however, it is the product of an entirely different stage in the development of first-world media economies, where deregulation and privatization (effects of what neoliberalism designates) have reshaped the BBC.

If one were to look even further at *Vicious* as a queer text within the formal parameters of the sitcom, as Adorno did with *Our Miss Brooks*, one would also emphasize a methodological faith in the micropolitical stakes of interpretation, despite well-founded macropolitical disappointment, if not despair. Adorno felt, and I still feel today, compelled to look closely at how creative works intervene. A more contemporary articulation of the possibilities of adventurous interpretation and experimentation comes from William Connolly, in *The Fragility of Things*:

> We must . . . become involved in experimental micropolitics on a number of fronts, as we participate in role experimentations, social movements, artistic displays, erotic-political shows, electoral campaigns, and creative interventions on the new media to help recode the ethos that now occupies investment practices, consumption desires, family savings, state priorities, church assemblies, university curricula, and media reporting. It is important to bear in mind how extant ideologies, established role performances, social movements, and commitments to state action intersect.[17]

In a critique of the neoliberal media that have emerged specifically from the 1980s changes in media policy, then, it is necessary to attend to these unpredictable intersections rather than engage in wholesale dismissals or appraisals. So, the second point I stipulate is this: insofar as we identify digital media (from so-called global television to Web 2.0) as corporate, voracious, consolidationist, hierarchical, advertiser driven, ecologically unsustainable, and antidemocratic, our response to it has to navigate, again to use Connolly's language, "loose ends, uneven edges, dicey intersections with non-human forces, and uncertain trajectories."[18] (Connolly's terms are, in my view, more helpfully capacious than something like Astra Taylor's critical condemnation of digital culture as unsustainable, particularly for the creative classes.)[19]

Today's media industries, in other words, are neither entirely new nor entirely knowable, even while they are often reflexive, allegorical, and self-referential. Television, for one, functions on multiple scales and durations: from platforms featuring the simultaneous broadcast of hundreds of channels to single-channel dominance, from programs that run for decades to segments of a few brief moments, from environments that cross terrestrial barriers to strictly contained national industries. Anna Cristina Pertierra and Graeme Turner's book *Locating Television: Zones of Consumption* makes this argument against convergence rhetoric, which tends to declare a brave new world over and over again, especially well.[20] So in approaching today's television, one must, I think, shuttle always between the macro and the micro, and also between surprising intersections and ingrained clichés. One place to focus such an inquiry, as I have intimated, concerns the proliferation of amateurism in digital media. I am using amateurism here as a kind of critical lever, one that allows us to shift attention from the ontology of television form to a set of practices, a techne, of televisual mediation, seeking to isolate those very transformations Adorno sought to track. They are now located elsewhere, not in a unified culture industry located in Los Angeles but in a more diffuse paraprofessional orbit that yields these multiple objects I want to gather still under the rubric of queer television.

Here perhaps is the place to underscore a point similar to the one Jameson is at pains to make in *Late Marxism* about "levels," about the importance of totality to any reckoning of Adorno's legacy.[21] I am similarly trying to stress a mode of analysis of television that traverses various levels, including textual analysis, industrial infrastructure, processes of spectatorship and reception, and both formal and informal networks of creators/artists/producers. It is a huge undertaking. If Adorno helped us to think about the television apparatus, his insights about its mechanisms of reification are no less apt today to the extent to which the overreaching imperatives of that apparatus remain constant: the commodification of attention, the routing of identification toward normative and constraining social roles (and the concomitant reliance upon types). But just think about how the locations of television's transformations have shifted and how much we are offered (or, alternatively, burdened with) in terms of a proliferating and uneven industry or paraindustry. Again, it is huge. Now, though, it is our friends and peers making television, many of them "out" and nuanced and imaginative. Where are they working?

Lines of Flight: Professionalism and Its Discontents

Amateurism has been cited, acknowledged, and even promoted by artists and media theorists alike. Joseph Beuys advocated social art or social architecture, in which "every human being must be an artist."[22] An admirer of Beuys, Bernard Stiegler diagnosed the destruction of processes of individuation by the program industry, emphasizing both amateur production and amateur or "general" publics in what he calls his "organology."[23] Even Goethe and Schiller's notes on dilettantism do not dismiss amateur attempts entirely; in fact, their promotion of its advantages includes a sense in which the domain of art might be *extended* by dilettantism. "Dilettantism is a necessary consequence of a general extension of art," they write, "and may even be a cause of it."[24]

Again, in these examples I want to show how queer television now presumes mobility across industrial/professional borders to create its objects; amateurism is not something to choose to examine but a condition of a horizon of intelligibility. "Creativity is to the cultural field what labor power is to the field of political economy," writes Thierry de Duve about Beuys.[25] To think about creativity as the capacity to produce in general (as Marx thought of labor power) is to raise vital questions about the ongoing transformations in the cultural field produced by capitalist subsumption: it is not just to oppose art to nonart but to find the particular spaces in the cultural field where we can glimpse these changes.

New casting practices for television series, as well as new models for financing them, may then result in surprising extensions wrought by amateurs, so I try to show how amateurism might rear its head in an unexpected way in today's television transformations. The wildly successful hybrid comedy-dramatic series *Orange Is the New Black*, moving from its second to its third season in 2015, offers an instructive example. (The series adapts Piper Kerman's prison memoir, focusing on the backstories of inmates of a women's prison and using Piper, the white upper-middle-class nominal protagonist, as a Trojan horse through whom to smuggle onto American and global television screens Latinas, lesbians, African Americans, and a transgender hairstylist, about whom more in a moment.)

Cast by Jennifer Euston, the production of *Orange* takes place in New York (even while, exceptionally, the writers' room and showrunner remain in Los Angeles), which allowed Euston to draw from the pool of New York theatrical talent and to extend her practice of "finding faces rarely seen on TV."[26] Euston is a lover of amateur uniqueness, and another favorite slogan of hers is "perfection is no fun!"[27] In practice, this means seeking character actors, or those who might otherwise work in unnamed one-off parts on cast-hungry shows such as *Law & Order*; in essence, however, it also means working with some actors on the fringes of professional broadcast media, actors who have not, or not yet, quit their day jobs. Because the series is produced under Netflix's syndication deal with Lionsgate Television, showrunner Jenji Kohan (previously the creator of *Weeds* for Lionsgate) received a thirteen-episode, straight-to-series commitment rather than an invitation to produce a pilot, providing the opportunity for a large cast of actors to create characters over time without fear of cancellation. Euston was recognized for her astonishing achievements in casting *Orange* with an Emmy Award in 2014, and it is thanks to her efforts that we have such a diverse range of queer characters to discuss here.

Sophia Burset, the character played by Laverne Cox, is one such character, a transgender hairstylist whose transition is part of her character's backstory. As Cox has become well known through her role as Sophia, she has gained a certain presence in the press, including the cover of *Time* in June 2014, a first for a trans person. What is notable about Cox is her growth into the role of trans celebrity from relatively recent invisibility: she has become an effective and passionate activist in the media spotlight only a year after quitting her job in a restaurant, and she has arguably had a more significant role in shaping the public discussion of transgender than the celebrity to the manor born, Chaz Bono. Cox even achieved some success in urging Katie Couric (who is the most clueless of interlocutors for a mass audience) to dwell less on spectacular surgeries and the prurient specifics of trans bodies in favor of a discussion of individuals' comprehension of their gender identities.

To pull back a bit, then, the particular industrial organization that makes possible a bicoastal production for an online distribution service with relatively unknown actors has consequences that are not easily mapped through the rhetoric of the program industries and that are not entirely contained by the televisual text either. Here we have to be attentive to slight transformations, loose networks, micropolitical adjustments. This cast is willing to take risks regarding onscreen nudity and queer sexuality, risks a union cast in Los Angeles would likely be unwilling to undertake. Those risks enable disruptive and edgy scripts that give density and life to characters (and faces) that do not usually populate serial comedy, even serial comedy produced through new content providers such as Netflix. And Cox, more than any other actor in the series, has taken the queer material of the series into a much broader spotlight, helping to determine the very terms under which trans communities are rendered legible and visible in broader public debates, whether over the language of the next *DSM* psychotherapy manual[28] or over the treatment of young children with gender identity disorders or other disordered relationships to their genders and bodies of birth. *These* are the effects of television's new locations, both figurative and literal, hard to map but crucial to note.

Despite the distance that would appear to separate *Orange Is the New Black* from comedic web-based work, to which I turn now, there is actually significant continuity in terms of participation in arts and activist communities. What distinguishes much of the web-based work is the relative illegibility of its amateurism. If we think in terms of assemblages, Laverne Cox becomes inserted into a highly diversified mediascape involving longtime industrial professionals (including showrunner Kohan and interviewers like Couric) that also reaches into on-the-ground networks and practices, from student groups to activist blogs. Moving in an opposite direction, amateur web-based serials often begin less coherently with unpaid labor and minor output, seeking to attract attention either from the queer arts and media community or from potential funders. *Falling in Love . . . with Chris and Greg* chronicled and ironized the real-life relationship between transgender film and video artist Chris Vargas and film studies scholar Greg Youmans. Made between 2008 and 2013, the series circulated at film festivals and is available in a DVD version online. Described by Damon Young, coeditor of this special issue, in a recent essay focused on the series, *Falling in Love* "is about [communication] problems, about navigating the groundless thing called love, an affective disposition toward the other or an ethical commitment, or a relation at once utterly conventional and generic and yet which feels unique and *sui generis* and even—in the case of a 'trans/cis[gay]couple'—avant garde, with few culturally available precedents."[29] In its first episode, for example, the more radical Chris has urged the more monogamous and liberal Greg to have sex outside of their relationship. Greg agrees and finds a willing Canadian, who is the butt of stereotypic humor about Canadians' ostensible blandness and earnestness. Chris and Greg's awkwardly scripted and acted conversations about their relationship and its twists form the core of the serial's action.

Formally, the series has only a few available precedents, as Young demonstrates in his essay, for its enunciation; the expressivity of its filmic narrator is, as you see if you watch but a moment, "halting and uneven, technically graceless, and rarely possessed of the clarity that would furnish an interpretive framework" for it.[30] It is, simply put, hard to know what to make of it. Certainly, it draws upon queer anti-aesthetics: Andy Warhol, Jack Smith, DIY YouTube videos, contemporary no-budget video. And its humor draws from a number of queer traditions, too: camp, parody, irony, and satire. What most clearly differentiates it, however, from these other traditions is, I want to note, its *televisuality*. For all of its distantiation and reflexivity, it is a sitcom, enlisting precedents like *Our Miss Brooks* and *Vicious*. Like those programs, *Chris and Greg* organizes itself around stereotypes (Canada), organized situations (the road trip), or topics of shame (food). What it makes of these, however, is in fact experimentally new and newly queer. In its particular brand of amateurism, *Chris and Greg* therefore might be said to assemble something out of these familiar traditions that we would be right to notice as continuous with those objects Adorno understood as serious, as consequential and meaningful and intense, even if this web-based incarnation of televisuality is not entirely consistent or legible. It rescripts—even through bad acting and deadpan undecidability—erotic and political performances, and it recodes televisual versions of domesticity and wit in innovative and creative ways.

In a similar vein of innovation, to take another example, Amy Rubin's series *Little Horribles* is, to use her tag line, "a darkly comedic web series following the poor decisions of a self-indulgent lesbian."[31] With considerably higher production values and far greater circulation than *Chris and Greg*, *Little Horribles* retraces ground laid in sitcoms such as *Our Miss Brooks* and *Vicious*, particularly shame attached to women's bodies, the politics of food, and familial dynamics surrounding emergence into queer adulthood.

A sort of digital bildungsroman in serial form, *Little Horribles* also incessantly references the world of the web out of which it emerged and in which it remains submerged. Amy Rubin, the actor/creator who has appeared in other queer television programs such as *Looking*, is, like that program's immersion in information technology, umbilically attached to a laptop in virtually every sequence, and the characters in *Little Horribles* are grounded as much in family sitcoms as in endlessly referenced virtual environments, where sociality becomes frayed and narrowed into commercialized corners. The series could therefore be understood, too simply I think, as a vacuous boutique production, featuring branded content and with blatantly commercial aspirations. Instead, I want to highlight its own lo-fi, intimate, awkward, everyday aesthetic: *Little Horribles* generally rejects brutality in favor of affection, and it sets its sights on a mode of queer existence, persisting through life's minor humiliations, that is perfectly scaled to the very web medium with which many of its personnel are professionally affiliated.

Its affinities are with the web's temporality, too, especially because each episode only runs four or five minutes, so the whole series can be consumed in a quick bite, not even a binge. The same temporality obtains for Ingrid Jungermann's series, like *The Slope* or her recent *F to 7th*, or any number of other productions whose entire "seasons" run for maybe an hour. Unlike the broadcast model of seasonal television (or even quasi-seasonal television, such as Amazon's *Transparent*, released as an entire "season" on its debut day), these serials are quick and easy to find and consume, making it possible as a spectator to engage critically a wide orbit of productions. Made collaboratively by groups of students and paraprofessionals rather than bona fide amateurs, these series reveal their commercial aspirations even while they generally rely upon informal networks of labor, financing, and audiences. In this mediascape, we see more clearly how the amateur and the professional intersect and crossbreed, how the intimate and the public are coimplicated even beyond textual form, how the hyperindustrial spawns para- and occasionally anti-industrial formations, and how micropolitical analyses of these complicated ways of saying no to mass synchronization might enable some measure of freedom.

F to 7th, Jungermann's most recent web-based serial, follows protagonist Ingrid from vignette to vignette of Brooklyn life and love, with each episode lasting five to eight minutes and mostly featuring dialogue between Ingrid and a recurrent or guest character. By featuring very short bits with extremely accomplished actors (including Olympia Dukakis, Amy Sedaris, and Gaby Hoffmann, now of *Transparent* fame), Jungermann tests her character's flat persona, derived in part from a lack of training as an actor, against much more robust characters developed for short bits (mostly shot on locations in and around her neighborhood). In an extended and familiar joke in the episode "Family," the lesbian who denies that she is one, Jungermann meets her Aunt Kate in a Brooklyn restaurant for a meal, and Kate (Sedaris) captures a Lacoste-shirted, Subaru-driving, quintessential golf dyke in a four-minute scene. Everything about Sedaris is characteristically expansive, from her leering gaze at the waitress and other lesbian patrons to her wink and repertoire of gesture and expression, while everything about Ingrid is slight, controlled, muffled, and self-effacing—in a word, humdrum. At times, in *F to 7th*, that constraint is associated with sexual style: Ingrid's soft butch anxiety that the series calls "homoneurotic." But it's also due to Ingrid's narrow range as an amateur actor, a range that is nonetheless fashioned into an appealing bemusement. In this episode, Ingrid mostly watches Amy Sedaris be the dazzling and over-the-top Amy Sedaris, scripted and directed by Jungermann but lovingly observed by our screen surrogate Ingrid. In this way, Ingrid Jungermann is refracted, as is Amy Rubin in *Little Horribles*, into presences and capacities that absorb the amateur into a queer style that one might, following Roland Barthes, describe as "the neutral," for what is this humdrum work if not, in Barthes's own words, "a manner . . . to be looking for my own style of being present to the struggles of my time."[32]

Conclusion

What I hope to have demonstrated is the persistence of multiple modes of transformation in the queer work I have collated as televisual, or in the televisual work I have collated as queer. Because the work presents itself in multiple locations, each with its own determinations and genealogies, the work asks us to temper our desire to decide between continuity or disruption with other aesthetic and critical projects. Instead, to respond adequately to this milieu, we need critical vocabularies, like Adorno's, that are supple enough to attend as rigorously to style as to production practices within variegated industries. But something *has* changed in recent years, namely, the proliferation of queer ways of being across small- and larger-scale televisual productions. The degree to which queerness (which especially should be understood to include a spectrum of trans experiences) now seems a desideratum of programming executives is simply striking, and it is one way to start to differentiate our moment from that of Reagan/Thatcher postmodernism. It *is* remarkable to me that we have this incredible array of queer storytelling available to us on our screens.

The reason, however, I belabored the micropolitical and microaesthetic ways in which queerness intervenes is not that I am too crabby to call this progress. "Too little of what is good has power in the world for progress to be expressed in a predictive judgement about the world," wrote Adorno in 1962, "but there can be no good, not a trace of it, without progress."[33] Sure, television is queerer now, with a visual and aural richness we would do well to appreciate, even celebrate. What is more important than celebration, in my view, is a kind of responsibility toward these lifeworlds that can appreciate what and where they are queer in a way that makes a televisual intervention. That means understanding the work beyond the text, the makers beyond the stars, the creative energies surging around the studio lots that are doing their thing despite the centripetal and destructive inclinations of capitalist culture industries. Maybe, just maybe, these folks have also read Adorno. In any case, these cultural workers are engaged in world making he did not anticipate, and we are damn lucky to write about it.

Notes

1. "Where Is Frankfurt, Now," Goethe Universität, Frankfurt, August 2014. See the conference call for papers at filmtheories.org/permanent-seminar-conference-2014-where-is-frankfurt-now/ (accessed 30 December 2014).
2. Villarejo, *Ethereal Queer*, 30–65.
3. Adorno, *Critical Models*, 331.
4. Thanks to Jonathan Flatley for his extraordinary reading of a draft of this paper, in which he proposed mimicry as an essential critical tool.
5. Heide Schlüpmann registered this critique of Marcuse, too, in her paper "The Unsettled Radicality of Adorno's *Kulturindustrie*" at "Where Is Frankfurt, Now?" See Villarejo, "Where Is Frankfurt, Now?"
6. Jameson, *Late Marxism*, 141.
7. Quoted in ibid., 148.
8. Ibid., 149.
9. Adorno, *Critical Models*, 127.
10. Hansen, Foreword, xviii.
11. Ibid.
12. Jameson, *Late Marxism*, 141.
13. Ibid.
14. Ibid., 142.
15. The full text of the act is available online: see UK National Archives, Broadcasting Act of 1990.
16. Lines transcribed by author from *Vicious*, season 1, episode 5.
17. Connolly, *Fragility of Things*, 38.
18. Ibid.
19. Taylor, *People's Platform*.
20. Pertierra and Turner, *Locating Television*.
21. Jameson, *Late Marxism*, 231–32.
22. Beuys, *What Is Money?*, 16.
23. Stiegler and Rogoff, "Transindividuation."
24. Goethe, *Literary Essays*, 75.
25. de Duve, *Sewn in the Sweatshops of Marx*, 11.
26. Sandberg, "How the Person Who Cast *Orange* Did It."
27. Lubin, "'Perfection Is No Fun.'"
28. The *Diagnostic and Statistical Manual of Mental Disorders*, periodically updated by the American Psychiatric Association, defines how and which psychiatric disorders are diagnosed.

29. Young, "Queer Seriousness."

30. Ibid.

31. The home page for this series is littlehorribles.com/, where the tag line appears.

32. Barthes, *Neutral*, 7–8.

33. Adorno, "Progress," in *Critical Models*, 147.

References

Adorno, Theodor. 2005. *Critical Models: Interventions and Catchwords*. With a new introduction by Lydia Goehr. New York: Columbia University Press.

Adorno, Theodor, and Max Horkheimer. 1972. *Dialectic of Enlightenment: Philosophical Fragments*. London: Continuum.

Barthes, Roland. 2005. *The Neutral: Lecture Course at the College de France (1977–1978)*. New York: Columbia University Press.

Beuys, Joseph. 2010. *What Is Money? A Discussion*. West Sussex, UK: Clairview Books.

Connolly, William. 2013. *The Fragility of Things: Self-Organizing Processes, Neoliberal Fantasies, and Democratic Activism*. Durham, NC: Duke University Press.

de Duve, Thierry. 2012. *Sewn in the Sweatshops of Marx: Beuys, Warhol, Klein, Duchamp*. Translated by Rosalind E. Krauss. Chicago: University of Chicago Press.

Fiske, John. 1989. *Reading the Popular*. New York: Routledge.

Goethe, Johann Wolfgang von. 1921. *Goethe's Literary Essays: A Selection in English*. Arranged by J. E. Spingarn. New York: Harcourt, Brace, and Company.

Hansen, Miriam. 1993. Foreword to *Public Sphere and Experience: Toward an Analysis of the Bourgeois and Proletarian Public Sphere*, by Oskar Negt and Alexander Kluge, translated by Peter Labanyi, Jamie Owen Daniel, and Assenka Oksiloff, ix–xli. Minneapolis: University of Minnesota Press.

Jameson, Fredric. 1990. *Late Marxism: Adorno; or, The Persistence of the Dialectic*. New York: Verso.

Lubin, Jaime. 2014. "'Perfection Is No Fun': Casting Director Jen Euston on TV's New Standard of Beauty," *Observer*, 20 November. observer.com/2014/11/perfection-is-no-fun-casting-director-jen-euston-on-tvs-new-standard-of-beauty.

Marcuse, Herbert. 1955. *Eros and Civilization: A Philosophical Inquiry into Freud*. Boston: Beacon.

Pertierra, Anna Cristina, and Graeme Turner. 2013. *Locating Television: Zones of Consumption*. London: Routledge.

Sandberg, Bryn Elise. 2014. "How the Person Who Cast *Orange* Did It." *Hollywood Reporter* 420, no. 28: 49.

Schlüpmann, Heide. 2014. "The Unsettled Radicality of Adorno's *Kulturindustrie*." Paper presented at the conference "Where Is Frankfurt, Now," Goethe Universität, Frankfurt, August.

Stiegler, Bernard, and Irit Rogoff. 2010. "Transindividuation." *e-flux*, www.e-flux.com/journal/transindividuation.

Taylor, Astra. 2014. *The People's Platform: Taking Back Power and Culture in the Digital Age*. New York: Metropolitan.

UK National Archives. 1990. Broadcasting Act of 1990. www.legislation.gov.uk/ukpga/1990/42/contents.

Villarejo, Amy. 2014. *Ethereal Queer: Television, Historicity, Desire*. Durham, NC: Duke University Press.

Villarejo, Amy. 2014. "Where Is Frankfurt, Now?" *Film Quarterly* 68, no. 2: 62–67.

Young, Damon R. 2014. "Queer Seriousness." *World Picture* 9. www.worldpicturejournal.com/WP_9/Young.html.

Beyond the "NGO Aesthetic"

Jennifer Bajorek

> Contemporary Africa is clearly *not* a featureless void defined only by its
> exclusion from the benefits of global capitalism, nor is it an informational
> "black hole."
> —James Ferguson, *Global Shadows*

Among the many unexpected insights of Sidney Kasfir's spellbinding
book *African Art and the Colonial Encounter* is that there has been no substantive change in the concepts, infrastructures, and systems governing
the flow of art from the African continent, where it is produced for the
express purpose of exportation and sale on the global art market, between
the period of what we might call "high" colonialism (Kasfir begins her
account with the Berlin Conference of 1884–85 and the start of the so-
called scramble for Africa) and the current conjuncture. Whereas the
former was characterized by "the specimen-collecting of natural history
museums" that was enabled by the acquisition of African colonies by
European states in the second half of the nineteenth century,[1] the latter
has been characterized by a vogue for contemporary African art in high-
profile museums and galleries in Europe and North America, and by the
increasingly visible presence of African art, artists, and curators on the
global biennial circuit.[2] Drawing on a meticulous body of comparative,
multisited research carried out in Nigeria and Kenya over several decades,
Kasfir presents a compelling argument for emphasizing the continuities
rather than discontinuities or ruptures in the market trajectory of "primitive" or "traditional" art and that of the "modernist and postmodernist
high-art genres" that, today, "form the most discussed and written-about
part of the global market for African art."[3]

Social Text 127 · Vol. 34, No. 2 · June 2016
DOI 10.1215/01642472-3467990   © 2016 Duke University Press

Figure 1. Sam Hopkins, *Logos of Non-Profit Organizations Working in Kenya (some of which are imaginary)*: "Bright Africa." 2010–ongoing. Silkscreen on canvas. 20 × 20 × 5 cm. ©Sam Hopkins. Courtesy of the artist

To be sure, the paradigms that once organized and legitimated the collecting of traditional African art in the West and North have succumbed to a certain conceptual static, thanks to the success of the new lexicons of African modernisms and the now ubiquitous category of "contemporary" African art.[4] Yet, if we accept Kasfir's analysis, which has been echoed by a generation of African/ist art historians, including those who (unlike Kasfir) have focused their analytical energies on the modern and the contemporary, this static can be minimized on the macro level—that of the market. In the galleries and collections of Western and Northern museums where it plays out, this static has been mitigated largely through minor shifts in institutional practice and can be played down as a problem largely of periodization and even of semantics. As Okwui Enwezor, Elizabeth Harney, Salah Hassan, Sylvester Ogbechie, and others have pointed out, art objects associated with rural or village-based practices and thought to have been produced by anonymous, long-dead artists (masks, statues, spears, etc.) now happily coexist, in these same museums, with contemporary art produced in radically heterogeneous urban contexts by artists with global brand recognition and encompassing a broad array of genres, media, and styles.[5]

This coexistence is predicated on the ongoing repression of African modernity in Western (colonial) historical consciousness, and on larger questions at the intersection of postcoloniality and postmodernity, two continents of the mind whose relationship remains, even today despite important work done by important scholars (including Pal Ahluwalia, Achille Mbembe, and Walter Mignolo), perversely undertheorized. As long as these objects stay in the galleries to which they have been assigned—primitive or traditional versus modern or contemporary—the challenges posed by African modernity to the sanctity of colonial knowledge systems or by African contemporaneity to the coherence of neocolonial geopolitics can be conveniently ignored, and we need not rock the boat (or the container ship) of the global export machine.

Kasfir's and others' arguments about a radical continuity in the market for African art over time have, or ought to have, theoretical consequences extending far beyond the disciplinary formations of art history and African studies to attain a much broader sphere of contemporary cultural analysis for two main reasons. The first is that art is, in many parts of Africa today, the only commodity produced for global export.[6] It follows that contemporary African art can lay claim to a privileged status in any attempt to analyze Africa's place in the contemporary capitalist system, and in our collective attempt, therefore, to understand contemporary capitalism's cultural logics on a global scale. The second reason is a distinction that Kasfir effectively makes between the system that was in place, in the colonial era, for sharing profits made from the sale of African art among sovereign European nation-states and the regime that replaced it: that of international nonprofit organizations, philanthropic foundations, and charities, what Kasfir calls "ex-colonial cultural organizations," and nongovernmental organizations (NGOs).[7] Both this exceptional visibility of African art as a global commodity and this unmistakable hegemony of the new, nongovernmental regime are, or ought to be, vital factors in any reflection on new possibilities for contemporary cultural analysis articulated from a Marxist vantage point.[8]

This article examines two projects by artists living and working in a single city in Africa: Nairobi. It pays particularly close attention to how these artists are visualizing or otherwise materializing the specificity of their contemporary geopolitical and geocultural situation in relation to capitalism. How might this specificity allow these artists to elucidate aspects of contemporary capitalism's cultural logic that are all too often invisible to people living in other parts of the world? How might it allow them to reframe or gain new traction on what Fredric Jameson once called a "radical cultural politics,"[9] an operation that presupposes, in much Marxist and post-Marxist analysis, an ability to represent one's location within the system of contemporary capitalism? My interpretation of these works unfolds against the horizon of a now widely received discourse about a generalized waning of criticality, which it nonetheless seeks to challenge.[10] At the same time, it will be informed by analyses of the global art market that have been ventured by African/ist curators, critics, and art historians who have, in recent decades, limned the contours of a collective project that is, despite myriad differences in individual approach, profoundly utopian in nature. This last group—typified by a younger generation of curators, such as Christine Eyene, Smooth Nzewi (who, together with Elise Atangana and Abdelkader Damani, curated Dak'Art 2014), and Elvira Dyangani Ose—has endeavored to rethink the place of Western/Northern exhibi-

Figure 2. Sam Hopkins, *Logos of Non-Profit Organizations Working in Kenya (some of which are imaginary)*: installation shot. 2010–ongoing. Silkscreen on canvas. 20 × 20 × 5 cm. ©Sam Hopkins. Courtesy of the artist

tions and global biennial culture as refractive or reflexive spaces that would allow contemporary African artists to interrogate and, in some versions of this project, reconfigure their relationship to global capital.[11] The word *utopian* should be understood in the strong sense here: despite the fact that the collective project is being framed by these curators and by the artists whose work they exhibit from a position "inside" the commercial art world, and one that is deeply conversant with its mores, practices, and institutions, it is oriented by a desire for radical change and by the dream of a future decolonization. One of the works that I discuss can be construed as coming from a position that is precisely "inside" the commercial art world, whereas the second project is not oriented by the market yet is working creatively with new tools and experiences emerging from the specific forms taken by contemporary capitalism in Nairobi's slums.

What Kind of Cognitive Map Is a Continent?

Artist Sam Hopkins, in his ongoing work *Logos of Non-Profit Organizations Working in Kenya (some of which are imaginary)*, reproduces the logos of nonprofit organizations working in Kenya, where the artist is from. As the title of the work suggests, the logos of real organizations are interspersed with the logos of fictional NGOs or nonprofits that Hopkins himself has invented. In the version exhibited at the 2014 Dak'Art Biennale (fig. 2), the logos were silk-screened on canvas, framed and glazed at modest dimensions (20 × 20 × 5 cm each), and wall mounted in three symmetrical rows of eight prints (twenty-four in total).[12] In an earlier version of the work, exhibited in 2010 in "Sketches," a solo show at the Goethe-Institut in Nairobi, the logos were digitally printed on a 3-mm plastic board in grid formation—small enough that there were one hundred of them. Four magnifying glasses were attached to the wall for viewers wanting to study the logos at close range. In neither installation was the viewer given any clues as to which logos were those of a real nonprofit organization and which were fake. Indeed, it is the central conceit of the *Logos* that the viewer not be able to distinguish real from imaginary.

Hopkins's *Logos* can doubtless be interpreted as a critique of the presence of the international aid and development industries in Kenya. *Logos* mounts this critique aesthetically, through its very form, and by virtue of the fact the logos exist in a critical relation *to* an aesthetic— what Hopkins himself calls the "NGO aesthetic." They appropriate this aesthetic precisely by appropriating the visual rhetoric, as well as discursive strategies, of the international aid and development industries, making visible their monopoly on images of Kenya. By choosing to work with the logos of nonprofit organizations— rather than, for example, with documentation of their activities (as has Kiluanji Kia Henda in a parallel context)[13]—Hopkins's *Logos* extend this critique to take aim, beyond the mere fact of its existence, at the decidedly consumerist inflection of the nonprofit industry. An anecdote that the artist recently shared with me about the work's recep-

Figure 3. Sam Hopkins, *Logos of Non-Profit Organizations Working in Kenya (some of which are imaginary)*: "Girl Child Africa." 2010–ongoing. Silkscreen on canvas. 20 × 20 × 5 cm. ©Sam Hopkins. Courtesy of the artist

Figure 4. Sam Hopkins, *Logos of Non-Profit Organizations Working in Kenya (some of which are imaginary)*: "Libyaid." 2010–ongoing. Silkscreen on canvas. 20 × 20 × 5 cm. ©Sam Hopkins. Courtesy of the artist

tion in its initial presentation at the Goethe-Institut, in 2010, only serves to underscore the need for a critical stance on the overwhelming nature of this industry's presence: at the exhibition opening, he noticed that someone was meticulously copying down, in a notebook, the names of the organizations represented among the logos—under the (mistaken) impression that they were the exhibition's sponsors.

The situation from which *Logos* emerges is, in this respect, deeply rooted in the lived experience of Kenyans and in the specific manifestations of contemporary capitalism experienced daily by people living in Nairobi. The banality and the pervasiveness of the NGO aesthetic become even clearer when we consider Hopkins's larger body of work. Beyond his solo practice, Hopkins has been deeply engaged in participatory and collaborative work, carried out since 2006 with artists and ordinary people living in Nairobi's slums. This work has, according to the artist, occasionally been funded by nonprofit organizations and NGOs.[14] Yet one need not live in Nairobi to recognize the banality and the pervasiveness of the NGO aesthetic. How else to understand the proliferation of bad visual metaphors that have saturated the global image ecology—trees for sustainability, light bulbs for progress, electrification for enlightenment? Hopkins fleshes out this already familiar list with images that perpetuate mystifying gender constructions (young girls must always be poor yet happy, powerful yet in need of "aid") and Western-centric ideas about friendship between nations. Why not Libya rather than Europe or America?[15]

A reflection on this aesthetic puts us in mind of Jameson, the foremost Marxist cultural critic to engage with the late twentieth-century "culture of the image" that was the hallmark of the postmodern.[16] At first glance, key elements of Hopkins's *Logos* do conform to Jameson's definition of postmodernism. *Logos* eschews "depth models."[17] It offers "new syntagmatic structures."[18] It delights in simulacra.[19] It exhibits an overt self-reflexivity on culture's (and therefore its own) status as a commodity, which is, according to Jameson, the most fundamental predicate of postmodern culture: "In postmodern culture, 'culture' has become a product in its own right," and "the sphere of culture is the sphere of commodities."[20] This conformity matters because, as I have suggested in passing, the periodization of African art as modern or postmodern (or contemporary) raises larger questions about the challenges posed by African modernity to Western self-perception or self-representation. In other respects, however, Hopkins's *Logos* departs from this formal resemblance to the postmodern. Within the logic of Jameson's *Postmodernism*, such a departure can be understood to announce either the restoration of a modernist impulse or some other, presumably more radical, departure from the critical impotence of postmodernism. One difference has to do with Hopkins's use of irony.[21] Another point on which this work diverges from both postmodernist and postcritical theories of art is connected with the question of instrumentalization. Here instrumentalization must be framed in the context of a highly specific historical and geopolitical situation—in which art and culture are instrumentalized as much (or more) by the international aid and development industries as by the market—from which (and this is the point) they are not distinct. In a published text, Hopkins describes the origin of his interest in nonprofit organizations, which he traces to the moment that he was cofounding Slum-TV, the well-known community media collective, in 2006, in Mathare. In this text, the artist remarks the role played by his own work in the larger schemes of contemporary "aid" and "development" in Kenya:

> During that time I co-founded Slum TV . . . and in the process of doing so I met with many NGOs. I was struck by the very particular language that these NGOs worked with. . . . Often this language seemed to reduce complex issues down to keywords such as *Sustainability, Capacity-Building, Synergies, Beneficiation,* and *Upscaling.* Whilst perhaps these keywords are useful in the context of Development, they did not seem suitable or helpful to the art project which we were developing, which was interested in setting up an experimental media project, without anticipated goals and outcomes, in Mathare.[22]

Logos, like almost all of Hopkins's solo work, understands the problem of its own instrumentalization by the contemporary capitalist system in a style that is nothing if not contemporary. Another example of Hopkins's solo work is *Tags of Some Services Offered in and around Nairobi* (fig. 5), in which public art is a "service" offered for sale around Nairobi.

What in "Cognitive Mapping" Jameson calls the "structural coordinates" of the "global colonial system" pose a problem for representation—and, therefore, it is implied, for contemporary Marxist analy-

Figure 5. Sam Hopkins, *Tags of Some Services Offered in and around Nairobi.* 2012. C-print. Dimensions variable. ©Sam Hopkins. Courtesy of the artist

sis.[23] In that essay Jameson explicitly discusses the problem of globalization in relation to visual and spatial representation, positing an exponential increase, under contemporary capitalism, in the difficulty of pinpointing one's place in "that great multinational space that remains to be cognitively mapped."[24] He alleges that the structural coordinates of the global colonial system are absent from individual experience and that they therefore escape existing modes of aesthetic representation—for people living in New York (or Boston, or Jersey City, or Los Angeles—the cities included in this initial formulation of cognitive mapping). But they are clearly not absent, Hopkins's work suggests, from the experience of people living in Nairobi. The Mathare slum in Nairobi in many ways resembles the situation of modern art, which, in the guise of Jameson's Van Gogh, in *Postmodernism*, emerged from a world threatened by primitive accumulation in the form of enclosure: "A world reduced to its most brutal and menaced, primitive and marginalized state."[25] But Hopkins's response to this situation is very different from that of the modernist artist, who attempts to represent the experience of primitive accumulation in isolation from a reflection on the commodity. His response entails a reflection on the responsibility of international actors for the specific forms taken by this brutality, marginalization, and poverty and the status quo that the aid industries and NGO culture, whether wittingly or not, maintain.[26] In this respect, *Logos* demonstrates, with considerable analytical and critical acuity, the ways in which Kenya, including but not limited to the slums of Nairobi, is in no way peripheral to contemporary capitalism and is, rather, an integral part of "that great multinational space" of contemporary capitalism.

We might consider, in this regard, Hopkins's reworking and reimagination of the "map" of Africa—a recurrent motif in *Logos*—not as a tool of empire but as a cognitive map of the totality of contemporary social relations. In particular, the representation of the African continent as a giant light bulb, in the "Bright Africa" logo (fig. 1), brilliantly illuminates the complicity of metaphors about electrification as enlightenment with developmentalist logics and, indeed, with the entire discourse of modernization. This discourse is based on ideas about progress and physical infrastructure derived from Western histories and experiences of industrialization, which have as their flip side certain ideas about primitive and premodern colonial others living on "dark" continents. Beyond the dialectical stranglehold that these concepts have on our understanding of the past, they constrain our understanding of the present, at the very moment when those living in extreme poverty are being reimagined as consumers, and when postindustrial reserve armies everywhere are being held out by venture capitalists and early-stage angel investors as the last frontier of capitalism, an "emerging market" par excellence that will have leapfrogged the old, familiar forms of industrial production and of social organization. Is it any wonder that these normative ideas about development, modernization, and infrastructure based on Western histories of industrialization have begun to be discredited and to seem increasingly irrelevant to people living without reliable access to electricity in African metropolises? It could furthermore be shown that many people living in large African cities, and particularly in the so-called megacities, live with rolling blackouts and an otherwise unreliable electricity supply, *not* because the infrastructural capacities to provide them with electricity are not there (the capacities that the NGOs tend to focus on) but because existing resources are routinely misallocated, usually through government corruption—a problem that, Hopkins's "Bright Africa" logo slyly reminds us, has proved rather more difficult for NGOs to fix.

To be sure, the imperial history of conventional cartographic representation is not Jameson's central concern in his discussion of cognitive mapping. Yet I am suggesting that we interpret Hopkins's deployment of conventional forms of cartographic representation in this work not as an uncritical acceptance of imperial cartographic conventions or even as an ironic commentary on those conventions but, rather, as an aesthetic representation of the distance or gap that inheres between the cultural logics of contemporary capitalism and those of earlier eras. Unlike representations of the continent designed to serve the needs of imperialist and colonialist expansion in an earlier era, Hopkins's representation of the continent in the "Bright Africa" logo can be seen as a species of cognitive map that is being drawn or envisioned from a place—Kenya—in which the cultural logics of contemporary capitalism require (in a way that previous logics did not) a reflection on the power of NGOs in the arena of culture. As such, this representation successfully locates Kenya as a place that is neither center nor periphery, and that only *seems* to be excluded from the space of postindustrial capital to those attempting to map the structural coordinates of the global colonial system from elsewhere.

It's a Pity We Only Exist in the Future

A project by the collective of artists and public space activists Urban Mirror called *I (Heart) Nairobi* approaches the representability—or, in the Jamesonian analysis, the supposed unrepresentability—of the totality of contemporary social relations from a different perspective.[27] Like Hopkins's *Logos*, Urban Mirror's project prompts a reflection on literal maps and techniques of visualization, but it also raises interesting questions about an emergent distinction between a tactics and an aesthetics within a given image culture or ecology, and, as befits the evolution of mapping technologies, it combines an array of mapping and mixed-media visualization techniques with public space activism.[28] This distinction between

Figure 6. Urban Mirror, *I (Heart) Nairobi*. 2009–ongoing. Documentation photograph.
©Silvia Gioiello. Courtesy of Urban Mirror

a tactics and an aesthetics, which I do not have time to develop at any length here, is nonetheless worth highlighting because it demonstrates that, if there is a new cultural logic of contemporary capitalism, the category of the aesthetic is necessarily evolving within it. At the same time, Urban Mirror's project will allow us to deepen our reflection on artists' concern with the local and with local experience, situating this concern in light of broader concerns about location, although, insofar as the project does not result in the production of an object or objects for export, it is not explicitly oriented by the global market for African art in the way that Hopkins's *Logos* so obviously is.[29]

Urban Mirror is a collective that formed in Nairobi in late 2008/early 2009.[30] The collective emerged from a workshop that was held in 2008 in Mombasa, called Urban Wasanii, with artists from both Nairobi and Mombasa.[31] *I (Heart) Nairobi* was itself a mixed media project, integrating performance, graffiti or tagging, and myriad forms of audience participation, including, in one of its iterations, crowd-mapping using Ushahidi, a well-known open-source crisis-mapping platform that was developed locally in Nairobi during the postelection violence that broke out after the contested December 2007 elections in Kenya.[32]

The figure you see in the documentary photographs (figs. 6 and 7) of the *I (Heart) Nairobi* project is named Upendo Hero. His name means, in Sheng, the "hero of love." Over several months in 2009, Upendo Hero performed and painted in public places in neighborhoods all over Nairobi—in Kibera, in Mathare (in the neighborhood known as Kosovo), in Ngara Market, and in Westlands—following a particular trajectory and logic: he was to visit, and to tag, places that had been identified by people living in these neighborhoods as meaningful or viable public spaces. He would go to a place that was rumored to be a public space, tag or stencil "I (HEART) NAIROBI" in or on that space, in this way identifying that space as public and making it visible to all. Urban Mirror dubbed him the world's first "Public Space Superhero."

The collective participated, along with other artists, in a February 2009 exhibition titled *It's a Pity We Only Exist in the Future*, at the Goethe-Institut in Nairobi.[33] The diverse artists in the exhibition and their many, otherwise disparate projects addressed complex global issues from a distinctly local vantage point: in addition to NGO-ization, they addressed the impact on public space of the growth of new hybrid private/public forms of property in urban development and the commercialization of the development sector globally. A description of *I (Heart) Nairobi* that was published in *another* exhibition catalog makes explicit a further dimension of public and political life in Nairobi to which this project responded: the reign of violence and terror that erupted in the slums and elsewhere in the immediate postelection period in 2007. The infamous postelection violence plunged many Kenyans into soul-searching about the role played by ethnic identity in threatening democracy in their country. The catalog text reads: "'I (HEART) NAIROBI' is a project and idea conceived of by [the] public space activists. . . . It was triggered by a local context which sees both a tight control of city spaces by the corrupt City Council and a dominant local and international image of a dangerous city. The idea was to challenge this image in a provocative and entertaining way and probe an emerging urban identity based on a city rather than ethnicity."[34] I think part of what I find so fascinating about *I (Heart) Nairobi* is that it unites this pushback against manufactured ethnic hatred with the mapping, remapping, or reimagining of public space.

Many factors inform the contested visibility of public space in Nairobi, some old and some new, some microlocal and some "glocal," in the sense that they are the result of systemic pressures connected with urban development globally. The local vantage point on global phenomena comes through particularly clearly in the words of participants in the 2008 Urban Wasanii workshop. When asked, what is public space?, these were their answers:

Public space in Kenya is something that there is and there isn't at the same time.

[Public space is] . . . a place where you can find freedom in the public.

[Public space is] . . . a place where I know I can go to share something with my friends, a place also where I can go and just chill.

Public space is: the police will come and start arresting us because there are a lot of us.

[Public space is] . . . something that only exists in the future.

The comparative dimension of the workshop that I mentioned earlier—the fact that participants came from both Nairobi and Mombasa—was extremely important in adding nuance to the discussion of public space, which participants observed functioned differently in each city. For example, they noted that in Mombasa it is possible to identify *Maskani*, or public spaces, even when they are unoccupied. (*Maskani*, meaning "dwellings" or "habitations," is the word that young people in Mombasa use for public space.) In Nairobi, by contrast, they noted that public spaces (or *bazes*, the Sheng word for public space used by young people in Nairobi) are invisible when unoccupied, and much more difficult to find.

In many respects *I (Heart) Nairobi* resembled the "I (Heart) NY" campaign of an earlier era, which it deliberately mimicked. At one point, it even included the selling of T-shirts (at Ngara market), stickers, and other "merchandise" branded with the "I (Heart) Nairobi" slogan. Yet that slogan is neither an ironizing of the "I (Heart) NY" campaign nor a pastiche of something coming from New York, and it works, in this project, in a significantly different way. Here, the slogan—or, rather, the slogan combined with Upendo Hero's live performances, in which the slogan was expressed *precisely as a tag*—worked as a kind of imprimatur of publicness, as well as a provocation lobbed at those perceived to be clamping down on public space. This performative dimension (in the sense intended by speech-act theory) of the tags furthermore enacted or engendered a spatial tactics in relation to the *visualization* of public space.[35]

Figure 7. Urban Mirror, *I (Heart) Nairobi.*
2009–ongoing. Documentation photograph.
©Silvia Gioiello. Courtesy of Urban Mirror

The performative and tactical dimensions of Upendo Hero's tags facilitated the incorporation of Ushahidi as a digital platform, which in turn allowed the artists to deepen and extend the scope of participation in the project, without, however, turning the digital platform into an object of technophilic desire. It is, in this respect, essential to underscore the ways in which Ushahidi opened up the potentialities of crisis mapping in the local context, where, for example, users need not have ready or continuous access to the Internet (intermittent access to the Internet is the norm in many African cities). The platform was designed, from its inception, to handle inputs from multiple data streams: meaning that SMS-based text messages (as distinct from later generations of messaging system) sent from a basic phone not connected to the Internet could also be used to map a location, as well as web-based inputs. Multiple data streams are vital in Kenya, where everyone has a phone but not everyone has a smartphone, especially in the slums.[36] What software developers call multiple data streams, the artists in Urban Mirror call a "media mix," and this mix was a big part of what drew them to the platform, for it allowed them to maximize the social element of participation.[37] When the artists observed that the inclusion of inputs via Ushahidi was presenting a financial barrier to participation in the project for many people, they made a decision to supplement the digital inputs that were being submitted via Ushahidi by setting up physical drop boxes at various locations in the slum. For those for whom the cost of a single SMS was too high and precluded their participation in the project, the drop boxes made it possible to contribute to the map on a piece of paper.

There are both collective and critical dimensions to Urban Mirror's *I (Heart) Nairobi* project. Artists enlisted the participation of denizens of Nairobi to make public space visible in their neighborhood. Using a diversity of tactics, including both tagging and crowd-mapping, that incorporated new technologies, their work had as its telos not a crowd-sourced "map" as an aesthetic or visual or spatial object but the work of remapping and reimagining public space in Nairobi for ordinary people who navigate the city daily. The point is not just the new spaces of negotiation that Upendo Hero's performances and tags effectively created, but the constitutive role played by a plurality of Nairobi's residents in this work of collective reimagination, which was here realized without succumbing to technophilic fantasies or the delusion that increased access to data will automatically be converted to a net increase in knowledge of the world or that denser maps will automatically mean more democratic ones.

Both Africanist art historians reflecting on the place of contemporary African art in the global art market and Marxist critics theorizing the cultural logics of contemporary capitalism might find considerable resources in these and other, similar projects coming out of contemporary Nairobi. These projects are deploying new digital technologies not to extend and intensify the global colonial system on an ever more mind-boggling scale but, rather, to respond to this system, in the diversity of its multinational expressions, in new ways. These projects furthermore allow us to glimpse in greater detail the immense imaginative and creative capacities emerging from cities, megacities, and slums of the Global South, which are challenging analytical frameworks arising from modes of aesthetic and cultural production associated with earlier phases of capitalism. Hence the ingenious nature of these artists' decision to plot themselves within the structural coordinates of contemporary capitalism under the aegis of the "NGO aesthetic" and to begin to develop a kind of tactics in relation to these new regimes of cultural production that are assuredly global, unfolding in the name of globalization, and yet experienced in decidedly local ways. The ingenuity with which this and other local experiences of contemporary capitalism are being expressed and represented both in work produced for export on global markets and in projects undertaken with and for local people living in Nairobi's slums suggests the inverse of the Jamesonian principle glossed by Alberto Toscano and Jeff Kinkle in their excellent, recent book *Cartographies of the Absolute*, when they write, "The privileges of domination are accompanied by a poverty of experience and a deficit of knowledge": there are certain privileges and a surfeit of knowledge with regard to contemporary capitalism that accrues to those living "elsewhere,"[38] that place (no place?) for which the word and concept *Africa* is so often a metaphor.

Notes

I am indebted to Nico Baumbach, Genevieve Yue, and Damon Young, organizers of "The Cultural Logic of Contemporary Capitalism" workshop, held at the New School for Social Research in New York, 21 February 2015, from which this article grew, and to the workshop participants for their many perspicacious questions and comments, particularly Jonathan Beller, Brian Larkin, Tavia Nyong'o, Neferti Tadiar, and Amy Villarejo. I also owe a debt of thanks to the two anonymous reviewers for *Social Text*, whose comments on an earlier version of the manuscript helped me to sharpen its focus. Above all, I am grateful to Sam Hopkins, Alex Nicolic, and Biki Kangwana for the crash course in Nairobi-based art and activism that they gave me over a series of public presentations and conversations about Slum-TV that took place in London in 2008 and 2009, and to Sam Hopkins for his extraordinary generosity in sharing both his work and his ideas in the intervening years.

I take the phrase "NGO aesthetic" from artist Sam Hopkins. Hopkins credits artist Alexander Nicolic with coining the phrase. Nicolic was a cofounder, with Hopkins and others, of the Slum-TV media collective in the Mathare slum in Nairobi.

1. Kasfir, *African Art and the Colonial Encounter*, 18.

2. Recent examples of the high visibility of African art, artists, and curators in the global commercial art scene and on the biennial circuit include the naming of Nigerian-born Okwui Enwezor as lead curator of the 56th International Art Exhibition at the 2015 Venice Biennale, titled "All the World's Futures," and the creation of an annual art fair dedicated to contemporary African art in London titled "1:54 Contemporary Art Fair," which ran in its first edition at Somerset House in 2013

and started a New York also in 2015. Also important to note is the opening of a spate of new galleries specializing in contemporary African art in both London and New York in recent years. In London, where October Gallery was once the only gallery routinely exhibiting work by living African artists, the scene has between 2010 and 2015 alone expanded to include Tiwani Contemporary, Gallery of African Art (GAFRA), Jack Bell Gallery, and most recently Tyburn Gallery. The growth of the New York scene during the same time period has roughly paralleled that of London: the trailblazing Jack Shainman Gallery was joined by the Walther Collection Project Space (specializing in African photography), Skoto Gallery, and Richard Taittinger Gallery. The year 2011 saw the creation of a new curatorial position at Tate Modern dedicated to contemporary African art, and 2013 saw two major monographic exhibitions at Tate Modern of two very well-known African artists who had previously been neglected by European and North American museums: Meschac Gaba and Ibrahim El-Salahi, from Benin and Sudan, respectively. On the limits of the "global" museums' self-proclaimed commitments to contemporary African art and artists, see Bajorek and Haney, "Guggenheim's MAP."

3. Kasfir, *African Art and the Colonial Encounter*, 24.

4. For an account of the vagaries of the term *contemporary* as it has been used in contradistinction to *modern*, see Enwezor and Okeke-Agulu, *Contemporary African Art since 1980*.

5. See the special issue of *South Atlantic Quarterly* titled "African Modernism," edited by Salah Hassan, particularly Enwezor, "Modernity and Postcolonial Ambivalence," and Harney, "Densities of Modernism." See also Ogbechie, "Ordering the Universe."

6. I use the term *commodity* here in the Marxian sense, to mean an object produced by human labor with an exchange value on the market, and not in the sense of a raw material used in industrial manufacturing, such as minerals obtained by extraction, or an agricultural product. According to the art market information aggregator Artprice, contemporary African art is estimated to account for less than 1 percent of all global auction sales (cited in Bloomberg Media, "Africa Trending"). Despite this relatively small market share, I take the fact that Bloomberg has covered African art as a topic, and the fact that this coverage refers to African art as a "growing asset class," as evidence of market growth. I am indebted to Sean Jacobs for calling the Bloomberg coverage to my attention.

7. Kasfir, *African Art and the Colonial Encounter*, 24. Kasfir underscores the outsized role played by these ex-colonial organizations, as well as by international curators, in creating the market for this art. The former, which include the British Council, Institut Français, Goethe-Institut, and the Gulbenkian Foundation, often operate as NGOs in their former colonies in Africa; the latter's activities on the continent are frequently supported by international nonprofits and philanthropic foundations, if not by NGOs per se.

8. This visibility is exceptional compared with other commodities produced in Africa for export on the global market.

9. Jameson, *Postmodernism*, 6.

10. Although this waning of criticality was first theorized by Jameson in his famous essay "Postmodernism," theories of the postcritical have enjoyed a recent resurgence and become strangely influential in the contemporary art world. Among the several prominent critics to have promoted, in some cases ambivalently, the postcritical turn are Nicolas Bourriaud and Claire Bishop, in their well-known work on relational aesthetics and participatory art, and, with a different emphasis, Jacques Rancière. See Bourriaud, *Relational Aesthetics*; Bishop, "Antagonism and Relational

Aesthetics" and *Artificial Hells*; and Rancière, *Emancipated Spectator*. Hal Foster in "Post-critical" has been particularly lucid in his arguments against the postcritical.

A more complete approach to the questions raised in this article would have to take into account the ways in which contemporary artists working on the continent are drawing inspiration from an earlier generation of artists' commitments to collectivism and to various forms of participation or social engagement that have not been taken up by Western/Northern theorists. These were undertaken in the wake of twentieth-century African liberation movements and were therefore highly compatible with modernism in ways that challenge core concepts of the contemporary discourse about participation articulated from a Western/Northern vantage point. Grant Kester is one of the few to have brought art from the Global South into conversation with the Eurocentric discourse about participation. See Kester, *The One and the Many*. For a recent example of the new work now being done on African collectivism, see Ose, "Enthusiasm." Finally, see Toyin Falola's discussion in "'Producing the Common'" of the influence of pan-Africanisms and the political projects of 1960s- and 1970s-era liberation movements on the Dak'Art 2014 curatorial agenda.

11. This younger generation has been most active in the curatorial arena. Eyene works as an independent curator, primarily in Europe, and was cocurator of Dak'Art 2012, as well as numerous smaller yet important exhibitions in European venues, such as Focus10 and Focus11 in Basel, Switzerland; Nzewi was appointed curator of African art at Dartmouth College's Hood Museum of Art in 2013; Dyangani Ose held the position of curator of international art at Tate Modern from 2011 to 2014 and has worked widely both as an independent and institutionally based curator in Africa and in Europe, including as curator of the 2015 Göteborg International Biennial for Contemporary Art (GIBCA), in Göteborg, Sweden.

12. A subset of the silkscreen prints has been produced in editions, ranging from four to fifteen. Sam Hopkins, Skype conversation with author, 3 June 2014.

13. See Kiluanji Kia Henda's, *O.R.G.A.S.M. [Organization of African States for Mellowness]* (2011–14), which takes the form of photographic documentation of the activities of a fictional NGO, an organization of African states dedicated to solving the problems of the First World. See also *The Samaritans*, a Kenyan television show. Chandler, "Kenya's First Mockumentary."

14. Sam Hopkins, multiple pers. comm., 2009–10, and e-mail message to author, 15 March 2015. See also Wanjiru, "Sam Hopkins."

15. Under Gaddafi, Libya was a significant provider of aid to many other African countries, and Gaddafi himself was beloved by people living all over the continent. I have seen several photographic portraits of Gaddafi displayed alongside family photographs and those of Sufi saints in private homes in Senegal, for example. The first version of Hopkins's *Logos* was exhibited in 2010, before Gaddafi was ousted.

16. Jameson, *Postmodernism*, 6–7.

17. Ibid., 12.

18. Ibid.

19. Ibid., 6.

20. Jameson, *Postmodernism*, x.

21. A constitutive element of the postmodern for Jameson is linguistic fragmentation, or the decay of language into forms of imitation, appropriation, and mimicry that preclude irony and become, instead, pastiche. Jameson, *Postmodernism*, 17.

22. Hopkins, quoted in Wanjiru, "Sam Hopkins."

23. Jameson, "Cognitive Mapping," 349.

24. Ibid., 356.

25. Jameson, *Postmodernism*, 7.

26. There have been many critiques of Northern/Western aid in postcolonial Africa. Economists have tended to focus on the ineffectiveness, as well as the relations of dependence, fostered by North-South donor-recipient relations. See, for example, Collier, *The Bottom Billion*. To be fair, Hopkins, quoted in Wanjiru's "Sam Hopkins," claims not to be competent to judge the value, success, or failure of the four thousand NGOs operating in contemporary Kenya. See also Chandler, "Kenya's First Mockumentary."

27. Hopkins is a member of Urban Mirror. The full list of artists operating as Urban Mirror is Alessandra Argenti, Abdalla Bakari, Vincenzo Cavallo, Ramadhan Chombo, Silvia Gioiello, Sam Hopkins, Abdalla Khamis, Michael P. Obach, Stephen R. Makula, Jackson M. Wambu, and Richard M. Mwawasi.

28. The idea of tactics that I invoke here owes a debt to the tactical media movement in Brazil but operates in ways that are specific to the work of artists using newer, and different, media in Nairobi.

29. Another project that is noteworthy for similar reasons is Terry Kurgan's massive collaborative multimedia and participatory art project *Hotel Yeoville*, undertaken with new migrants living in the Yeoville neighborhood of Johannesburg. The exhibition catalog, although it does not include comprehensive documentation of the project, nonetheless conveys key aspects of its exploration of the physical, technical, and social infrastructures of new information and communications technologies in a migrant community. See Kurgan's *Hotel Yeoville*.

30. Hopkins curated the 2008 Urban Wasanii workshop—one in a series of workshops bringing together artists from Kenya and from the international Triangle Arts Trust network and sponsored by Kuona Trust—and it was Hopkins who proposed to situate the workshop in a city with a focus on public space. Sam Hopkins, e-mail message to author, 15 March 2015.

31. *Urban Wasanii* means "urban artists" in Swahili.

32. The election took place on 27 December 2007; violence broke out on 2 January 2008. In the presidential election (there was also a parliamentary election), both Kibaki (the incumbent, a member of the Kikuyu linguistic/ethnic group) and Odinga (the challenger, with a Luo coalition behind him) had used ethnicity as an explicit part of their political campaigns, and when the postelection violence exploded, people took up the politicians' ethnic rallying cries. Many Kenyans were appalled by the interethnic nature of the violence, which they believed was manufactured and manipulated by the politicians.

33. The description of the exhibition I give here is based on multiple personal communications, e-mail messages, and Skype conversations of Hopkins and Alexander Nicolic with the author, which took place in 2009 and 2010. Nicolic is a founding member of African Maximalism, another collective, which curated the exhibition. See also the many exquisite texts published in the exhibition catalog: African Maximalism, *It's a Pity We Only Exist in the Future*.

34. Quoted in Hopkins and Hossfeld, *Sam Hopkins*, 78.

35. The tags were, as an act of visual signification, also an aesthetic gesture or trace. I emphasize this point about the visual dimensions of the tags' signification because a consensus has emerged in contemporary art discourse about participatory art that images and visuality have been displaced or at least demoted in participation.

36. The population of Kenya is estimated at 45 million people, and mobile phone penetration is estimated at above 80 percent; smartphone penetration is, however, less than 1 percent.

37. Hopkins credits the idea to use Ushahidi to Vincenzo Cavallo, a member of Urban Mirror and founder and director of the Cultural Video Foundation, which took part in the 2008 Urban Wasanii workshop.

38. Toscano and Kinkle, *Cartographies of the Absolute*, 17.

References

African Maximalism. 2010. *It's a Pity We Only Exist in the Future: Regaining Public Space*. Nairobi: Goethe-Institut.

Bajorek, Jennifer, and Erin Haney. 2012. "Guggenheim's MAP: Where Is the Rest of Africa?" *Africa Is a Country* (blog), 25 April. africasacountry.com/2012/04/guggenheims-map-where-is-the-rest-of-africa.

Bishop, Claire. 2004. "Antagonism and Relational Aesthetics." *October* 110: 51–79.

Bishop, Claire. 2012. *Artificial Hells: Participatory Art and the Politics of Spectatorship*. London: Verso.

Bloomberg Media. 2014. "Africa Trending: Investing in African Art." *Bloomberg TV Africa*, 22 September. www.youtube.com/watch?v=tMlAIcM9iug&feature=youtu.be&t=1m47s.

Bourriaud, Nicolas. 2002. *Relational Aesthetics*. Dijon: Les presses du réel.

Chandler, Caitlin L. 2014. "Kenya's First Mockumentary Takes on the NGO World." *Africa Is a Country* (blog), 10 February. africasacountry.com/kenyas-first-mockumentary-takes-on-the-ngo-world.

Collier, Paul. 2008. *The Bottom Billion*. Oxford: Oxford University Press.

Enwezor, Okwui. 2010. "Modernity and Postcolonial Ambivalence." *South Atlantic Quarterly* 109, no. 3: 595–620.

Enwezor, Okwui, and Chika Okeke-Agulu. 2009. *Contemporary African Art since 1980*. Bologna: Damiani.

Falola, Toyin. 2014. "'Producing the Common': Dak'Art 2014 and Dr. Ugochukwu-Smooth." African Studies Association blog, 12 June. www.africanstudies.org/blog/118-june-2014/379-producing-the-common-dak-art-2014-and-dr-ugochukwu-smooth.

Ferguson, James. 2006. *Global Shadows: Africa in the Neoliberal World Order*. Durham, NC: Duke University Press.

Foster, Hal. 2010. "The Post-critical." *Brooklyn Rail*, December 10. www.brooklynrail.org/2012/12/artseen/post-critical.

Harney, Elizabeth. 2010. "The Densities of Modernism." *South Atlantic Quarterly* 109, no. 3: 475–503.

Hassan, Salah, ed. 2010. "African Modernism." Special issue. *South Atlantic Quarterly* 109, no. 3.

Hopkins, Sam, and Johannes Hossfeld, eds. 2011. *Sam Hopkins*. Contact Zones NRB 2. Kenya: KSH 1000.

Jameson, Fredric. 1998. "Cognitive Mapping." In *Marxism and the Interpretation of Culture*, edited by Cary Nelson and Lawrence Grossberg, 347–60. Champaign: University of Illinois Press.

Jameson, Fredric. 1991. *Postmodernism; or, The Cultural Logic of Late Capitalism*. Durham, NC: Duke University Press.

Kasfir, Sidney. 2007. *African Art and the Colonial Encounter: Inventing a Global Commodity*. Bloomington: Indiana University Press.

Kester, Grant. 2011. *The One and the Many*. Durham, NC: Duke University Press.

Kurgan, Terry. 2013. *Hotel Yeoville*. Johannesburg: Fourthwall Books.

Ogbechie, Sylvester Okwunodu. 2005. "Ordering the Universe: Documenta 11 and the Apotheosis of the Occidental Gaze." *Art Journal* 64, no. 1: 80–89.

Ose, Elvira Dyangani. 2014. "Enthusiasm: Collectiveness, Politics, and Aesthetics." *Nka: Journal of Contemporary African Art* 34: 24–33.

Rancière, Jacques. 2009. *The Emancipated Spectator.* Translated by Gregory Elliott. New York: Verso.

Toscano, Alberto, and Jeff Kinkle. 2015. *Cartographies of the Absolute.* Winchester, UK: Zero Books.

Wanjiru, Kimani wa. 2014. "Sam Hopkins: Deconstructing Logos." *Contemporary And*, 14 May. www.contemporaryand.com/de/magazines/deconstructing-logos -of-non-profit-organisations.

The World Is Already without Us

Alberto Toscano

Figures in a Human-Altered Landscape

News outlets recently featured a scientific debate that could, with some irony, be dubbed Jamesonian.[1] In the context of the widespread conviction that we now inhabit the Anthropocene, an epoch in which mankind has risen to the dubious stature of "geological agent," as the anarchist geographer Elisée Reclus had already anticipated in the nineteenth century,[2] some earth scientists have cut through the periodizing controversy—did the Anthropocene begin with the human discovery of fire? with the industrial revolution?[3]—by dating the onset of mankind's geological maturity with disconcerting precision: 16 July 1945, the first test detonation of an atomic bomb.

The (unconsciously) political character of periodization as an act of both representation and totalization could not be more clearly illustrated. While the atomic age fades uneasily from cultural consciousness, it resurfaces here in the paradoxical dating of a process whose extension along an unexperienceably long duration would seem to defy the urge to name the event and thus to assuage one's ontological and methodological anxieties. Dating the Anthropocene according to what many have regarded as the apex of Promethean hubris seems to imply that the epoch be understood as that of nature's collapse into history—in a discourse that projects human agency on a vast temporal and spatial scale at the very moment when mankind's political capacity to master or even attenuate its material fate appears to be at its lowest ebb. The end of nature (as autonomous from human agency) here coincides with the end of history (as the inability to articulate that agency as a common project), and postmodernity receives a kind of geological imprimatur, by the same token losing its own temporal contours. "We" make nature, but in the act of recognizing this we also

Social Text 127 · Vol. 34, No. 2 · June 2016

DOI 10.1215/01642472-3468002 © 2016 Duke University Press

confront our inability to act historically, as natural processes inextricable from our historical agency threaten to make and unmake history—to thoroughly unmake it in the very process of finally and truly making it. If we place the terminological and periodizing debate over the Anthropocene in our conjuncture of interminable crisis—political, economic, ecological— it is hard not to see it as an implicit theory of species alienation, if by the latter term we grasp a kind of speculative identity between mastery and impotence, agency and subjection.

However, the narrative of irreversibility that dominates this discourse appears to occlude any horizon of disalienation, a process that has frequently been conceived as a kind of inversion or reversal. The ultra-humanism, so to speak, of the Anthropocene, where natural-historical agency is ascribed to humanity (irrespective of actual incarnation, in the atomic event in question, in the US military-industrial complex) also renders obsolete the political and philosophical humanisms that envisaged the end of alienation in a recognition and reappropriation of collective praxis. In narratives of the Anthropocene, the geological agency of mankind seems instead to overwhelm and obliterate the actions of human beings, especially by confecting a discourse of responsibility and guilt that is improbably intended to interpellate all equally. The periodizing and representational choice of the Anthropocene as the name of an epoch that seals the indiscernibility of history and nature—and threatens to absorb and collapse all historical or political periodizations—has already been met with trenchant challenges, some of which I touch on below. At their core lies the claim (variously articulated) that this formation of natural history is the outcome of the material agency of capital, as conceived in its natural, historical, epistemological, and logical aspects.

To treat the Anthropocene as a notion that exceeds in its very act of periodization any univocal material referent (say, a given quantity of isotopes of carbon dioxide in the earth's atmosphere, or a certain threshold of deforestation) is simply to be attentive to its status as a representation that strives to totalize and inform our natural history. From this vantage point, it would be instructive to consider how it has been prepared by a long and complex history of planetary consciousness, but especially a welter of discursive and aesthetic developments broadly congruent with, and even formative of, the cultural logics of postmodernity and globalization as delineated in Fredric Jameson's writings—from Buckminster Fuller's *Operating Manual for Spaceship Earth* to Stewart Brand's *Whole Earth Catalog*. The 1960s flourishing of "globe talk"[4] can be seen as an optimistic precursor to today's rather more anxious acknowledgments of geological difference. Our own representational conundrums are arguably much closer to those crystallized in the very title of a landmark exhibition from 1975, *New Topographics: Photographs of a Man-Altered Landscape.*[5]

That show, bringing together photographic series by Lewis Baltz, Robert Adams, Joe Deal, and others, continues to inform photographic practices that try to picture humanity's footprint in the terrains, built forms, logistical infrastructures, energy complexes, and sheer waste that simply *are* the landscape of an increasingly urbanized species—witness the work of the Canadian photographer Edward Burtynsky.

There is a rich, critical literature on *New Topographics* and its aftermath. What I wish to ask here is a disarmingly simple question: why are photographs of manufactured landscapes so often depopulated? This question was polemically advanced by Allan Sekula, in his militant skepticism about the aesthetics of what he termed the "neutron-bomb school of photography." In his postscript to his photo essay "School Is a Factory," with the aim of questioning the ambiguity of images that were poised between documentary and abstraction, Sekula dwelled on an image by Lewis Baltz taken in the same landscapes of the industrial park that Sekula himself had grasped as the occasion to reflect on the corporatization of minds and bodies.[6] The waning of reference often ascribed to a late-modernist aesthetic was taken to task for combining a complaisant representation of late-capitalist logistical posturbanism with a compulsion to repeat or imitate the coordinates of modernist abstraction. Reference slipped from social space to aesthetics itself, as the photography performs a kind of nostalgia for pictoriality, an affiliation or aspiration to painterly abstraction.[7]

Sekula's critique of this depoliticizing modernist haunting, present in much of his critical writing on photography's history, is powerful, but it also includes a more sympathetic caveat, as he credits Baltz's ambiguity with the capacity to echo "an ambiguity and loss of referentiality already present in the built environment."[8] This built environment, this logistical landscape of business parks, this abode (both hidden and ubiquitous) of capitalist reproduction—in which as Baltz noted you do not know whether what is being manufactured is pantyhose or megadeath, or, we could add, anything at all—is itself ambiguous in the sense that it is a really abstract space, shaped to an unprecedented extent by imperatives of accumulation and standardized integration that strip it of discernible singularity. A dialectical reading of Sekula's twofold critique of capitalist and (late) modernist abstraction, which takes Baltz's new topographic photography as its occasion, could in turn be the object of a further dialectical twist, as we come to recognize that to a large extent the falsity of Baltz's representation is a falsity in the things themselves. That much, together with a specific anchoring in the atomic inception of the Anthropocene, is present in Baltz's own writings.[9]

In a review of the fellow new topographics photographer Robert Adams's influential *New West*, Baltz noted how the serried sprawl of tract houses that are the subject matter of much of Adams's work are no longer the kind of structures we experience and perceive as true homes or shelters but, rather, resemble "the test structures built at ground zero."[10] This doesn't just point us toward the intimate relation between the process of suburbanization and the postwar nuclear state; it gestures toward a kind of lethal abstraction, a convergence between the human-altered landscapes generated by the urbanization of capital and the ultimate human capacity to alter landscapes beyond recognition, beyond its very possibility. A preliminary answer to our question could then identify the aesthetic identity between human-altered and the human-absent landscapes, so to speak, as a combined product of Western traditions of landscape imagery, a late-modernist photographic harkening for pictorial abstraction, and the real abstraction of suburban, productive, destructive, and logistical spaces in late capitalism—which are in turn predicated, especially in the "new West," on ongoing if often occluded histories of settler colonialism and racialized dispossession.

Extinguishing Labor

The work of the new topographics photographers, and of their many contemporary epigones, can be usefully framed as an answer—irrespective of the artists' and curators' motives—to the question of how capitalism is to be represented. It is in this light that Sekula's comment about the ambiguity (between documentation and abstraction) that pervades Baltz's photographs gains its full scope. Yet this world in which mankind (that imposing if precarious abstraction here standing in for a congeries of profit imperatives, legal apparatuses, settler-colonial dispositions, racial ascriptions, etc.) has altered humans out of the picture is a representation (of capital) that appears to block the path to anything like the aesthetic of cognitive mapping that Jameson called for in the 1980s (and not by name well before that) to provide an answer—at once political, artistic, and ideological—to a predicament in which a situational representation of one's place within the totality of the capitalist mode of production had become for all intents and purposes impossible.[11]

Taking as their very object the phenomenon that elicited from Kevin Lynch the planning notion of cognitive mapping in his *Image of the City* (the text later transcoded by Jameson), namely, the US postwar sprawl, those photographs of a human-altered landscape were precisely not photographs of landscapes that men and women could themselves alter, in the sense of a directed collective action. By the same token, they are not spaces for an oriented life but, rather, ones that, though not shorn of a certain specificity (the new West, by which we can understand both the US West and the planetary one), defeat the imagination of any possible praxis through their homogeneity, depopulation, and, not least, blank beauty. We could perhaps add these depopulated landscapes and the production of space they evince to the catalog of interlocking sources of the problem of cognitive mapping as variously posed by Jameson. They are not simply a crucial, antimonumental pendant to the justly famous reflections on Portman and Gehry's hotels and homes in *Postmodernism*;[12] they can also supplement Jameson's attention to such disorienting and depoliticizing processes as containerization and financialization, and to what in a more philosophical (Sartrean) vein he arrestingly terms the "demographic plebianization of my subjectivity"[13] (the postcolonial realization that one lives amid a sprawling multitude of others) and, in a more firmly periodizing and Marxist vein, to imperialism itself[14] (such that attention to the landscapes of the new West and their repressed histories demands inquiry into the place of settler colonialism in fantasies and foreclosures of historical agency).

Though its concern with the representation of capital is not conveyed in explicitly aesthetic terms, Jameson's recent commentary on the first volume of *Das Kapital* contains what is arguably his most articulated theoretical answer to the problem of cognitive mapping, conceived as a product of the temporalizing and spatializing logic of capital. It also harbors a possible solution to the riddle posed by the persistence of depopulation as a trope in images that explicitly thematize our human-altered world, our Anthropocene without an *anthropos*. In a suitably dialectical twist, this illumination of the capital's infrastructures and their representations comes in a chapter devoted to the time of Marx's *Capital* (and of capital). Earlier in his commentary, Jameson sets the stage for this investigation by directing our attention to the crucial role that living labor power plays in resurrecting the dead labor sunk or congealed in fixed capital, in a duality between resurrection-production and extinction-destruction that he posits as fundamental to capital itself (and, a fortiori, to its representations and representability). He observes how

> resurrection no doubt entails the extinction of the past of death as well, in one of those Biblical negations of the negation in which death is itself killed off. Yet there is here an unavoidable contradiction in tonality between the celebration of resurrection and the "extinction" of the past. I think it expresses Marx's deep ambivalence about his immediate subject here, in a figural excitement that celebrates the productive or regenerative power of labor as such, accompanied by a sober assessment of capitalist temporality which ruthlessly extinguishes the past of the labor process in order to appropriate its present as a commodity: which forgets that qualitative past, the existential nature of the work, its origins and contexts, "the traces of labour on the product," in favor of the quantitative present in which alone it is to be sold in pristine form and itself "consumed."[15]

The quantitative past represents past labor precisely by erasing its very traces. And yet this drive to extinction is also behind the overpowering of our praxis and our imaginations by dead labor—or capital spatialized and experienced as the absence of labor, the absence of "us."

In Jameson's reading of volume 1 of *Capital*, this dynamic pivots around the Marxian verb *auslöschen*, "to extinguish," identified as the linchpin of capitalist temporality and revealing "the present of production" as a restless negativity that "immediately converts [its] objectal result into the raw material of some other production" in what appears as an "apocalyptic process"[16] (we will return in a moment to how this restless extinction-resurrection can be squared with the megamachines and megaruins—as well as the quotidian infrastructure—of capital that make up our human-altered landscapes). This dialectic of extinction directly concerns the question of how, or indeed if, capital as a movement can be represented, since the capitalist process, as Marx famously notes, appears to disappear in its product.

The matrix for the periodizing or figural search after the problem of cognitive mapping, and its multiple aesthetic answers, is thus anchored in a simple if momentous observation of Marx, which will spawn multiple visual inquiries, from Sergei Eisenstein to Alexander Kluge: "The taste of the porridge does not tell us who grew the oats, and the process we have presented does not reveal the conditions under which it takes place, whether under the slave-owner's brutal lash or the anxious eye of the capitalist."[17] Reification can thus be seen to define the everyday reality of commodity production. Stepping into the "hidden abode" itself, contrary to a widespread realist instinct, will not break the spell of this violently endless present, since when products of past labor enter a new production process (as means of production or processed raw materials), the fact that they are indeed products of past labor is, in Marx's colorfully crude metaphor, "as irrelevant, as, in the case of the digestive system, the fact that the bread is the product of the previous labour of the farmer, the miller and the baker."[18]

When living labor power seizes these products, these things, and "awaken[s] them from the dead," as Marx declares,[19] it is not as past but as present use values within a labor process overdetermined by the empty, homogenizing time of exchange value. As Jameson notes, the pastness, which is to say the thingness of these products, is only revealed—in Marx's anticipation of the phenomenological doctrine of failure as ontological revelation, made famous by Heidegger's hammer—when they break. Otherwise, the labor of resurrection, labor as resurrection (itself extinguished in the product, extinguished in and by resurrection), exists in a "supreme present of time."[20] This is the time of labor as a paradoxically "extinguishing fire," as (productive) consumption, which, when it comes to constant capital fixed in machines and raw materials, must (in a twofold process and temporality) both preserve and transfer the value that will retroactively be shown to have slumbered within them, raising them from the dead (and thus resurrecting them as something other than what they originally were, indeed resurrecting them in full indifference to their past as anything but potential values).

Yet this temporality of labor's form-giving and form-taking fire is itself, according to Jameson, nested in the logical-historical temporality of absolute surplus value (and formal subsumption).[21] Notwithstanding the fact that it makes the past of production representable only in its very extinction, it makes the present (and arguably the future, what will have been made) intelligible within a horizon of human praxis. This changes irreversibly (for now) through what Jameson calls "the dialectic of scale embodied in machinery itself."[22] As the organic composition of capital shifts ever higher ratios toward constant rather than variable capital, though the dialectic of labor's extinguishing fire is not terminated, it is in a sense overwhelmed by "the immense quantity of . . . past labour now deployed."[23] In Jacques Camatte's lucid formulation this is an effect of the critical dynamic whereby "in capitalism, immediate labour, the labour of the living, enters production in a decreasing proportion, while the labour of the dead enters in an increasing proportion."[24]

Now, although Jameson noted the reifying erasure of the past that defines the social ontology (and aesthetics) of the commodity itself, he holds that in the "earlier moment" (before manufacture), "the past labor embodied in the raw materials and in tools stood in a ratio to the human labor power which was certainly exploitative, *but nonetheless relatively mappable or representable*, relatively thinkable in human terms."[25] As the individual laborer becomes but an adjunct, a supervisor (when not simply superfluous), dead labor takes center stage, or rather, it becomes the stage, the human-altered landscape in which men and women increasingly appear as supplements, extras, or surplus. (Fears and representations of a Malthusian catastrophe, say, in the demographic horror of the 1973 movie *Soylent Green*, are but the obverse of this, finding their pivot in Marx's account of surplus populations: viewed through the prism of labor's absorption and repulsion, of its own extinguishing, the aesthetics of depopulation and overpopulation are intimately, if antinomically connected.)

In a crucial and arresting passage, Jameson advances what I think is the nucleus of a powerful and far more precise (if not exhaustive) updating of the problem of cognitive mapping than the one advanced in *Postmodernism* and contiguous texts,[26] which links the spatializing dynamics of constant capital, and of capital's accelerating disproportion in its organic composition, directly to the collapse of time as experienced individually and historically, thereby neutralizing the widespread temptation to treat cognitive mapping as a primarily spatial problem:

> At the same time, the dead labor embodied in machinery suddenly swells to inhuman proportions (and is properly compared to a monster or a Cyclopean machine). It is as though the reservoir, or as Heidegger would call it, the "standing reserve" (*Gestell*), of past or dead labor was immensely increased and offered ever huger storage facilities for these quantities of dead hours, which the merely life-sized human machine-minder is nonetheless to bring back to life, on the pattern of the older production. The quantities of the past have been rendered invisible by the production process outlined above, and yet they now surround the worker in a proportion hitherto unthinkable.[27]

In the context of our discussion of the new topographics, the irony of Jameson's slippage from a Gargantuan, plethoric accumulation of dead labor to "huger storage facilities" is not lost, but I wish to pause on that "quantities of the past" that so pithily encapsulates the collapsing of time into space that belongs to this dynamic. In this light, the manufactured landscapes of contemporary photography can be seen to make visible these quantities, but not as past. In this sense they accompany, rather than reveal or orient, that vast spatiotemporal estrangement that Jameson thinks in line with Sartre's vision of an antipraxis in the *Critique of Dialectical Reason*: man altered, alienated by man-altered landscapes, in which all praxis seems to be snuffed out, abstracted, extinguished.

The disappearance of the past is an objective appearance, but it is also the form of its massive if unconscious presence. The dialectical transformation linked to the rising organic composition of capital, this silent rise of the machines, can thus be seen, in what only appears as a paradox, as a way in which the past (of production) is "immensely more present at the same time that it is invisible, having been effaced in the process of its own 'extinguishing.'"[28] And while we could speculatively correlate the rising organic composition of capital to a waning of history, viewed from the standpoint of capital, there "is more of the past now (in the form of dead or stored labor) to be resurrected."[29] In other words, the past can never be experienced as past, but by that very same token, it dominates the present—as that which operationally and retroactively exist as resurrected value. Manufactured landscapes—along with the "ruin porn" photography that so fascinates the contemporary imagination and the entire "world without us" franchise—thus stand revealed as ciphers of this conjuncture of the hypertrophy of the material past with the seeming vanishing of the *historical* past.

Anthropocene or Capitalocene?

The social ontology of the material past and the (anti)aesthetics of constant capital sketched out in Jameson's Marx commentary can also provide a different angle on the mainstream debate about a human-altered geology and climate. That debate is one that orbits around a notion of species agency and a representation of history that, in most versions, lend themselves rather easily to ideology critique. As already intimated above, the ascription of geological agency to humanity treats by analogy with an individual act—and its customary matrix of intention, responsibility, and perhaps reparation—a widely and extremely unevenly distributed (in space and time, geography and history) multitude of actions, whose potentially catastrophic consequences are here used to unify the species as a subject of nature, precisely when the subject of history has long become an object of tired mockery. The thesis whereby the most ideologically mystifying acts are the ones that posit a false universalization here seems to find poignant corroboration.

In this vein, Andreas Malm and Alf Hornborg have diagnosed the fallacies and fetishisms of the Anthropocene with great lucidity, noting how in light of the staggering variations in energy usage and the social relations underlying it, "humanity seems far too slender an abstraction to shoulder the burden of causality."[30] Moreover, in the Anthropocene narrative's elision of the social agencies of capital accumulation, colonial and racial domination, patriarchy, and class conflict, the very articulation between historical agency and natural causality creates a kind of false immanence of man to nature, in which the price to be paid for acknowledging human society's impact on nature is no longer to treat it as society. Or, in the authors' dialectical formulation: "Climate change is *denaturalised* in one moment—relocated from the sphere of natural causes to that of human activities—only to be *renaturalised* in the next, when derived from an innate human trait, such as the ability to control fire."[31] The forgetting of unevenness is also the forgetting of the real historical conditions of energy exploitation—and not the "trivial" conditions of humanity's burning of wood, which have no teleological bond to CFCs or shale oil, for instance—that can make sense of the phenomena classed under the heading of the "Anthropocene," to be sought in the "globalized technological systems [that] essentially represent an unequal exchange of embodied labour and land in the world-system."[32] The authors soberly conclude, also in light of the massively unequal effects of climate change on axes of class, race, and empire that "if climate change represents a form of apocalypse, it is not universal, but uneven and combined: *the species is as much an abstraction at the end of the line as at the source.*"[33]

Inspired by a related Marxist critique of prevailing ecological discourse—though dissenting from Malm and Hornborg on the question of periodization, and seeing the long sixteenth century as the historical watershed rather than the Industrial Revolution's nexus of coal and capital—Jason W. Moore has proposed that we dub our epoch the Capitalocene, thereby identifying the social relation best suited to stand in as the agent (itself a very limited concept) for irreversible geological and climactic change. Against the grain of some of Jameson's pronouncements on the end of nature, Moore's proposal depends on trying to articulate the immanence of capital and nature, to break through what he perceives as the dissonance in a green thought that oscillates between a theoretical assumption of the idea of humanity-in-nature and a rhetoric and praxis that rely on their separation. This is not to say that Moore simply rejects that separation; it is a real appearance, a real abstraction: capital reproduces itself by producing an abstract social nature. In Moore's alternative formulation: "Capitalism, *as project*, emerges through a world-praxis that creates external natures as objects to be mapped, quantified, and regulated so that they may service capital's insatiable demands for cheap nature. At the same time, *as process*, capitalism emerges and develops through the web of life; nature is at once internal and external."[34]

Moore's proposal is very rich and redolent with challenges not just for mainstream ecological thought but for Marxism itself, especially in what concerns the latter's theories of value and labor. While I cannot do it any justice, I think that, in critical dialogue with the arguments advanced by Malm and Hornborg and other Marxist critics of contemporary ecological narratives, Moore allows us to reflect on the specific ways in which today's thinking of ecological catastrophe and human agency conspires in not representing capital. The visible, palpable, disastrous—but also abstract and uncertain—mutation of the conditions of society-in-nature is totalized in the Anthropocene by a kind of pseudoagency that is all the more perplexing in that it simultaneously signals the collapse of all the humanist ideals of progress and enlightenment that saw mankind's mastery over history and nature as both possible and desirable. And while consequent collective historical action in the present—not even by humanity but by a class, a nation, a community, even a single municipal administration—appears as increasingly fantastical, mankind rises to the status of a geological agent. The debate around the Anthropocene event, its date of inception, with which I began, ironically marks this short-circuit between supposedly being able to think a geological time scale and being entirely rudderless when it comes to cognizing historical difference in the present.

It is theoretically vital, though it largely exceeds the confines of this essay, to bring this ideological and political-economic critique of the dominant narrative of the Anthropocene into dialogue with those projects of historical epistemology that—often in the wake of Foucault's *Order of*

Things—have traced the emergence and phases of mankind as a subject of history and thus of material and natural mastery. This process, reliant on the epistemological and political inclusive exclusion of others dispossessed of rational agency and personality—whether as merely natural, inferior, subaltern, or abject—profoundly conditions the very parameters through which we envision or represent the geological agency of humanity. The false horizon of planetary human agency depends on (to return to the new West) neglecting to define, for instance, who is doing the depopulating and who is suffering and resisting it. In this respect, the arguments of Malm and Hornborg and of Moore could be revisited in light of Sylvia Wynter's effort to propose an "embattled humanism" (the formulation is David Scott's) on the basis of a diagnosis, itself borrowing from Frantz Fanon, of our "sociogenic code": the "principle/code that is constitutive of the multiple and varying genres of the human in the terms of which we can alone experience ourselves as human."[35] This "code of symbolic/life that institutes our genres of being human"[36] is one whose humanism is profoundly restrictive; it is "an ethno-class or Western-bourgeois form of humanism, whose truth-for at the level of social reality, while a truth-for-Man, cannot be one for the human."[37] Wynter's question regarding the interlinking of race and humanism is one that resonates profoundly with the critique of the Anthropocene sketched herein: "What if, following up on Marx, we were to propose that this insistent degradation, this systemic inferiorization, is an indispensable function of our ongoing production and reproduction of our present bioeconomic conception of the human, of its governing sociogenic principle?"[38]

Communism and the Resurrection of Dead Labor

I conclude, in light of the above arguments, with how Jameson's reflection on the time of *Capital* may also hold some further clues for those wishing to consider the emergence of this strange new name for our present. That geological rather than historical time dominates our consciousness testifies to the pervasive formal and material apparatus of forgetting that Jameson tracked down to the rising ratio of constant over variable capital. The past of production is extinguished of its historical dimension in the process of valorization, and when it is expelled from its circuits it appears as a melancholy trace whose apparent legibility hides our own mystification about its origins.

Some of the theories that accompany our prurient gaze over the ruins of Detroit are almost as arbitrary as those that ufologists posit about the Nazca lines of Peru. The manufactured landscapes that serve as the aesthetic correlate of narratives of the Anthropocene join together two separate moments that Jameson highlights in the exposition of *Capi-*

tal—the revelation of a product in the breakdown of its use value to the labor process, and the looming sublimity of the unthinkably vast quantity of constant capital commanded by contemporary capital accumulation. The landfills, airplane graveyards, coal mountains, and landscapes of extraction that populate (or depopulate) Edward Burtynsky's volume of photographs *Oil*, for instance, could be read as so many planetary projections of the broken tools of which Marx spoke in *Capital*—except that they and their viewers don't often do the representational work of revealing or recovering the past labor (paid and unpaid, free and forced) that had entered into their production. Labor's extinguishing fire is itself representationally extinguished (adapting Sekula on Baltz, we could say that some, though not all, of this extinction is real). Marx himself, in the very passage that Jameson had indicated as a precursor of the "phenomenological doctrine of the relationship between consciousness and failed acts," had observed that "a machine which is not active in the labour process is useless. In addition, it falls prey to the destructive power of natural processes. Iron rusts; wood rots. Yarn with which we neither weave nor knit is cotton wasted. Living labour must seize on these things, awaken them from the dead, change them from merely possible into real and effective use-values."[39]

Many of the human-altered landscapes of the present appear to be landscapes beyond resurrection. Much of the reason for this could be sought in the vanishing of labor from the visual field of northern capitalist ideology, from the political aesthetics of the present. The ruins of Detroit are thus readable as an objective allegory of the twin deaths of living and dead labor (apparent deaths of course, since the great undead, capital, lives in and lives on these very appearances, not least through property speculation). But the call to restore the practical and representational rights of living labor—against the death of agency or the pseudo-agency of the *anthropos*, which will always find itself represented by one capitalist avatar or other—is powerless if it does not traverse the problem that Jameson has captured as that of the "quantities of the past" all around us. It is those quantities that do not just lie behind our visual need to tarry with human-altered landscapes and our attraction to the superficially unified agency of the species; they also account, at least in part, for what the German philosopher Günther Anders termed the "Promethean imbalance" (and its ensuing "Promethean shame"):[40] we are humiliated by the very machines and technologies we have produced. Their seemingly limitless power of production, but especially destruction (the nuclear bomb), reveals our pitiful embodiment. Where Anders continues to treat the agency of humanity as potentially unified, even in the negative image of its humiliation and collapse, Jameson's Marx interpretation provides a way of thinking through the origin of our power and our impotence, through the sources of our Promethean imbalance and the often paralyzing shame that our representations of production entail.[41]

Instead of simply conjuring workers out of the shadows of their own seclusion or superfluity, such a thought, were it to orient itself toward reflecting on the meaning of praxis in our human-altered landscape, might want to approach the question from the inverse direction, that of dead labor—provided that we conceive of that labor not only as dead waged labor but as the multiple "work" that has been appropriated by capital through various strategies of dispossession and of what Wynter called "insistent degradation" and "systemic inferiorization."[42] As capital continues to exploit the congealed work of past generations, but also to abrogate use values no longer fit for exchange, we may need to reflect further on the practical implications of Jacques Camatte's heretical definition of communism as "the resurrection of dead labour."[43] This intuition has been developed at some length by Moishe Postone, who, in an interesting counterpoint to Jameson's reading, considers the emancipation from labor in the horizon of a world of dead labor no longer framed as the direct embodiment of living labor but as "the objectification of historical time," the possibility of "the full utilisation of a history alienated no longer."[44]

Yet one must resist the temptation in such accounts—an effect of emphasizing capital's production of sameness at the cost of its production of difference—to unify communist agency (or postcapitalist praxis) in a way that, while not as mystified as the positing of an agency of the human as such, nevertheless also occludes the present and future existence of unevenness and difference. As Henri Lefebvre taught us, the abstract landscapes of dead labor are both homogeneous and broken, simultaneously.[45] Efforts to resurrect dead labor, to use accumulated historical time and agency beyond the imperatives of capital, will perhaps need to invent forms of being both heterogeneous and united.

Notes

An earlier version of this article was delivered as a talk at the Museu Coleção Berardo in Lisbon in April 2015. I thank the museum and the organizers for their kind invitation, and my dear comrade Jürgen Bock for his hospitality. I also thank the anonymous *Social Text* reviewers for their perceptive suggestions.

1. See, e.g., Hooton, "Anthropocene."
2. On Reclus, see Toscano, "Fighting Ground."
3. As Daniel Hartley astutely notes in a sharp intervention into this debate: "The temporality of the Anthropocene as a periodising category is bizarre indeed, shifting as it does between the present, a retroactively posited past and an imagined future." "Against the Anthropocene," 107.
4. See Boal, "Globe Talk," and Diedrichsen and Franke, *Whole Earth*.
5. See Salvesen, *New Topographics*; Foster-Rice and Rohrbach, *Reframing the New Topographics*.

6. See Sekula, "Postscript to School Is a Factory."

7. I have taken inspiration from Sekula's critical framework in addressing the representation of capital in Isaac Julien's video and installation work *Playtime*, which also flirts with the pictorial aesthetics of depopulation. See Toscano, "Maid and the Money-Form."

8. Sekula, "Postscript to School Is a Factory," 252. See also Toscano and Kinkle, *Cartographies of the Absolute*, 229–32.

9. See Baltz, *Texts*.

10. Baltz, "Review of *The New West*," 41.

11. Jameson, "Cognitive Mapping."

12. Jameson, *Postmodernism*, 39–44, 108–30.

13. Jameson, "End of Temporality," 710.

14. Jameson, "Modernism and Imperialism."

15. Jameson, *Representing Capital*, 59–60.

16. Ibid., 93–94.

17. Marx, *Capital*, 290–91, quoted in Jameson, *Representing Capital*, 96.

18. Marx, *Capital*, 289–90, quoted in Jameson, *Representing Capital*, 96–97.

19. Marx, *Capital*, 289–90, quoted in Jameson, *Representing Capital*, 97.

20. Jameson, *Representing Capital*, 97.

21. Ibid., 101.

22. Ibid.

23. Ibid.

24. Camatte, *Capital and Community*, 126.

25. Jameson, *Representing Capital*, 101 (my emphasis).

26. Jameson, *Postmodernism*, 51–56.

27. Jameson, *Representing Capital*, 102.

28. Ibid.

29. Ibid.

30. Malm and Hornborg, "Geology of Mankind?," 65. See also Malm, *Fossil Capital*.

31. Ibid.

32. Malm and Hornborg, "Geology of Mankind?," 64.

33. Ibid., 66–67 (my emphasis).

34. Moore, "Capitalocene—Part I," 12. See also Moore, *Capitalism in the Web of Life*.

35. Scott, "Re-enchantment of Humanism," 183.

36. Ibid., 186.

37. Ibid., 196.

38. Ibid., 201.

39. Marx, *Capital*, 290, quoted in Jameson, *Representing Capital*, 97.

40. Anders, *Die Antiquiertheit des Menschen 1*.

41. On the way in which Promethean shame is shaped by capital, see also Cavalletti, *Classe*.

42. Quoted in Scott, "Re-enchantment of Humanism," 200. I am taking the term *appropriation* roughly in the sense proposed by Jason W. Moore: "Appropriation . . . names those extra-economic processes that identify, secure, and channel unpaid work outside the commodity system into the circuit of capital." *Capitalism in the Web of Life*, 17.

43. Camatte, *Capital and Community*, 126.

44. Quoted in Slater, "Toward Agonism."

45. Lefebvre, *De l'Etat*, 290. See also Toscano, "Lineaments of the Logistical State."

References

Anders, Günther. (1956) 2009. *Die Antiquiertheit des Menschen 1: Über die Seele im Zeitalter der zweiten industriellen Revolution*. Munich: Beck.

Baltz, Lewis. 1975. "Review of *The New West*." *Art in America* 63, no. 2: 41–43.

Baltz, Lewis. 2012. *Texts*. Göttingen: Steidl.

Boal, Iain. 2007. "Globe Talk: The Cartographic Logic of Late Capitalism." *History Workshop Journal* 64: 341–46.

Camatte, Jacques. 1988. *Capital and Community: The Results of the Immediate Process of Production and the Economic Work of Marx*, translated by David Brown. London: Unpopular Books. www.marxists.org/archive/camatte/capcom/camatte-capcom.pdf.

Cavalletti, Andrea. 2009. *Classe*. Turin: Bollati Boringhieri.

Diedrichsen, Diedrich, and Anselm Franke, eds. 2013. *The Whole Earth: California and the Disappearance of the Outside*. Berlin: Sternberg.

Foster-Rice, Greg, and John Rohrbach, eds. 2013. *Reframing the New Topographics*. Chicago: University of Chicago Press.

Hartley, Daniel. 2015. "Against the Anthropocene." *Salvage* 1: 107–17.

Hooton, Christopher. 2015. "Anthropocene: Earth Is Already in a New Epoch, Has Been since July 16, 1945, Scientists Claim." *Independent*, 15 January. www.independent.co.uk/news/science/anthropocene-earth-is-already-in-a-new-epoch-has-been-since-july-16-1945-scientists-claim-9981042.html.

Jameson, Fredric. 1988. "Cognitive Mapping." In *Marxism and the Interpretation of Culture*, edited by Cary Nelson and Lawrence Grossberg, 347–58. Champaign: University of Illinois Press.

Jameson, Fredric. 1991. *Postmodernism; or, The Cultural Logic of Late Capitalism*. Durham, NC: Duke University Press.

Jameson, Fredric. 2007. "Modernism and Imperialism." In *The Modernist Papers*, 152–69. London: Verso.

Jameson, Fredric. 2011. *Representing Capital: A Commentary on Volume 1*. London: Verso.

Jameson, Fredric. 2013. "The End of Temporality." *Critical Inquiry*, 29, no. 4: 695–718.

Lefebvre, Henri. 1978. *De l'Etat*, vol. 4. Paris: UGE.

Lynch, Kevin. 1960. *The Image of the City*. Cambridge, MA: MIT Press.

Malm, Andreas. 2016. *Fossil Capital: The Rise of Steam Power and the Roots of Global Warming*. London: Verso.

Malm, Andreas, and Alf Hornborg. 2014. "The Geology of Mankind? A Critique of the Anthropocene Narrative." *Anthropocene Review* 1: 62–69.

Marx, Karl. 1976. *Capital*, vol. 1, translated by Ben Fowkes. London: New Left Review/Penguin.

Moore, Jason W. 2014. "The Capitalocene—Part I: On the Nature and Origins of Our Ecological Crisis." www.jasonwmoore.com/uploads/The_Capitalocene__Part_I__June_2014.pdf.

Moore, Jason W. 2015. *Capitalism in the Web of Life: Ecology and the Accumulation of Capital*. London: Verso.

Salvesen, Britt, ed. 2013. *New Topographics*. Göttingen: Steidl.

Scott, David. 2000. "The Re-enchantment of Humanism: An Interview with Sylvia Wynter." *Small Axe* 8: 119–207.

Sekula, Allan. 2003. "Postscript to School Is a Factory." In *Allan Sekula: Performance under Working Conditions*, edited by Sabine Breitweiser, 251–54. Berlin: Hatje Cantz.

Slater, Howard. 2006. "Toward Agonism: Moishe Postone's *Time, Labour and Social Domination*." *Mute*, 28 June. www.metamute.org/editorial/articles/toward -agonism-moishe-postones-time-labour-social-domination.

Toscano, Alberto. 2013. "The Fighting Ground." In *The Anarchist Turn*, edited by Jacob Blumenfeld, Chiara Bottici, and Simon Critchley, 158–71. London: Pluto.

Toscano, Alberto. 2014. "Lineaments of the Logistical State." *Viewpoint* 4, 28 September. viewpointmag.com/2014/09/28/lineaments-of-the-logistical-state.

Toscano, Alberto. 2014. "The Maid and the Money-Form." *Mute*, 25 April. www .metamute.org/editorial/articles/maid-and-money-form.

Toscano, Alberto, and Jeff Kinkle. 2015. *Cartographies of the Absolute*. Winchester, UK: Zero.

History Is What Hurts

On Old Materialism

Alexander R. Galloway

"In our time exegesis, interpretation, commentary have fallen into disrepute"—the year is 1971, but the observation could easily be applied to the
present day.[1] For many humanists and cultural critics, Fredric Jameson's
work in the 1970s and early 1980s typified a particular kind of Freudo-
Marxist inquiry, a materialist approach to the investigation of politics and
aesthetics that would remain influential through the turn of the millennium. Yet the status of criticism and theory has changed subtly in recent
years, with many in the field seeing a crisis of legitimacy in the face of
competing methodologies such as cognitive science, neuroscience, or the
statistical techniques deployed by digital humanities, not to mention the
widespread triumph of neoliberalism, which, among other things, pro-
fesses an end to competing methodologies as such. Many have wondered
whether cultural theory has a future at all and, if so, whether "exegesis,
interpretation, commentary" have any role to play in it.

   Published in the winter of 2004, *Critical Inquiry*'s special issue on
"The Future of Criticism" was one of several publications that tackled
these questions directly. Based on papers delivered at the journal's editorial board symposium in Chicago on 11–12 April 2003, the issue included
contributions from such authors as Homi Bhabha, Teresa de Lauretis,
Miriam Hansen, Mary Poovey, and Lauren Berlant, along with Jameson's
own contribution, "Symptoms of Theory or Symptoms for Theory?"[2] To
fan the flames, the editors ran Bruno Latour's anticritical diatribe "Why
Has Critique Run out of Steam?" as lead article ahead of the special dos-
sier on the future of criticism.

   While the so-called crisis of theory is complex and irreducible to
a single theme or trend, I will nevertheless focus here on materialism,

Social Text 127 · Vol. 34, No. 2 · June 2016
DOI 10.1215/01642472-3468014   © 2016 Duke University Press

a theme particularly relevant to Jameson and twentieth-century cultural Marxism as a whole. Having fallen out of fashion, materialism is once again a topic of debate thanks to so-called new materialism and the ontological turn in contemporary theory. A capacious if also overly vague appellation, *ontological turn* has been used to describe the work of thinkers as diverse as Karen Barad, Manuel DeLanda, Elizabeth Grosz, Bruno Latour, and Quentin Meillassoux, many of whom have achieved prominence in the last ten to fifteen years. *New materialism,* also broad and often difficult to define, indicates a newfound interest in nature, matter, reality, being, and ontology, as opposed to what it sees as the irredeemably culturalist tendencies of postmodern theory, with its penchant for text, discourse, subjectivity, ideology, and epistemology.

Such pat distinctions are challenging to defend, however, and the "new" materialism is often difficult to separate from its "old" counterpart. For example, in the second half of the twentieth century, "old" cultural Marxists such as Louis Althusser and Pierre Macherey helped spark a renaissance of interest in what were called radical materialists, chief among them Spinoza. Even poststructuralism, often unfairly caricatured as unmoored from material reality, placed a special emphasis on the material specificity of, say, the diacritical mark, the gestures of the body, or the way power flows through society. Nevertheless, today's new materialism often defines itself in opposition to materialism's previous caretakers, particularly those like György Lukács or Raymond Williams, or Jameson himself, who were working under the banner of the cultural turn in Western Marxism. Indeed, amid recent calls for a return to materialism and ontology, one often hears various strains of post-Marxism, if not anti-Marxism, along with a variety of reasons for doing away with interpretation and criticism altogether, as if the warm presence of being were nourished in equal proportion to the waning of the critical apparatus.

For instance, in "Why Has Critique Run out of Steam?" Latour has argued stridently against the critical stance, that type of rationality inherited from Kant's critical philosophy but also, more pointedly, the critical stance passed down via Marx's critique of commodity fetishism. For Latour critique is a form of pernicious deception in which an elite specialist (the critical intellectual) demonstrates to naive believers that what they believe is wrong. Critique creates the very conditions of mental trickery precisely so that it can valiantly overcome them. In the end, according to Latour, intellectuals use critique to make themselves look better, while showing how audiences, readers, and subjects of all kinds can be redeemed from false consciousness. "Do you see now why it feels so good to be a critical mind?" Latour asked sarcastically. "Why critique, this most ambiguous *pharmakon,* has become such a potent euphoric drug?

You are always right! . . . Isn't this fabulous? Isn't it really worth going to graduate school to study critique?"[3]

Contra critique, Latour urges his followers to pursue more material concerns rooted in a realist ontology. "What I am going to argue is that the critical mind, if it is to renew itself and be relevant again, is to be found in the cultivation of a *stubbornly realist attitude*"—realism (along with empiricism) being Latour's preferred form of material ontology.[4] Latour's indictment is thus an indictment against cultural theory as a whole: cultural critique *or* ontological realism.

Latour is just one thinker, of course, albeit a hugely influential one. And, given more time, it would be useful to delve into the details of the recent ontological turn, along with new materialism more generally. Suffice it to say that something is afoot and that here, in the context of this special issue, the time is ripe to reassess an old materialist, Jameson, in the context of today's new materialism. Much has already been said about Jameson's writings on utopia, art, dialectics, allegory, history, and totality. Yet this article explores a different side of Jameson's work, not new materialism so much as old materialism: historical materialism and its often fraught relationship to ontology. By the end I hope to demonstrate that this choice—critique or ontology—is in fact a forced choice and a false one. Jameson resolves this dichotomy, in my view, by showing that it never existed in the first place, instead furnishing his readers with a kind of criticism that can only be called ontological.

Such an end, however, requires a counterintuitive beginning, for on the surface it appears that Jameson has little interest in ontology. Like many Marxists, Jameson tends to avoid discussions of essence, existence, presence, and other ontological topics. In an echo of Althusser's distinction between theory and philosophy, if not Karl Korsch's assertion that "Marxian theory constitutes neither a positive materialistic philosophy nor a positive science," Jameson typically shuns the kinds of grand systemic claims made by metaphysics, ontology, and other branches of philosophy.[5] "Marxism is not an ontology, and should be neither an ontology nor a philosophy," Jameson stated flatly in a 1995 interview with Xudong Zhang; "there is not a philosophical system of Marxism that you can write down. . . . Marxism is not a recipe."[6] On the one hand, ontology and metaphysics devote themselves to the most fundamental questions of existence and presence, organizing their discourse into a coherent system of being. "Theory," on the other hand, "makes no such systematic or philosophical claims."[7]

So stands the record. And our time will not be spent contesting Jameson's own claims about the nonrelation between Marxism and philosophy, much less dissolving the distinction between theory and philosophy;

on the contrary, the distinction should be reexamined and made all the more relevant for our times. Yet being so thoroughly influenced by Hegel's dialectic and the representational logics of cultural Marxism, Jameson indeed promulgates a very specific ontological structure, if not in word then in deed. This article makes the argument explicitly: Jameson is an ontological thinker; he proposes a specific structure of being, a structure that, while rooted in the Kantian tradition, nevertheless inverts that tradition in favor of a more materialist core.[8]

And thus—to reveal the ending before hardly having gotten under way—Jameson's Marxism is not so much a repudiation of philosophy as a rejection of one particular kind of philosophy, an influential kind to be sure, in favor of an alternative relation between thinking and existing. Such an alternative has something to say about ontology, while at the same time it maintains a fidelity to the core political commitments of Marxism.

The key lies in Jameson's critique of method. Ostensibly against method, in that he denies the existence of any kind of pregiven Marxist method perfected and honed for all circumstances, Jameson defines Marxism instead in terms of a material condition. In other words, there exists no Marxist method as such, yet there exists a material condition that structures the horizon of interpretability for all society and culture. The outlines for such a position were laid down early on by Jameson, as evidenced by two key methodological pieces, the concluding chapter "Towards Dialectical Criticism" in *Marxism and Form* published in 1971 (along with the above-cited essay "Metacommentary" also published that year), and the 1981 book *The Political Unconscious*, the latter, in a famous line, claiming that "the political perspective [is] the absolute horizon of all reading and all interpretation."[9]

This "absolute horizon"—or what, in a phrase borrowed from Sartre, he sometimes calls the "untranscendable horizon"—remains somewhat elusive. Nevertheless it resides at the heart of Jameson's method and will serve as our first principle, *there is an absolute horizon.*

Representation

What is this horizon? Where does it reside? And why is it absolute? History is one part of the answer, materiality another, "that absent thing called the social" yet another.[10] And while Jameson's fundamental Freudianism is sometimes overlooked in the secondary literature, the unconscious is still another way of thinking through the problem of the absolute horizon. Jameson's interviews bear this out: "One comes to Marxism at least partially with the conviction that convictions themselves are formed at some deeper place than sheer opinion by realities other than conscious choices—realities of social class and of the unconscious."[11] Or as he put it once during an interview in reference to the work of architect Rem Kool-haas, we must be sensitive to "the presence of some rigid, inhuman, non-differential form that enables the differentiation of what goes on around it."[12] So there is an absolute horizon, a "deeper place" conditioned by history, materiality, social class, and the unconscious. And this absolute horizon has a relationship of necessity, determinism even, vis-à-vis the normal facts of society and culture. "History is necessity," Jameson wrote in his essay-length reflection on the long decade of the 1960s, and we must be attentive to "objective constraints" and the "determinate historical situation."[13]

There is an absolute horizon, then, even if Jameson avoids more extensive reflection on the nature of being, existing, and other ontological questions. But asserting the absolute horizon is quite sufficient; that hoary question of being now surrounds us, with its ground and foundation, its limit and possibility, its totality and prescription. This leads to a second principle, closely related to the first, having to do with *the determining nature of the material conditions of existence*—indeed, the influence of Sartre's existentialist Marxism is evident in both of these initial principles. The absolute horizon thus inflects and sculpts all things taking place within it. And inside such a structure is forged a fundamental relationship of correspondence: the "realities of social class and of the unconscious" condition the everyday life of individuals; the "determinate historical situation" conditions social relations and cultural production.

Or, in the punchiest line from *The Political Unconscious*, "history is what hurts."[14] An evocative expression, it means two things at once: when history is reified or mystified, it sets real limits on individual or collective practice, yet at the same time history is the badge people wear designating the struggle or hurt endured. History hurts because history is full of the violence of capitalism, or what Jameson described as "the scars and marks of social fragmentation and monadization, and of the gradual separation of the public from the private" and "the atomization of all hitherto existing forms of community or collective life."[15] History hurts because of unemployment, proletarianization, and "pauperism."[16] History hurts whenever material necessity wins out over social collectivity.

Yet Jameson's role is not simply that of doomsayer, predicting the continued degradation of life under capitalism. His significance lies elsewhere, in what can only be described as a full-scale metaphysics, manifest in that most vivid of metaphysical structures, the structure of representation. Is there a Marxist ontology after all, and if so, what does it look like?

"If there is an ontology of Marxism," Jameson observed once, breaking the implicit taboo against thinking Marxism in terms of ontology, "it lies in that, through praxis and its determinate failures, one confronts the very nature of Being itself (provided you grasp Being as a historical and changing, evolving process)."[17] Three points are important to underline in this observation. First is the fundamentally Hegelian conception of being as historical evolution ("historical . . . changing, evolving"). Second is the importance of the dialectic, unnamed but clearly evident, as the primary structure and mediating apparatus of the world ("praxis and its determinate failures"). Third is the notion of a confrontation with being in which, through the dialectic, being is revealed (confronting Being, grasping Being). Taken together, these points describe a structure of representation in which a world, understood as an "historical and social substance itself in constant dialectical transformation," is revealed to an individual attempting to confront or grasp it.[18]

Hence a third principle, *historicity means thinking the mode of production*.[19] An Althusserian or Foucauldian might articulate this principle in terms of the "conditions of possibility" for thinking anything whatsoever—a fact that reveals how there can be no ontological claim that is not also implicitly an epistemological one and, vice versa, how there can be no claim about knowledge that does not already assume something about existence. (It also reveals the essentially modern, even Kantian, nature of Jameson's project, a topic addressed presently.) But how does this actually work on the page? I have already summoned the most essential Jamesonian axiom, that "the political perspective [is] the absolute horizon of all reading and all interpretation." And Jameson goes to great lengths to amalgamate three crucial ingredients in almost every sentence that he writes, whether on a novel or film, or on a work of philosophy or theory.[20] The text itself (as narrative), its sociohistorical context, and the critic's own interpretive stance are all three triangulated in Jameson, through a kind of dialectical supergrammar in which three structures of representation, (a) manifest narrative/latent narrative, (b) reading/interpretation, and (c) inscription/world, are superimposed one on the other, all before the concluding punctuation is reached.[21] Hence, the layers of allegorical meaning embedded in a text structurally resemble the critic's own interpretive layering, superimposed over the text as criticism, which themselves likewise resemble the text's own relation to a larger sociohistorical context. Aesthetics and politics are related, therefore, by way of a shared representational structure.

As evocative as this might be, thus far we have only scratched the surface of Jameson's method and its relationship to ontology. The above observations serve merely to broach the question, without yet being able to answer it. We must step back, then, and reexamine a larger picture that includes Jameson's relation to the theoretical enterprise as a whole.

The Dialectic

A burning question: why is the dialectic *so great*? Answer: "The only truly original solution, which does not claim to resolve anything but rather to incorporate the dilemma of oppositions and binaries into its very structure and method, remains the dialectic, which posits a permanent gap between subject and object within all our thoughts as well as in reality itself."[22] No other term or concept in all of Jameson is so well revered, neither class nor culture, neither literature nor allegory. Essentially unclassifiable and irreducible to other concepts under discussion (form, figuration, historicity, material conditions), the dialectic is something like a physical law in Jameson, something akin to the normal physics of the world. It plays roughly the same role in Jameson that the machinic plays in Gilles Deleuze or the process of revealing in Martin Heidegger. Yet there is nothing grandiose about the dialectic and, likewise, nothing so humble or insignificant as to be overlooked by it. The dialectic keeps the world humming along, like the vibrations of atoms or the gravitational pull of the earth and planets. Thus the fourth principle: *the dialectic governs the world.*

Here the young Hegelian from Durham is on full display. So influenced by Althusser in other ways, Jameson has willfully ignored one of his master's central tenets. Hegel should not be exorcised from the annals of modern thought like some unwelcome spirit. How foolhardy to hope to expel the spirit of the spirit doctor himself. The problem with modernity is not Hegel; Hegel *is* modernity, or, rather, only Hegel provides the philosophical tools with which to think the fundamental contradictions of modernity. "The dialectic is an injunction to think the negative and the positive together at one and the same time, in the unity of a single thought," wrote Jameson in his recent long compendium on the dialectic.[23] And this form of contradiction—a suspended unity, but still resolved, and the negation repeated—is the very heartbeat of modern life.[24]

This makes the question of a valuation of the dialectic so difficult, for in its very ubiquity the dialectic resists localization within any particular real phenomena or any particular human endeavor (Marxism as opposed to, say, marketing). The dogged persistence of the dialectic, with its many inversions and negations, is precisely what summons forth a whole host of secondary phenomena (representation, allegory, mapping, interpretation), not so much to instantiate the dialectic into particular logical arrangements—part to whole, self to world, this to that—but to supersede it via a series of interminable externalizations, which doubtless is the dialectical machination par excellence.

Still, let us broach that vexed question of value—morality even—so steadfastly avoided by Jameson, but that nevertheless reappears in other ways. From Nietzsche on down, moral value has been rightly condemned for its retrograde effects, to both the personal and the social body. As distasteful as the term might be, it seems impossible to conceive of a Marxism without some admixture of morality, some component attuned to the level of obligation, to the level of *want* and *ought*. Can Marxism ever cease to pose that age-old question: what should be done?

So even as Jameson states flatly that utopia "cannot be imagined at all,"[25] there are sprinklings here and there of an actual dream that ought to be realized, whether it be "socialism as a vision of freedom—freedom from unwanted and avoidable economic and material constraints, freedom for collective praxis,"[26] or the encomium to Marx's chapter on cooperation, "the most full-throated affirmation of history and production in all of Marx and the one moment which one might be tempted to read as a metaphysics or a proposition about human nature as such,"[27] or Jameson's modest proposal that a new communist America might be forged from, of all institutions, the army.[28]

Marxists are a fretful bunch, on the whole, and I imagine the great court of history judging all political authors based on nothing but a compendium of the concluding paragraphs to their written works, wherein the most profoundly hopeful grammar often houses a boundless, if all too invisible, pessimism about the state of world affairs, as if two hundred words of utopian pep could change the course of the preceding two hundred pages of sober assessment. This is precisely the stylistic trap that Jameson avoids, resisting in each written line the sufficiency of the sober assessment—an ideological style, if there ever was one, owing much to the tradition of Anglo-American empiricism and pragmatism—and suspending the rousing peroration in favor of a continuous stream of dialectical contradiction in which both the most demeaning proletarianization and the most utopian liberation appear mixed together like some strange metal alloy.

Regardless, if he skips a valuation of the dialectic, Jameson still wishes to think the dialectic in terms of value, not as much an absolute value as a valence, a provisional direction or vector of value, as with electrons or subatomic particles that carry a particular valence or spin. Hence, the dialectic is both natural law and political strategy. The very impermanence of valence makes it so useful, for one can simply invert the spin, switch from negative to positive, or "change the valences on phenomena."[29]

In an eye-opening chapter from Jameson's recent *Valences of the Dialectic*, even that most odious site of hypercapitalism, Walmart, is read in terms of its utopian potential. That such an unlikely institution might provide important insight into the logic of utopia might strike some as counterintuitive if not altogether misguided, casting doubt on the very utility of the dialectic with its many twists and turns. Still, those scandalized by such an approach might be surprised to learn that Jameson has been doing this with the dialectic all along—Peter Sloterdijk's cynical reason is utopian, Gary Becker and the Chicago School are utopian, Hollywood popcorn movies are utopian, and so on. Indeed, with the dialectic "the most noxious phenomena can serve as the repository and hiding place for all kinds of unsuspected wish-fulfillments and Utopian gratifications."[30]

The Political

This brings us to the problem of postmodernism and the vexed question of Jameson's relation to it: Is he? Is he not? Admittedly Jameson's method sometimes appears to align with postmodernity, to the extent that postmodernity, that steadfast foe of method, can claim to have one. His occasional commentary on the difference between philosophy and theory bears this out. Philosophy hails from an older time, if perhaps not entirely modern then part of the old regime. And the break precipitated by theory is one in which the old canons of philosophical truth cede territory to a new kind of discourse unfettered by ground, truth, and other forms of permanency. Once refigured as theory, "'philosophy' thereby becomes radically occasional; one would want to call it disposable theory, the production of a *metabook*, to be replaced by a different one next season, rather than the ambition to express a proposition, a position or a system with greater 'truth' value."[31] Jameson's vocabulary in this passage—the disposability of culture, a meta- or ironic stance, social construction rather than universal truth—all point to a postmodern sensibility.

Yet I suspect Jameson's methodological kinship with postmodernity is not as entirely close-knit as it seems to be. And, with this in mind, we can revisit an assertion made earlier in passing, which while perhaps not obvious at the time should now fit more properly, much like plot points that snap into focus but whose narrative arc could never have been foretold: *Jameson thinks like a modern* (which serves as principle number five). Indeed, he might be aptly labeled a modern critic in the strict sense of the term, no matter how frequently his name has been paired with postmodernism or that more appropriate label, late capitalism, and no matter how much time he devotes to the first great gesture of modernity, realism. In fact, I want to argue—with Jameson against Jameson—that his conception of theory is not at all postmodern and that, of the three basic modern sites (realism, modernism, and postmodernism), Jameson's method is firmly rooted in the middle position, modernism. Jameson is not a realist who has opted to think modernity, or a postmodern embarking on the same; Jameson thinks the modern epoch in general from the perch of theoretical modernism in particular. And so we may ask of him what he asked of Alexander Sokurov: Is Jameson the last modernist, the last great modernist thinker?[32]

Consider four different aspects of Jameson's approach, all central to the modern paradigm: (1) history and temporality; (2) shock, break, or rupture; (3) critique; and (4) the materialist reduction. There is a long-standing tension in Jameson's work that the dialectic is simply unfit for any other historical period than the modern. (By extension, the postmodern is the time in which it becomes difficult if not impossible to think dialectically any more, hence Jameson's attempt to invent novel iterations of the dialectic under postmodernity, the "spatial dialectic" for one.) The dialectic is so characteristically modern because it is unthinkable except in terms of temporality and break, those classic avant-garde categories of shock and reinvention so integral to the modern subject. "Shock indeed is basic, and constitutive of the dialectic as such: without this transformational moment, without this initial conscious transcendence of an older, more naïve position, there can be no question of any genuinely dialectical coming to consciousness."[33] Narratives of beforeness and afterness are the very stuff of the dialectic, even if modernity's "ontology of the present" neuters the narrative of its potency.[34]

Postmodernity is thus not a word to describe a series of years or decades, beginning in the 1970s or what have you, but rather the name of a condition of stylistic overdevelopment in which the modernist break no longer obtains, the assumption being that such a condition, a medical condition almost, can appear and reappear at various points in history, a kind of motile mannerism or rococo (or what the Greeks in their own very different context called cleverness or sophistry), in the same way that the modern break itself has reappeared in any number of historical guises: the Socratic break, the Galilean break, the Duchampian break, and on and on. Postmodernity, then, is better understood as a kind of depressive state, a psychological Thermidor in which militancy becomes well-nigh impossible on the existential plane. It is no surprise, then, that the greatest thinker of militancy in our times, Alain Badiou, emerged in the Anglophone world precisely at the point when postmodernity outgrew its utility, his project formulated on the basis of a reinvigorated modernism in which all subjects are militants of some form or another. The break is everything, and everything, to the extent that it deviates from the state of the situation, is a break. Jameson's modernism is thus no anachronism, even in the twenty-first century, given that modernism describes more a subjective stance than a historical period.

The break in Jameson is categorizable. Not an aesthetic break (from one style to another, such as Adolf Loos proclaiming there will be no more ornament, or Lars von Trier that the camera must be hand-held), and not so much a political break (from one form of government to another, bourgeois to communist), the break in Jameson is an epistemological break. Dialectical critique is "thought to the second power"; it involves thinking at "a higher level," at a level that is "one floor higher."[35] Is this not the most fundamental definition of modern critique, evident in Marx and others, that in the absence of any transcendental anchor, earth-bound and secular humanity must be able to think its own metaconditions?

In this sense, critique is defined simply as the self-grounding of the conditions of possibility of thinking. The fundamental Jamesonian move is to shift from a discussion of the things themselves to a discussion of the conditions of the things themselves. Thus, it is not the particularities of one interpretation over another that is ultimately at stake, or an attention to the various levels of allegory—as in Northrop Frye, the literal, formal, mythical, and anagogic levels—but the condition of interpretability as such and the condition of allegorical levels as such. "One does not necessarily solve this fragmented reality in existential terms," Jameson observed during a conversation about the complexities of late capitalism; "one does not map that out or represent it by turning it from fragments into something unified. One *theorizes the fragmentary*."[36] In other words, cognitive mapping is not fundamentally a question of orientating, grounding, fixing, or resolving a subject's position. The fundamental issue for Jameson is the fact of needing a map as such, not the supposedly grounded subjectivity that results or, as in this quotation, the fact of fragmentation as such. Indeed, the "as such" is the key indicator for these Jamesonian conditions.

To be sure, this is not a form of modern thought akin to that of Kant or Descartes in which the transcendental takes over. Jameson has spoken of a "Gödel's law of social class" in which there is "no foundational position outside the system."[37] Under such a law, it is difficult if not impossible for an intellectual to "legitimate his own practice" by providing a foundation or ground from which to speak authoritatively and "look down with glacial indifference at these interminable mortal struggles."[38] Yet Jameson's grievance has to do with the abstract or external nature of such a hypothetical position, not the fact that it is grounded. Even as there is "no foundational position outside the system," there is still a system, and Jameson's Marxist reduction is to found the position not so much inside the system but superimpose it on the system itself. Or as he put it in an early text: "We have always shown that for Marx political economy is not just one type of research among others, it is rather that on which the others are founded."[39]

We find ourselves again at the heart of the matter, already mentioned at the outset. Jameson is ultimately a thinker of the foundation, of the ground, of the condition of grounding, so much so that we may say of him what Luce Irigaray said of Heidegger, that his metaphysics "always supposes, in some manner, a solid crust from which to raise a construction."[40] Thus, in a discussion on periodization, a perennial theme for him, Jameson characterized periodization in terms of absolute beginnings and first instances: it is "an absolute historiographic beginning, that cannot be justified by the nature of the historical material or evidence, since it organizes all such material and evidence in the first place."[41] How frequently Jameson uses the expression "as such." How frequently he ends an idea with "in the first place." These are some of the linguistic indicators of grounding.

Such an ontological ground requires the elaboration of a sixth and final principle: *materialism is an exceptionalism, but a properly justified exceptionalism*. At issue is what Jameson simply calls dialectical criticism or what we might label the critical reduction, conceived as a kind of impossible antonym to Edmund Husserl's idealist *epokhē*. Recall again the oft-cited passage from *The Political Unconscious*, used to define the first principle above, only now quoted in context to show how the critical suspension operates: "This book [*The Political Unconscious*] will argue the priority of the political interpretation of literary texts. It conceives of the political perspective not as some supplementary method, not as an optional auxiliary to other interpretive methods current today—the psychoanalytic or the myth-critical, the stylistic, the ethical, the structural—but rather as the absolute horizon of all reading and all interpretation."[42] The properly materialist or critical *epokhē* is thus a suspension not of the world but of the "supplementary" and "auxiliary" varieties of thinking. And through such suspension, the many possible interpretive methods are reduced to a single "absolute horizon," which is nothing more than the fact of interpretation itself. In other words, despite the lofty aspirations of scientific Marxism, materialism *is* an exceptionalism. It is folly to argue otherwise in a quixotic attempt to overturn exceptionalism at all costs, the reason being, materialism's exceptionalism is properly justified.

In sum, Jameson's position on the determinate conditions of modern thought indicates not a dismissal of traditionally metaphysical or onto-logical questions, toward which, to be sure, Marxism has had an entirely valid historical and theoretical aversion, but rather a reinvention of those questions along different lines. Still, Jameson is not as much a metaphysical thinker as a *reverse* metaphysical thinker. Instead of the "absolute horizon" being the essence or form or noumenon that withdraws to the perimeter, leading to all manner of philosophical orientalisms from Kant to Hegel and beyond, Jameson's absolute horizon remains, as it were, at the center, for it is nothing more than the real matter of history whose presence is deliverable only by way of representation, figuration, or forms of appearance.

If materialism means anything, it means this: Instead of the noumena withdrawing from the phenomena, instead of the transcendental residing through or beyond matter and appearance thus constituting the very stuff of existence, materialism shows how the phenomena withdraw from the noumena, how the "in itself" is the most real, the phenomena the least real. The noumena-phenomena relation is then explained through the structure of allegory, a structure in which one narrative layer may convey the manifest phenomena, while another parallel layer conveys the real truth of history.

Viewed in this way, old materialism might not be so incompatible with new materialism. Both approaches have a way of accounting for ontology, even if historical materialism has traditionally tried to mute, even discard, some of the more speculative, metaphysical approaches inherited from the philosophical legacy. And indeed, there might not be as large a gap on the political question as some might fear, with many thinkers of the new materialism devoting their political energies to climate change, the nonhuman, and other branches of materialist inquiry. Where the gap remains, however, is on the question of criticism or interpretation of the world, that intractable debate in which both culture and nature play a part. Much of the new materialism tends to elevate empirical, descriptive, even pragmatic approaches in its quest to unlock material reality, while denigrating hermeneutic pursuits to a kind of useless culturalism, or what Quentin Meillassoux in a different context labeled "correlationism."[43]

Such a dramatic step is wholly incompatible with Jamesonian Marxism. As we have seen, Jameson's "ontology"—disclaimers surrounding the use of this term notwithstanding—requires a reduction to material conditions, a determinism (no matter how weak or strong) of these material conditions, and indeed ultimately an accounting of the absolute horizon that conditions the world as a whole. Hence, the dialectic of reduction-and-expression is absolutely necessary, as are the structures of figuration like allegory and metaphor engendered by them, along with the interpretive techniques required to parse them.

This also furnishes a partial explanation for the close alliance forged historically between Marxism and other political movements such as feminism and antiracist struggles; Marxism is not so much the "reduction to class," a move that might seem to exclude other forms of subjugation, but the reduction as such, the "reduction to reduction," or the desire to ground ideology and antagonism in the generic continuum of collective life.

Against the idea that reduction is essentialist or otherwise limiting—against both Latour's "irreduction" and the tradition of antifoundationalism common on the theoretical left—Jameson demonstrates that such reduction is not to be feared. His lesson is that ontology, properly conceived, is critical and, likewise, that critique itself follows an ontological structure. The reduction of one to the other is simply more evidence of the dialectical machine, that aforementioned "dilemma of oppositions and binaries" that governs the world.

Such dialectical inversions are the very stuff of the Jamesonian method. "We're all idealists, all materialists," he once said, a hyper-Hegelian stance that only a dialectician can appreciate, "and the final judgment or label is simply a matter of ideology, or, if you prefer, of political commitment."[44] Still, such commitment remains key, and it helps to differentiate Jameson's Marxism from those other modes of thought (empiricism, realism, pragmatism) in which the world is described for what it is. Marxism is not that. And, following Jameson, I suspect that the future of dialectical criticism will rest not on the changing winds of commitment, this ideology or that ideology, but an unvarnished appraisal of the conditions of all ideologies and an encounter with the absolute horizon that, so far, has been eclipsed from view.

Notes

1. Jameson, "Metacommentary," 9. That essay was reprinted, most recently, in Jameson, *Ideologies of Theory*, 5–19.

2. The special section in the journal, edited by W. J. T. Mitchell, was entitled "The Future of Criticism—A Critical Inquiry Symposium," 324–479.

3. Ibid., 238–39. Latour is fighting a straw man here; the "false consciousness" position was refuted and amended decades ago within critical theory by any number of thinkers from Stuart Hall to Jameson as well.

4. Ibid., 231. See also Latour's recent treatise on ontology, *Inquiry into Modes of Existence*.

5. Korsch, *Three Essays on Marxism*, 65, emphasis removed. Marx's early writings, particularly the "Letter to Ruge" (1843) and the theses "Concerning Feuerbach" (1845), serve as the locus classicus for the distinction between philosophy and critique. See Marx, *Early Writings*.

6. Jameson, "Marxism and the Historicity of Theory," 363–64, 371. This, the definitive Jameson interview, is reprinted along with a number of other revealing interviews in Jameson, *Jameson on Jameson*.

7. Jameson, *Hegel Variations*, 52.

8. Robert Kaufman has written on Jameson as a "Red Kant," a label evoked by Xudong Zhang in Jameson, "Marxism and the Historicity of Theory," 379. See Kaufman, "Red Kant."

9. Jameson, *Political Unconscious*, 17.

10. Jameson, "Symptoms of Theory or Symptoms for Theory?," 407.

11. Jameson, "On Contemporary Marxist Theory," 126. This interview was reprinted in Jameson, *Jameson on Jameson*.

12. Jameson, "Envelopes and Enclaves," 33. This interview was reprinted in Jameson, *Jameson on Jameson*.

13. Jameson, "Periodizing the 60s," 178. This essay was reprinted, most recently, in Jameson, *Ideologies of Theory*, 483–515.

14. Jameson, *Political Unconscious*, 102.

15. Jameson, *Signatures of the Visible*, 101, 102.

16. Jameson, *Representing Capital*, 88. Jameson's short book on capital contains a meditation on unemployment and the "general law" of overwork and unemployment; see 2, 71, 125, and 147–51.

17. Jameson, "On Contemporary Marxist Theory," 128, punctuation modified.

18. Jameson, "Periodizing the 60s," 186.

19. For more on this principle, including the concept of totality as historical knowledge, see the chapter "Marxism and Postmodernism" in Jameson, *Cultural Turn*, esp. 35–43. Some of the material from that chapter, which forms part of Jameson's response to critics on the left, also reappears in the conclusion to Jameson, *Postmodernism*.

20. Jameson's notorious dialectical sentences, a stylistic convention borrowed from Theodor Adorno, are a source of wonderment to some and consternation to others. For more, see Wegner, *Periodizing Jameson*, 18, 222n68.

21. For an example of this at work, see Jameson, *Political Unconscious*, 31.

22. Jameson, "How Not to Historicize Theory," 574–75.

23. Jameson, *Valences of the Dialectic*, 421. The singular importance of the dialectic within Jameson's corpus may be seen in the very fact that this formidable book is excluded from his six-volume collection *The Poetics of Social Forms*, as in a painting where the reversal of figure and ground reveals, via absence, the ultimate importance of the negative space.

24. The dialectic is not modern tout court, as any classicist will quickly attest, and Jameson has shown how the dialectic plays a similar role to peripeteia (reversal) in Aristotle, as evidenced in the long final chapter of *Valences of the Dialectic*. In taking up Aristotle's terminology from the *Poetics*—peripeteia, anagnorisis, and pathos—Jameson has attempted to adapt these classical terms "to a modern and materialist historiography" (565).

25. Jameson, *Valences of the Dialectic*, 612.

26. Jameson, "Five Theses on Actually Existing Marxism," 3.

27. Jameson, *Representing Capital*, 53.

28. Jameson, "American Utopia."

29. Jameson, *Valences of the Dialectic*, 434.

30. Ibid., 416.

31. Jameson, "Periodizing the 60s," 193.

32. See Jameson, "History and Elegy in Sokurov," 10.

33. Jameson, *Marxism and Form*, 308.

34. See Jameson, *Singular Modernity*, where he is not at all bullish on the political potential of modernism. On beforeness and afterness see also the final chapter in *Valences of the Dialectic*, esp. 475–82.

35. Jameson, *Marxism and Form*, 307, 308.

36. Jameson, "Marxism and the Historicity of Theory," 369, emphasis added.

37. Jameson, "How Not to Historicize Theory," 577.

38. Ibid.

39. Jameson, *Marxism and Form*, 377.

40. Irigaray, *Forgetting of Air in Martin Heidegger*, 2.

41. Jameson, *Singular Modernity*, 23.

42. Jameson, *Political Unconscious*, 17.

43. Meillassoux, *After Finitude*, 5.

44. Jameson, *Jameson on Jameson*, 3.

References

Irigaray, Luce. 1999. *The Forgetting of Air in Martin Heidegger*, translated by Mary Beth Mader. Austin: University of Texas Press.

Jameson, Fredric. 1971. *Marxism and Form: Twentieth-Century Dialectical Theories of Literature*. Princeton, NJ: Princeton University Press.

Jameson, Fredric. 1971. "Metacommentary." *PMLA* 86, no. 1: 9–18.

Jameson, Fredric. 1981. *The Political Unconscious: Narrative as a Socially Symbolic Act*. Ithaca, NY: Cornell University Press.

Jameson, Fredric. 1984. "Periodizing the 60s." *Social Text* 9–10: 178–209.

Jameson, Fredric. 1990. "On Contemporary Marxist Theory: An Interview with Fredric Jameson," with Sabry Hafez, Abbas Al-Tonsi, Mona Abousenna, and Aida Nasr. *Alif: Journal of Comparative Poetics* 10: 114–31.

Jameson, Fredric. 1991. *Postmodernism; or, The Cultural Logic of Late Capitalism*. Durham, NC: Duke University Press.

Jameson, Fredric. 1992. "Envelopes and Enclaves: The Space of Post-civil Society (an Architectural Conversation)," with Micheal Speaks. *Assemblage* 17: 30–37.

Jameson, Fredric. 1992. *Signatures of the Visible*. New York: Routledge.

Jameson, Fredric. 1996. "Five Theses on Actually Existing Marxism." *Monthly Review* 47, no. 11: 1–10.

Jameson, Fredric. 1998. *The Cultural Turn: Selected Writings on the Postmodern, 1983–1998*. London: Verso.

Jameson, Fredric. 1998. "Marxism and the Historicity of Theory: An Interview with Fredric Jameson," with Xudong Zhang. *New Literary History* 29, no. 3: 353–83.

Jameson, Fredric. 2002. *A Singular Modernity: Essay on the Ontology of the Present*. London: Verso.

Jameson, Fredric. 2004. "Symptoms of Theory or Symptoms for Theory?" *Critical Inquiry* 30, no. 2: 403–8.

Jameson, Fredric. 2006. "History and Elegy in Sokurov." *Critical Inquiry* 33, no. 1: 1–12.

Jameson, Fredric. 2007. *Jameson on Jameson: Conversations on Cultural Marxism*, edited by Ian Buchanan. Durham, NC: Duke University Press.

Jameson, Fredric. 2008. "How Not to Historicize Theory." *Critical Inquiry* 34, no. 3: 563–82.

Jameson, Fredric. 2008. *The Ideologies of Theory*. London: Verso.

Jameson, Fredric. 2010. *The Hegel Variations: On the Phenomenology of Spirit*. New York: Verso.

Jameson, Fredric. 2010. *Valences of the Dialectic*. New York: Verso.

Jameson, Fredric. 2011. *Representing Capital: A Reading of Volume One*. New York: Verso.

Jameson, Fredric. 2014. "An American Utopia." Lecture presented at the CUNY Graduate Center, New York, 14 March.

Kaufman, Robert. 2000. "Red Kant; or, The Persistence of the Third *Critique* in Adorno and Jameson." *Critical Inquiry* 26, no. 4: 682–724.

Korsch, Karl. 1972. *Three Essays on Marxism*. New York: Monthly Review Press.

Latour, Bruno. 2004. "Why Has Critique Run out of Steam? From Matters of Fact to Matters of Concern." *Critical Inquiry* 30, no. 2: 225–48.

Latour, Bruno. 2013. *An Inquiry into Modes of Existence: An Anthropology of the Moderns*, translated by Catherine Porter. Cambridge, MA: Harvard University Press.

Marx, Karl. 1974. *Early Writings*, translated by Rodney Livingstone and Gregor Benton. London: Penguin.

Meillassoux, Quentin. 2008. *After Finitude: An Essay on the Necessity of Contingency.* Translated by Ray Brassier. London: Continuum.

Mitchell, W. J. T., ed. 2004. "The Future of Criticism—a Critical Inquiry Symposium." Special section, *Critical Inquiry* 30, no. 2: 324–479.

Wegner, Phillip. 2014. *Periodizing Jameson: Dialectics, the University, and the Desire for Narrative.* Evanston, IL: Northwestern University Press.

Revisiting Postmodernism

An Interview with Fredric Jameson

Conducted by Nico Baumbach, Damon R. Young, and Genevieve Yue

Editors' Note: This interview was conducted with Fredric Jameson on 13 March 2014 in New York City and has been lightly edited for clarity. On the occasion of the thirtieth anniversary of the publication of "Postmodernism; or, The Cultural Logic of Late Capitalism" in the New Left Review, *Jameson looks back at the essay and considers the current state of capitalism, theory, art, and culture in relation to the concepts he adopted in 1984. Jameson is Knut Schmidt-Nielsen Professor of Comparative Literature, professor of romance studies (French), and director of the Institute for Critical Theory at Duke University. He is the author of many books, including* The Political Unconscious: Narrative as a Socially Symbolic Act *(1981),* Postmodernism; or, The Cultural Logic of Late Capitalism *(1991),* A Singular Modernity: Essay on the Ontology of the Present *(2002), and, most recently,* The Ancients and the Postmoderns: On the Historicity of Forms *(2015).*

Social Text: *If you were to think through the project of defining* postmodernism *today, following the basic framework in the 1984 essay or the 1991 book, which constitutive features would you emphasize? Are there aspects you emphasized thirty years ago that seem less relevant today, and have others emerged as more significant in recent decades? If there has been a shift, how do we account for it?*

Fredric Jameson: The first thing I would do is to separate these terms *postmodernity* and *postmodernism*, because people have often thought that my first description of it was a sort of aesthetic inventory of stylistic features. In part it was that, but I had understood it in terms of periodization and social structure. And now I realize that it would have been much clearer

Social Text 127 · Vol. 34, No. 2 · June 2016
DOI 10.1215/01642472-3468026 © 2016 Duke University Press

had I distinguished *postmodernity* as a historical period from *postmodernism* as a style. I should say that I don't care what people call these things. It seems to me that everybody recognizes some kind of postmodern break, whatever name they give it, that takes place around 1980 or so, in the Reagan/Thatcher era, with the advent of economic deregulation, the new salience of globalization, and so on. I still call it *postmodernity* because it does seem to mark the end of the modern in all kinds of ways, from communications technologies and industry all the way to forms of art. I don't think that postmodernity is over. You can say that postmodernism is over, if you understand postmodernism in a narrow way, because art has certainly changed in many respects since the '80s. But I don't think that you can say that the whole historical period—the third stage of capitalism, I would like to call it—has come to an end, unless you are able to specify what has followed it.

To take art: what I was ascribing to the postmodern period was a kind of art that wished to escape from the high seriousness of modernism, in favor of the entertaining and the relaxing and so on. We're probably beyond that stage in art, and what strikes me about recent art is that, in a sense, everybody's political. But that does not mean that our "political" art *works* as politics. I don't think anybody knows what a successful political—truly political—art would be, one that would have an effect. But I think that everybody nowadays recognizes that capitalism is an omnipresent form of our existence, and I would say it's a continuation of the process that was called, in the famous missing chapter of *Capital*, a "subsumption." That is, everything has been subsumed under capital to a much greater degree than ever before. Remember that in the '80s there was still such a thing as a socialist block, not that it was very successful as a form of resistance or as an alternative to capitalism; and there were other forms of art or of experience itself that seemed to exist outside the system, that resisted commodification, however provisionally or temporarily. Indeed, whole aesthetics, from Adorno's notion of the negative to Left ideas of subversion, were based on the premise that there could be some kind of noncommodified art. Now everything seems subsumed, in that sense; people seem resigned to the idea that everything is commodified.

It seems to me that capitalism—or late capitalism, if you like, or perhaps finance capital is a better way of naming it, or globalization—at any rate, it seems to me that everyone has had to come to terms with the omnipresence of this far more wholly subsumed kind of social and economic structure. And that, I think, leaves its traces on or in art, much of which wants to be oppositional; but do we know any longer what oppositional means in this total system, or what might "subvert" it, or even function as its critique? Those were the synonyms for Adorno's negativity in the modern period, and I don't think anyone really understands what form they would take today. Just as there was a struggle over the meaning of the word *political* itself (in recent French theory), so there is today a feeling that even the negative has been co-opted by the system—indeed, that the system needs negative critiques to keep itself going (this is the meaning of the ingenious saying, communism is the dream of capitalism). So that's one basic change. I would call it cynicism, this totalized form of awareness of capitalism. I don't think I mean quite the same thing as what Sloterdijk meant, because that book of his was really a book about Weimar [*Critique of Cynical Reason*], but I do think this is an age of generalized cynicism, in the sense that everybody knows what the score is. There is nothing surprising to anybody about this system, and in that sense, maybe *cynicism* is the best term for it.

As for other features, one of the things I have written about is the effects on temporality. The French have invented this word *presentism*—I don't like it very much, but it fits. I have written a lot about the disappearance of history, of historicity, about the becoming simulacrum of the past, the reduction to the present. I also call it a reduction to the body, because if you're in the present that's really all you have. This has its effect on all kinds of artistic forms, which used to be able to draw on longer and larger temporalities but which now seem incapable of doing that. I have given the example of action films, but there could be many other examples.

One way I've thought of characterizing such changes has to do with theory or interpretation—namely, the predominance (and everybody in art history talks about this; it's not new with me) of the curator. We have conferences on the curatorial. Curators' shows are a little bit like derivatives: they put all these different elements or entities together, they last for a minute, and then they're gone again; the individual work is no longer very significant. Those ephemeral connections in the present correspond to a new form of the collective, which you can call, if you like, the "multitude." Baudrillard already wrote long ago about how the very nature of the museum has changed, and we know that in the old days you could go to the great museums and nobody was ever there. Nowadays these are big shows, you pay a lot of money, you sometimes have to make a reservation—so there's a transformation in the way museums have become public, and that has to do with shows and the rise of the curatorial.

Theory is also essentially a curatorial process. We've got various texts from the past, say Aristotle or Kant, and we put them all together in an ephemeral combination. Deleuze is the great master of this. You have a theoretical show in which these various things are plugged into each other, and then another one comes on line later on. Since theory is not philosophy—something I want to insist on—the question of what it is becomes an interesting one; it approaches the situation of art as much as it does anything else. But if you put it that way you can see that what's collective about the public in museums, and about the fashions in theory I suppose, is itself really the multitude. That is, these big demonstrations like Tahrir Square, and so forth, are also ephemeral. It's pretty clear from many of these examples that they are not enduring; they are not political events in the old sense: they don't produce constitutions, they're not political events with lasting institutional consequences. They are "events" in the stronger philosophical sense of that word, and like events, they then disappear, so they too are in the present. This "presentism" has to do with finance, too, and with communications. That would probably be the major feature that I would try to examine in terms of the evolution of what once was postmodern or what was art after the modern.

Since you brought up the theory/philosophy distinction, we wanted to ask about how these terms are viewed today. In the preface to Singular Modernity, *you referred to "regressions of the current age," including, for example, the return to "ethics." You end that section by asking: "Can metaphysics be far behind?" It seems to us that the last decade has, as you anticipated, seen a metaphysical turn in the kinds of English language theory or philosophy that have their origins in Continental thought. And it seems to us that, increasingly, there's a sense that people no longer like this word* theory *much anymore.*

Just as in postmodern art there was a recourse to the pastiche of older forms of art, so that finally there's a pastiche of the modern itself, a lot of what constitutes the reaction against theory has become a pastiche of philosophy, which I continue to think is not really possible. Let me put it this way, because I think it's a better way of talking about it: I want to say philosophy has to be metaphysics, or else it remains theory. You have a metaphysics in Deleuze that is a kind of vitalism. It comes and goes in his various books, but it's always there. And his attacks on idealism are part of a philosophical framework, and he was professionally linked to philosophy—philosophy departments, philosophy books, the form of the philosophical treatise, and books like *What Is Philosophy?* stage an apologia for philosophy as such. Nonetheless, I think we read the other part of his work as theory.

Why don't people like this word, *theory?* Little by little there's been a return to various forms of empiricism; this is no doubt related to a reaction against so-called high theory, but I would put it another way. As I said, it seems to me that any proper philosophy, anything that really is philosophy, is a metaphysics. That's why Nietzsche is so ambiguous, because it's not clear whether that's a philosophy or not. Nietzsche was, in that sense, maybe the first theorist.

You have a metaphysics when you try to answer two questions: what is the meaning of life, and what is the meaning of nature or the world or something to that effect. Any attempt to give either of those things an answer becomes metaphysical or, to use another word, ideological. Ontology, unless it's a description of these brief flashes of being and so forth that you get in Heidegger, is necessarily a kind of ideology or metaphysics. And theory is something which attempts maybe vainly to avoid that, because probably we can't avoid ideology or metaphysics. We can try to evade it. Derrida evades it by never really taking positions. One of the remarkable, formal characteristics of Derrida's work is that it always was parasitical on another text, which it took apart or deconstructed without constructing any positive terms. Now when you take the analytic terms or neologisms of Derrida, like "writing" or "logocentrism," and turn them into slogans, you've turned them back into a system, into a metaphysics, into a philosophy. Derrida was struggling to *not* have a philosophy, but it's something that's very difficult to avoid, because of intellectual reification. It is almost impossible for any systematic work not to get reified in the terms of slogans and in terms of some form of basic thematics or metaphysics. That's the logic of the commodity system: it's virtually impossible for us to escape it, except for brief moments.

In the past, philosophers have been tempted to turn their own philosophies into systems. It seems to me that's what finally happened to Hegel. He invents something called "Hegelianism." And he makes it into his own system and his own metaphysics, which incidentally climaxes not so much in "absolute spirit" but in "life" at the end, and so we have there the beginnings of some kind of vitalism. In the case of Marx, it's Engels who creates Marxism as a philosophy, and then Stalin. So dialectical materialism is not in Marx, but it is a philosophy. Marx and Freud are each one what I would call a unity-of-theory-and-practice. That is, they're not philosophies or systems. You want to call them theories? Well, I don't know. Contemporary theory is a very unique form in which you attempt to de-ideologize your positions by relating them to your situation or your practice in both of those cases; that's not something that one can do on any permanent basis. I think both Marx and Freud had their metaphysical moments. But those were rather different kinds of "thought assemblages," let's say. Although that's not a good word either because *assemblage* is another word for what I earlier referred to as the curatorial. You curate an assemblage. In modern times whether you like it or not, it's been rather difficult to escape this dilemma.

Now as for ontology, I should say that I am constantly rediscovering I'm still a Sartrean rather than a Heideggerian. I do believe there's an experience of being. Sartre calls it "nausea." It is also an experience of not-being which some call anxiety or freedom. In Heidegger, I think there is a lot of metaphysics, but Sartre did not really make a mysticism out of his philosophy as I think Heidegger did. So finally, my own position is closer to Sartre. Or, let's say Vico: the *verum factum*. I don't think we can know nature. That is to say, I think that life and the world are meaningless accidents. On the other hand, we can know history, that history, society, events, the human world are meaningful. And that's the way I would define myself with respect to ontology, or metaphysics, or philosophy.

Your own work has stood for the persistence of dialectical thinking, which includes the persistence of negativity and more broadly of critical thought, as well as the call for both historicization and interpretation. At the same time, in the attempt to register the novelty of contemporary aesthetic or cultural forms, you have also suggested that the works worth paying attention to tend to formally avoid negativity, the requirement of interpretation, or the sense of historical time found in the great modernist works. Increasingly, theory itself has followed this trend, and there appears to be an emphasis on affirmation and an increasing resistance to hermeneutics. Do you see this as merely a negative symptom of post-modernism itself? Or can you consider a point at which the categories such as interpretation, historicization, and critique really do become outmoded in light of current cultural realities?

It's paradoxical, because after all, let's say you want to think very crudely of art as somehow reflecting the real. Okay. And let's say that the real has become ahistorical, has been reduced to the present, has lost its historicity, and so on. Well then, the art that reflects it is also going to be reduced to the present, ahistorical, and all the rest of it. We can only take an ambiguous relationship to this. In order for contemporary art to have some profound relationship to lived reality—David Foster Wallace's *Infinite Jest*, for example—it has to reflect that reality. The mode of interpretation required for a representation like that necessarily changes. When years ago I talked about surface, lack of depth, and so on, well then, in order to be a proper reflection of social reality, the art has to be a surface art without depth, and therefore the older hermeneutics of depth analysis—whether they're of a Freudian or Marxian kind—are no longer appropriate. But I do think that one can interpret this art in another way as a kind of diagnosis whose form can be described, and whose description is then itself a kind of clue to the weirdness of contemporary social reality. I consider that still a form of interpretation. Does a diagnosis still find some deeper meaning behind the surface? Or does it simply register a new reality?

I think we can still specify relationships to an underlying social situation. In *The Political Unconscious*, I tried to isolate three levels of such interpretation. One would have to do with historical events. I once heard a wonderful Hong Kong film critic who showed how each one of a group of Hong Kong films that we think of as completely cinematic products reflected a certain year in the crisis that was leading up to '97. So there is a case in which actual historical contexts and events themselves leave their mark in the work and—even if they are not exactly the meaning of the work—we can find the trace of a symbolic event or response. On a second level, we can often detect a more generalized struggle of groups and classes. And on the third level, it's the pattern of the mode of production itself that becomes legible; that is, it's this third moment of capitalism that gets inscribed in the work, and one can recover that inscription and use the work to explore it in new directions. That's still what I call interpretation. Now, the attacks on interpretation—Deleuze is again one of the great examples—those attacks also reflected a situation in which we didn't want any more depth, realities, and essences; we wanted surfaces. And therefore Deleuze's—how can I say—his method, his polemics, and so forth, were themselves a faithful recognition of the turn that history itself or that social reality had taken. The old kind of ideological analysis where one attacks a certain kind of ideology or idealism in the name of a certain kind of materialism or vice versa—I don't think that's what ideological analysis is anymore. But it still may be the attempt to locate the way in which a certain kind of work is characteristic of a present situation.

I guess the big Hegelian question would be what about the next step, which is locating the contradictions. The problem is that older works of art or literature had a certain self-sufficiency to them, and one could locate a contradiction in an individual work. I think the newer artistic production is more of a field as opposed to an isolatable individual work in the same way. The example I always use is installation art. As T. J. Clark has said, painting is, well, dead. Now we have bunches of objects that are put together or assembled, to use a popular word. Well, it's not going to be in any one of those objects that one locates fundamental contradictions anymore, but I wouldn't for that give up the kind of criticism that's looking for contradictions. I've written an essay on *Neuromancer*, for example, which really does locate a contradiction in the two kinds of operations that are going on in the mechanics of that book. What are our contemporary contradictions? Local and global is a good one. There are all kinds of formal dilemmas and antinomies that one can find embedded in works and that can be studied. But that is not the same process as finding the contradictions in a modernist writer like Flaubert, let's say, or in an older kind of genre like Greek tragedy. It's a different kind of operation. One hesitates to use the word *hermeneutics*, but I still think that's a good word despite its overtones of digging under and finding hidden treasure.

What are your thoughts about reading practices as taught in universities today and practiced in academic journals, and the extent to which there is a resistance to, or at least a turn away from, close reading and deconstruction, but also ideological analysis and symptomatic reading? One finds new terms proposed; for example, a journal issue a few years ago was devoted to "surface reading," or another example might be Franco Moretti's idea of "distant reading." Close read-

ing gets replaced by data mining. So we're interested in hearing you say a little more about this trend away from the text-based approach. You say that there are reasons that the individual text can no longer be necessarily taken as the primary object of analysis, and yet as you're suggesting, in some cases it is still useful to draw out contradictions in a single primary text.

Yeah, it does seem to me difficult to do any kind of real criticism unless one begins with a text or maybe several texts. Comparison and comparative work are always safer and more revealing than being locked in one particular text. Yet, criticism today is a very free form. And I think that's as it should be; we have everything to gain from people doing all kinds of different things. I wouldn't want to impose any particular approaches or "methods." But, on the other hand, it is the institution that imposes that: it still wants articles, it still wants books, some of which the publishers won't print anymore, like single-author studies. There's obviously a reason for that. I have the feeling—and I don't think I'm the only one—that what's succeeded literary studies, namely, cultural studies, is itself greatly weakened today. It's a convenient way of lumping a lot of different things together, but I'm not sure there really is such a thing as "cultural studies" anymore; it's no longer a movement or a vanguard.

Criticism should minimally involve some sense of history, even if it is only a heightened sense of the present. On the other hand, we have global history now, and it's very hard for anybody to have a really enlarged sense of all that history. And then there's also English as a global language and what remains of an older kind of English. Think of those long sentences of George Eliot. I would be interested to know whether students would be more receptive to Proust's long sentences than Eliot's and, if so, why. It has been claimed, for example, that reading electronic texts like on a Kindle makes it more and more difficult to follow plots, to remember what happened, but above all, more and more difficult to read long sentences. I suppose that this is one of things that history is: a history of our retention of sentences and their structure, which is actually the very topic of Auerbach's *Mimesis*. Still I do think that something is lost when people are not trained to sustain that kind of temporal attention. The same goes for music and really for all of the art of the past.

I tend to still have some sympathy for the old humanities courses and so-called great books courses. But people have to be attracted to them in some way. I know that when my daughters were growing up a whole run of Jane Austen movies came out, and they all sat down and read Jane Austen's novels. So that seems to me fine, but if people want, after seeing them, to read five-volume fantasy novels, I think that's fine too. It's a question of reading itself. On the other hand, I wouldn't stridently defend "reading" or the classics in the familiar reactionary way (what Brecht called the good old things, as opposed to the bad new things). Pedagogy is not inflicting discipline but awakening interest.

Is this sympathy for these arts of the past why in your recent work you returned to questions of modernism and realism?

The series you are alluding to [*The Poetics of Social Forms*] was always planned that way. I mean, I started with utopias, that is, science fiction and the future; then I went to postmodernism, which is the present, and so I'm making my way back into a certain past—to realism and then on to allegory and to epic and finally to narrative itself, which has always been my primary interest. Maybe indeed I have less to say about contemporary works than about even the recent past; or let's say I have built up a certain capital of reading but am not making any new and exciting investments any longer. It's a problem: you can either read or write, but time intervenes, and you have to choose between them. Still, I feel that I always discover new things about the present when working on these moments of the past. Allegory, for example, is both antiquated and surprisingly actual, and the work on museum pieces suddenly proves to make you aware of present-day processes that you weren't aware of.

Has that tracing backward from The Modernist Papers *to* The Antinomies of Realism *in any way make you rethink questions of postmodernism?*

No, not in the sense of revising my description, but perhaps in enlarging it: thus, all the new work on affect and emotion has allowed me to see certain things in a different way. I suppose it would be inevitable that this process would allow you to be able to articulate some new problems that you hadn't really thought of in those terms before. And certainly the affect material was one of those.

Following from that, we would like to ask you explicitly about your use of the word affect *today compared to thirty years ago. Of the various tendencies associated with postmodernism that you highlighted in 1984, it is "the waning of affect" that has often been taken to be the most at odds with the current cultural climate, or at least current theoretical assumptions. Do you see "the waning of affect" as still a constitutive feature of contemporary culture? How so? How do you understand the current theoretical emphasis on affect (which, of course, has a number of variations, from Eve Sedgwick's influence on the use of the term in queer theory, to the more Deleuzian and/or Spinozist forms, to phenomenological or cognitivist uses of the term)?*

I used the wrong word in that passage. It was written in the early 1980s, before the term *affect* had the voluminous theoretical attention it has since; I did not then have a binary opposition to guide me, and I simply took the word *affect* as a synonym for emotion. Today, however, I see the situation as involving an opposition between *affect* and *emotion* or, better still, *named emotion*, as I prefer to call it: where affect as an emergent and bodily sliding scale of feelings and *Stimmungen* (Heidegger's word for it) is radically opposed to a system of named emotions which in one form or another has been in place since ancient times (in the West). This system is at one with a whole aesthetic, a rhetoric, and a psychology of expression and expressiveness, whereas affect has not been visible aesthetically until recently and is resistant to the operation of naming—I'm not sure we yet have the right terminology to describe its manifestations. So to sum up, what I really meant at the time was the waning of emotions, but I didn't yet have that opposition between affect and emotion available, which I've deployed in more recent work. I develop it really only in a one-sided way in *The Antinomies of Realism* because my allegory book will deal more with named emotions. I see affect and emotion almost as opposites, and that opposition suddenly allows one to see the historical position of affect as, if you like, a kind of reduction to the body, which I mentioned earlier. I'm not sure that I'm using *affect* the way other people are nowadays. But certainly the whole emergence of "affect theory" has forced me to rethink that word and to recognize how useful it is in the context that I was trying to develop.

We were asking you this because we feel like what you called "the waning of affect" does still correspond to something even if, as you say, you may have chosen the wrong word for it. The term you posed at the time in opposition to affect was "intensity" . . .

Yes, and now I identify those two things. It seems to me intensity is another word for affect in the Deleuzian or Lyotardian sense. But on the other hand, I think the point about waning in connection with affect—you could talk about it in terms of intensities too, of waxing—is that it's something that is temporal, is ephemeral, chromatic, if you like, and one has to think of it that way.

Whereas emotions of the older variety nowadays play a lesser part in narrative and in what narrative tries to do and therefore in the way people think about their lives. If you're isolated in the present, then it's affects and intensities that you're aware of, more than the dominance of some fundamental emotion. What would be the dominant emotion today? Ressentiment, perhaps, or something like that? Well that's not exactly an emotion either. But things like ressentiment, hatred, maybe even some of the positive emotions . . . Proust already showed that grief was—how did he put it?—an intermittency. Maybe emotions are now only used to organize characters around a certain kind of emotion, which would make for a kind of static character of some sort, or secondary character.

On the other hand, affect is very difficult to organize into a narrative. And, whatever the status of our temporality today, we still have to think of things somehow in terms of narratives. That's maybe really the most interesting problem of postmodernism. Whereas the representational problem in the modern was very present—the impossibility of representation and so on and so forth—modernist artists and authors thought it could be overcome. They thought that something could be constructed that could even stand as the impossibility of representation—even Lukács says that, oddly enough, in *The Theory of the Novel*—whereas I think that in postmodernism everybody knows that it's impossible and nobody cares. So the problem of representation is there, but maybe it's no longer a crisis the way it was in the modern period, and you can connect that to the social too. If capitalism is everywhere, there's no great urgency about describing it, whereas if it's still isolated and comes into being alongside other modes of production, or older forms of life, then it suddenly is seen as this strange new, frightening, even monstrous thing that you need to describe.

We'd like to return to the question of the global. If, as you just said, capitalism is everywhere, is it accented differently in Asia, Africa, Latin America, or the Global South more generally?

Yes, of course, and those are also incompletely capitalized, financialized, colonized areas. There are still lots of very poor peasants in China. What we think of as China, especially the "new China," is right on the coast in the old concession areas. So there is bound to be a much more uneven kind of temporality in some parts of the world. On the other hand, people have said the same thing about the United States, which is supposed to be the most advanced country, and yet we also have immense pockets of poverty which have become areas that are perhaps no longer completely subsumed by capital.

I do think the national framework is still very important. First of all, it's what organizes globalization. I always use the example of New Zealand; it was Chomsky who brought it to our attention. If you want to lower salaries and create worker givebacks and so on and so forth, you do that by saying, "Look, we can't compete in the world." The national framework is indispensable for that kind of propaganda operation, because the "we" who have to make sacrifices, take pay cuts and payoffs, and so forth, are of course the national workforce. We're still in that situation. Meanwhile, there is a representational problem of globalization: what are the fantasy characters that all these countries are playing in our unconscious? I mean it's obvious from a much cruder standpoint that Russia's a villain, China's some kind of ally but let's not trust it too much, et cetera. And each country or culture has its version of this, which is Carl Schmitt's "friend or foe," of course, but which is not fixed but shifts and changes according to the national and international context.

And then there is tourism. Tourism was always a matter of going back to the past. When it began in the nineteenth century, you wanted to see older modes of production. You went to North Africa or even to Italy. For a while, it was also seeing the future; that was the role of Japan in the '90s in *Neuromancer*, for example. Japan was this future, though it seems not to be anymore. That kind of tourism, which was a kind of time travel, has gone away. Meanwhile everything looks alike, all airports look alike, all hotels look alike, like motels; I mean these non-places, to use Marc Augé's term. Well, I think that's quite a useful way of describing something that is neither global nor local but that is certainly allegorical.

Since we're talking about terminology, what about the terms we use to describe contemporary capitalism? Is the phrase late capitalism *still the key term for you? Earlier you mentioned "finance capitalism," and there is also "flexible capitalism"* . . .

I don't like "flexible" because that sounds too positive somehow, but you could also say post-Fordism, disorganized capitalism, the knowledge economy, cognitive capitalism, and so forth (I get these terms from Mezzadra and Neilson's useful *Border as Method*), but I still like "postmodernity" best.

And neoliberalism?

Neoliberalism is for me a strategy and an ideology. I wouldn't call the system itself neoliberalism, because that hasn't been doing so well either lately. Late capitalism is the term I got from Ernest Mandel, and I think it's a good term for it. It has some suggestive overtones. Certainly finance capital is a much more precise way of underlining what's unique about this combination of communications and finance and abstraction that's taken over the system of postindustrial production. And then I think one can still say *globalization* except it doesn't seem to sound like a word for a social system exactly. But all of those things express an aspect of this new system. Whatever people want to call it, by now almost everybody recognizes that from the '80s on a fundamental change took place.

A friend of mine who has looked into this said that the last moment in which government was still planning utopian projects was the Carter administration. So that's one interesting temporal index, but there are many other ways of dating the shift. It has to do with the peculiar kind of abstraction that finance involves: autonomy of finance as opposed to that of production. People have analyzed the way in which money is different in these two systems: value of production is very different from the value or nonvalue of all these crazy figures. So abstraction becomes itself a very interesting philosophical question. And I think that has something to do with this newer art that you ask about.

I suppose the equivalent of abstraction in art or literature would be the *simulacrum*, which everybody is probably tired of, but which was really the definitional moment for this art, because it both looks like reality and somehow is also abstract at the same time. If there is another fundamental characteristic of this art, it would be its relationship to that and how it invents some new mode of dealing with that impossible representation. Because representation of the simulacrum means you have a complete realism, none of which is real. That's rather different from what the modernists did. I also have the feeling that much of contemporary literature is a kind of first-person literature which approaches these changes through a different kind of subjectivity. That is, you don't have somebody telling about their feelings or affects or whatever in a stream of consciousness. You have somebody testifying to their flow of experience. It isn't really subjective anymore in the same way.

Postmodernism, as a term, emerged from architecture, but visual media seemed to provide the paradigmatic examples; for example, Debord's idea of spectacle and Baudrillard on the simulacrum became some of the most used and abused concepts to mark the shift to the postmodern. You, of course, highlighted the notion of a shift from time to space or, indeed, a spatialization of time as a primary feature of this new cultural logic. Do you think this diagnosis holds for contemporary culture? It seems as if the sense of a perpetual present, the loss of an ability to think historically, et cetera, is as true as ever if not more so, but what do you say to the idea that, increasingly, cultural forms seem to be moving away from the visual and that the word that seems to have replaced spectacle *is* information? *Do you think there has been a shift away from visual culture in recent years toward something else? And how do you understand the trend toward information becoming the primary category through which to read everything—not just the images and texts that make up cultural forms but also everything that makes up the human as such?*

So you're seeing the image itself as a form of information?

Yeah, or at least that might be one way in which digital culture can be seen to have changed the way we think about the image.

I'm not sure I understand enough about digital culture to answer that properly. I do think that this is where film comes in because in some sense, photography and film are neither subjective nor objective, which might become the answer. As Cavell said, it's the world without people. So from a Kantian standpoint, what would film be? I mean, you're not getting the thing in itself, but you're not getting a point of view on the thing, and you're not there either. And so I think that film becomes a very different kind of nonsubjective, but also really nonobjective, medium in which that strange no-man's land can be conveyed. Now how does that change when you pass from film stock to digital media? I'm not clear. It seems as if literature becomes a sort of voice-over of that contemporary experience.

But meanwhile I think that art exhibitions as such are no longer visual in that sense. Painting—the great age of painting—all the way up through abstract expressionism was an autonomization of the visual, a way in which everything was translated into the visual. And that's clearly not the case anymore. But is spatial the right word for this? I guess space in this context presupposes the temporality of the present, so it's not exactly geographical. But it's also not exactly visual. I'm not sure quite how to characterize that. And probably the relationship of music and space and music and time has something to do with that too. But we have different—you can use Rancière's slogan if you like—we have different ratios of the senses to each other in this case.

Can you elaborate on this idea that art today is less visual? It seems today that moving image art is everywhere, as if cinema has bled out into the spaces of the gallery and the museum. Does this say something about the state of contemporary cinema?

Well, this first raises the issue of photography. There were a lot of combinations of painting and photography, and photography itself became a very fundamental kind of art for a while. But I wouldn't say it's film; I would rather say it's video that has effected this change, or that is present in all these ways. But I'm not sure about the dominance of video either, since it too is reduced to an aspect. So it isn't visuality of that older, autonomous kind; it is the integration of a different kind of sensation into the mix, so to speak. I looked at video art a long time ago, and I thought it was very interesting in itself, but now it's really everywhere. In the beginning it was also autonomous. It used to be a separate medium and a separate branch of art. I don't think that's true anymore. It seems to me that a lot of gallery installations include video, in the form of loops and so on, something which reduces the autonomy of all of the components, including the visual.

In The Antinomies of Realism, *you write, "The weakening of the fictional undermines its opposite number, the category of the factual; and . . . this is the point where we find ourselves on the threshold of a new world." You are writing about Alexander Kluge but suggest that this has much larger implications. Can you say a bit more about what you think might be happening with the breakdown of the fact/fiction distinction and how it might relate to the kinds of shifts you see taking place in the function or understanding of the aesthetic more generally? Thirty years ago, you hinted at the sense of an emergent shift in our understanding of aesthetics and culture more generally that perhaps could not yet be clearly articulated.*

I think that's right. I mean we still use this word *art*, and we have museums and what we call works of art, but the whole function of the thing has changed. That is why the revival of aesthetics is not a good idea, because it isn't dealing with works anymore—it isn't dealing with the same kinds of objects, and these are not really objects anymore anyway. I don't know whether people use the word *fiction* very much anymore, either. Let's just stick to a Freudian approach here: if fantasy is so important and omnipresent, then it becomes a fact, too. I mean, if people keep talking about the *narrative* of things—all the news commentaries use this word now, which is a relatively new word in that context—then everything's a narrative and everything goes.

But I wouldn't want to be thought to be promoting the primacy of the "fact" either, as in documentary. If now we know that the fact is constructed, as so many people have taught us, then the very power of the fact has lost out. Is this simulacrum? You see it; it's there. Is it a fact? Well, but it isn't really a fiction either. . . . So the whole opposition has faded in some sense. Has it been replaced by something else? I do think that art and art's autonomy have also disappeared in everyday life. If everything in everyday life is becoming images, and simulacrum, then art ceased to occupy a separate sphere.

Art still occupies a separate sphere in that it can be sold for a lot of money . . .

Well, but you can sell everything else for a lot of money, too. So in a sense, it's drawn into the world, the commodity world, by the way of its price. In another sense by way of its number if you're talking about these astronomical figures. I don't think that should necessarily lead us to the triumphant conclusion that all we're interested in now is reality, as is suggested by a book like *Reality Hunger* [by David Shields], because reality itself gets lost in all that. So people's memoirs and their accounts of things are just as fictional as anything else. But that does devalue the act of writing novels: the crisis of the novel! In film you get the same thing with the documentary. Film follows the same evolution. I always think of *Eclipse*. You're seeing something real in that fictional film. Film is still photography. Well, okay, special effects throws a monkey wrench into this question. Maybe that's why I don't care much for special effects. I think everybody's a little annoyed because they would like their simulacrum to have a little reality, and the more they know that somebody's got a machine that just produces this, the less they can have their sense of the disappearance of the real. I mean that's certainly fictive, but it's not the fiction of the storyteller, it's some damn engineer who has produced it and so it loses its jouissance. The news also becomes this fictional thing. It doesn't mean that those things are not real, but maybe there are more things that are real now than before. Or maybe we need a more capitalized word like Lacan's *Real* to distinguish some other relationship to it. But the Real of Lacan didn't refer to facts either. That was an existential distinction between truth and science, lived experience and fact. But it does mean that experience itself has become transformed, modified in its structure.

Regarding the issue of distinguishing lived experience from fact, how do you take the concept of "cognitive mapping" today? Is it different from when you first used it?

There too, the map has to be understood as a representational problem, and a representational impossibility. Everybody is writing about maps today, for and against. Really the concept has to do with the representation of globalization. It also relates to how we situate our own individual consciousness in a larger situation. It might be better to just consider it a form problem, and when it makes for new representations, it's interesting. When people manage to think of something new, whether it's film or the novel or something else, then I think we know that something interesting, something relevant is going on. But, on the other hand, I don't think I imagine the artist can do that just by thinking about it. Something in their own psyche, in their own experience or situation has to make those kinds of discoveries possible and unexpected.

Faulkner once said that the best novels had to draw on three things: imagination, observation, and experience (any two of which would do in a pinch). Maybe that's the starting point for us both in terms of literature and theory, these three questions: what can we experience in the US? What can we observe from the US? How far can an American imagination take us?

You were speaking earlier about the possibility of the political in the artwork being different now than it was in the past. Are there any cultural forms— movies, works of literature, art—being made right now that are exciting to you?

We always have to reckon our class position into these forms of personal taste; the kind of revelations that we got from naturalism on don't have the same kind of impact now. Or maybe we don't know them in the right way. I think it's harder to shock people, it's harder to stun people, with new kinds of realities that they didn't know. But maybe we're not doing it right. Or maybe the documentaries or newsreels and so on are not doing it right.

One is always looking for newer kinds of texts and films, and newer kinds of art as well.

I think the most interesting painter around right now is Neo Rauch. I hope to write something about him someday, and that's certainly a case where narratives are fundamental, maybe reinvented, combined in weird assemblages. It's not surrealism anymore, not exactly fantasy or magical realism; it's more like pieces of the past are being superimposed in some new sense.

In terms of film, I think that the most interesting examples come from outside the West. I hesitate to mention specific examples off the top of my head, but there is [Nuri Bilge] Ceylan, for example, and in other ways, Béla Tarr or Aleksei German. There used to be good Chinese films before Tiananmen, though perhaps less now. People like Tsai Ming-liang were doing weird and interesting things, but I haven't seen his latest films. Jia Zhangke has been interesting to me. I'm somewhat more interested in fiction films, despite there being no such thing as fiction, and then subgenres like detective stories and science fiction sometimes. I wrote about *Cloud Atlas*, the novel, which I think was a real breakthrough. The funny thing is detective stories are coming out everywhere. They're a new form of tourism—there isn't a major city in the world that doesn't have somebody writing a detective story. And then it often ceases to be so productive.

What about TV? Around the time you were working on Postmodernism *(the book), you also seemed to focus a great deal on cinema. Today certain kinds of TV shows (no longer necessarily watched on a TV) seem to be displacing films as the dominant narrative cultural form at least within a certain elite culture. Meanwhile, new kinds of viewing and reading practices are getting shaped by the centrality of the computer in so many current forms of cultural consumption. Is there anything that seems new here that might inform how we think about the "cultural logic" of capitalism today? You've written, for example, about* The Wire, *but do you see other significant features in some of these new TV series?*

I am sure people will produce that kind of analysis. I wasn't so crazy about *Treme*, and I didn't like the war thing, but if he [David Simon] only did *The Wire*, that's still something (and I don't underrate *Homicide*). The problem is that there aren't any plots anymore. So you have to work very hard to put a lot of different strands together in a way that operates like a plot. But otherwise all you get in popular culture is serial killers and terrorists. That's about it. Pedophiles, but we don't really show them much. Well, I guess maybe those fit under serial killers. It is to *that* that plot has been reduced.

I read something recently about the disappearance of the family novel. I think that's an interesting thought. That some of it still exists in other countries where you still have families. I don't know whether we're interested in families anymore here; Franzen's families, for example, are fairly restrictive, besides being dysfunctional. But these other things were dynastic novels really . . . in China, in India I think too, to a certain degree. I think that for me generally the good things—whether films or novels—are coming from the non-Western world right now. But one doesn't want to rule anything out. One has to keep looking for it. That I'm willing to do.

Printed and bound by CPI Group (UK) Ltd, Croydon, CR0 4YY

03/11/2024

14584905-0001